MASTERS OF MYSTERY

A Study of The Detective Story

by

H. DOUGLAS THOMSON

WITH A NEW INTRODUCTION BY
E. F. BLEILER

DOVER PUBLICATIONS, INC.
NEW YORK

To

A.D.T. and M.D.T.

This Dover edition, first published in 1978, is an
unabridged republication of the text as published
by Wm. Collins Sons & Co., Ltd., London, in 1931.
A new introduction has been specially written for
the present edition by E. F. Bleiler who has also
furnished a number of new footnotes.

International Standard Book Number: 0-486-23606-4
Library of Congress Catalog Card Number: 77-92479

Manufactured in the United States of America
Dover Publications, Inc.
180 Varick Street
New York, N.Y. 10014

INTRODUCTION

Masters of Mystery by Henry Douglas Thomson [1905–1975] is the first book in English devoted to the history and aesthetics of the detective story. Before Thomson's work there had been only a few scattered periodical essays on special topics or individual authors by such men as Chesterton, Arnold Bennett and Valentine Williams; a couple of anthology introductions by Dorothy Sayers and E. M. Wrong; and a fine chapter, but only a chapter, in Frank Chandler's *Literature of Roguery*. With Thomson's book, however, began the serious history and serious criticism of the detective story both as entertainment and as a literary form.

Seen nearly fifty years after its first publication in 1931 *Masters of Mystery* has many strengths, and it is still worth reading for, at the very least, its panorama of the British detective story as of 1930 or so. It covers the foremost practitioners, the noteworthy books and the prevalent critical standards. It offers many good summaries of books that are now difficult of access, and gives a nice brief history of key moments in the various subforms loosely grouped together under the term "detective story." Indeed, very often a modern reader can go to Thomson and discover an insight or a telling phrase that sums up a phenomenon, or a point of view to which we are only now reverting.

It must be frankly admitted, of course, that Thomson's work has many of the forgivable weaknesses inherent in pioneer work. While Thomson is accurate and the reader need not worry about error, Thomson omits much, particularly in the earlier periods of the detective story. But this can certainly be forgiven, for these areas were not known at the time Thomson wrote, and even today there is no good survey, in any language, of the early detective story.

More important, for the modern reader, is the change in aesthetics that has taken place since Thomson did his reading. While detectives have practiced their craft endlessly since the 1920's, they have evolved, and any study of the form must face this question: what constitutes a detective story, and, emergent from this answer, what are the formal patterns by which it must be judged.

Around 1930 the prevailing detective story in Great Britain and (to a somewhat lesser extent) in the United States was the "house party" crime: a closed circle of suspects is associated with a murder, and a formal detective, whether amateur or professional or both, must find a solution to the mystery surrounding the murder. This was a rigorously conscribed form, hyperclassical in its rigidity, and Thomson, along with most of his contemporaries, accepted this pattern as an absolute and worked out his judgments within its parameters.

One of the conventions within the house party story was the literary device known as "fairness." Although "fairness" is by no means inherent in the detective situation, and is only an accident, authors and critics of the 1920's and 1930's made a great to-do about it, R. Austin Freeman and S. S. Van Dine even codifying it. "Fairness" meant that the reader should have access to all the information that the detective has, and that at a certain point in the story something should crystallize in the reader's mind, so that he can anticipate the fictional detective. In other words, the detective story had to be a puzzle story, and the author, like a carnival booster, perforce had to deceive the reader yet remain reasonably honest, or he would suffer a bad review.

Today, "fairness" does not seem so important, indeed, it even seems illusory or self-deceiving. It was a very temporary development in the history of the detective story, something that was not present in the earlier works and that is not always present in the better modern works. The importance of "fairness," of course, is a matter of opinion, and the reader can accept as much of Thomson's criticism from this point of view as he wishes.

Writing a critical history of the detective story in 1930 was a dangerous task, since this was a period of transition, during which new themes, new techniques, and new aesthetic judgments were emerging, particularly in America. Thomson did not appreciate the importance of this. The peripheral wash of novelty was beginning to strike England during Thomson's day, in the form of pulp magazines with sensational gangster stories, and as can be seen, the British were bewildered by it and did not know what to make of it. On the side of theory Dashiell Hammett wrote book reviews that savagely slashed the aesthetics of S. S. Van Dine and J. S. Fletcher (two typical authors whom Thomson admired) and somewhat later Raymond Chandler in his "Simple Art of Murder" provided a glowing apologia for the new romanticism of American crime. One need not agree with their positions, either, to see that Thomson was often parochial.

Thomson's critical standards were often a function of his day, but two more personal flaws in his work must be mentioned. His worst gaffe, of course, is his failure to estimate Hammett's work adequately. While Hammett-worship may be excessive at the moment, it is still perplexing that Thomson could have missed Hammett's imagination, powerful writing, and ability to convey a social or moral message. Related to this lacuna is Thomson's lack of awareness of the other better American writers of his day, men who stood just as high as the better English writers that he praises. It was inexcusable to be unaware of the work of Melville D. Post, F. I. Anderson and T. S. Stribling. It is also surprising, since all three men were writers of world reputation at this time.

Yet all in all, the strengths of H. D. Thomson's *Masters of Mystery* outweigh its weaknesses. Since so much of Thomson's subject matter is nearly unique, it is difficult to imagine anyone seriously interested in the history or aesthetics of the detective story who would not profit from reading *Masters of Mystery*. We can only regret that Thomson did not see fit to enlarge it and keep it up to date.

On the whole I have not commented on Thomson's judgments, since they constitute a field consistent within themselves, even though I sometimes disagree with them. In one or two instances, however, I have called attention to bad guesses and estimations, and have corrected a very few errors of fact.

E. F. BLEILER

CONTENTS

Overwork means undue congestion of certain lobes of the brain. In order to draw the blood from these lobes, other contiguous lobes must be stimulated. A week in the country merely means that you brood on your work. Detective novels act like iodine on a gum and serve as a counter-irritant.
—LORD BALFOUR.

FOREWORD

I HAVE had a twofold object in writing this book. Despite the universal appeal of detective fiction, only recently has serious attention been paid to its technique. It is surely high time that criticism " placed " detective fiction and officially recognised the conscientious craftsmanship that beguiles our leisure hours. Secondly, I have attempted to provide a comprehensive, though an unavoidably incomplete, guide to the best detective stories. The lives of even the detective classics are often curtailed owing to the voraciousness of the gourmand and to the absence of any records on the subject. It is my hope that the following pages may help a little to repair that loss to the occasional reader and also to those newly addicted to the sport.

York Street,
Baker Street, W. 1

CHAPTER I

THE DETECTIVE STORY

I

" Poor worm, thou art infected."

THOMAS DE QUINCEY was responsible for the inclusion of Murder in the sisterhood of the Fine Arts. Literature resented the intrusion and devoted herself to the castigation of the parvenue, claiming that if a fine murder was artistic, the detection of it was equally artistic—all ethical considerations apart. Thus there came into existence a new genre in literature.

Contemplate, if you please, the catholicity of the detective story's popularity. During a recess Prime Ministers do not as of old hie themselves to the Classics and thank their God for Virgil. They batten instead on the works of Mr. Edgar Wallace. Hence, " The Prime Ministers' Detective Library." The clergy have damned the consequences and have abandoned themselves to the dissipation. Conformists and Nonconformists alike have cudgelled their brains to provide the public with this particular form of profane entertainment. Likewise the professors at our universities, for detective fiction thrives in the quietude of the cloisters. Probably the most extensive library of detective stories is owned by a professor of philosophy in the north. And there philosophy is philosophy indeed. Lawyers, whom one might expect to be supercilious from their esoteric familiarity with criminals and criminal procedure, are yet voracious readers.

What loss of dignity can there be to them, when the Lord Chief Justice has set the precedent ?

The records of any circulating library will attest that the man in the street shares this predilection. Still further proof is furnished by the growing membership of the recently established Crime Club. Each month the club's selection committee of three chooses and recommends to its members the best detective stories submitted to them. On this august panel sits none other than Dr. Alington, the Headmaster of Eton.

Nor is this movement confined to our own country. A fillip has recently been given to " crime fiction " in America by some very competent work in the genre, and by the activities of her Crime Club and her Detective Story Club. On the continent France, the creator of the *roman policier*, has never wavered in her affections. Germany has only just discovered the delights of the *Kriminalroman*, thanks largely to the wide distribution of the translated works of Mr. Edgar Wallace ; but she can with justice claim to have made in *Espione* (*The Spy*) the best detective film yet screened.* In Scandinavia a popular series of translations of detective stories, chiefly English, is meeting with large sales.

Before the present " peak season " the general attitude towards detective fiction may be expressed in Philip Trent's words, " I have a sort of sneaking respect for the determination to make life interesting and lively in spite of civilisation."

An enjoyment of detective stories was in these days a " weakness " to which we " confessed," as we might confess to a partiality for mustard with mutton. For some reason or other we thought we ought not to delight in this type of literature, that our sensibility was being outraged by a Philistinism. The only cure

---

* *Spione* (Spies), UFA, a Fritz Lang film based on a novel by Thea von Harbou.—E. F. B.

for the disease was a prolonged course of Meredith or
a volume of some politician's reminiscences. I am not
for a moment saying that this purgative was not an
eminently commendable or even a reformatory pre-
scription. I condemn, however, the fallacious diagnosis
of the symptoms which called for this treatment. It
was hastily assumed that this modern genre to which
we so joyously responded had no art in it at all, but
was a specious ostentation of Blood and Thunder.
Our unalloyed enjoyment was left unexplained. It
might be the comfortable sensation *alterius spectare
laborem* (ten years hard!), or it might be the fascination
evil has for us owing to our canker of original sin.
Public opinion has since veered. Mayfair and Chelsea
have come to Tooting. But the curious fact is that
for the most part the æsthetic of our genre is not
recognised, far less appreciated.

Most of us are seldom sure of our tastes, and literary
criticism has not aided us here to have the courage of
our convictions. Apart from Mr. G. K. Chesterton's
A Defence of Detective Stories, in *The Defendant*, and a
Preface to Mr. Masterman's *The Wrong Letter* ; the
late E. M. Wrong's Introduction to *Stories of Crime
and Detection* ; Miss Dorothy Sayers' Introduction to
Great Short Stories of Detection, Mystery and Horror ;
and some few *obiter dicta* uttered by such authorities
as Father Ronald Knox and Mr. Arnold Bennett,
there has been little or no attempt to account for the
popularity of the detective story, or to give a systematic
analysis of it.

In the centenary edition of *The Spectator* Edith
Wharton wrote : " I am convinced that the reviewer
should be as helpful to the author as to the reader,
and what he can be to the latter is still to be learned
from Sainte-Beuve, and these minor successors of his

who continue to maintain in France the tradition that
a work of art is something worthy of the attention of
a *trained* intelligence."

Can it honestly be affirmed that the average reviewer
is trained (supposing that the average reader is not),
and that he is by way of being an expositor of the art
and craft in this age of educational publicity, when
science is made easy and art difficult ? Are our critics
eager to show a sign or disprove a myth ? It is a sad
admission to make, but really Momus, the old genius
of criticism, must be nodding. Poor fellow, he has too
much work to do nowadays, so he has started an agency
and turned over detective fiction to his publicity man.
The newcomer, translated from his proper sphere of
action, is pathetically complaisant, and seldom, if ever,
barks out a word of protest. Certainly it is not his
business to spoil like Jeffrey. Therefore there is little
to be said, and apparently there is only one way
to say it.

Thus, once upon a time reviewers were chary of
saying either too much or too little, and found sanctuary
in jargonistic ready-to-wear. Detective stories were
never anything else than "tense," "baffling," "rousing,"
" ingenious." Invariably one was advised on no account
to read them before going to bed ; and one was hotly
challenged to lay them aside unfinished. New ground,
it is true, was covered from time to time. By the
Glamorgan County Gazette, for example, in its notice
on the Sherlock Holmes tales :—

" The Adventures of Sherlock Holmes should be
read by all who desire to improve their faculty of
observation. Fathers would do well to make it a
birthday present to their boys, and if they do this,
they certainly may have the comforting thought that
the book will be read from beginning to end " !

But it was distressing to read in the *Saturday Review's* critique on Mr. F. Wills Crofts's *The Cask*: " If detective novels were a new genre, we should call this a great book." As if novelty of subject or an exploitation of literary types were the " Open Sesame " to great writing.

A new spirit happily prevails. The giants are now on our side. *The Times Literary Supplement* for one has no compunction in sparing a column now and again. Generally speaking, not only is more space devoted to our genre, but the criticism itself is vastly more entertaining.

Indeed any antagonism to our much maligned Press on this score is, perhaps, unfair. We impose a condition of secrecy and then expect a criticism instead of an advertisement. Whereas criticism thus fettered cannot be genuine. The true criticism of any detective story can only take place *in camera*, where the critic expounds his views to an audience *already* familiar with the subject. That is obvious—a truism applicable to criticism in general. *N'importe*, it is certainly true of the detective story.

Now, while admitting the truth of the submission that the detective story enjoys a catholic popularity, you may be militantly reprehensive of the general attitude. This is only, mark you, taking a hypothetical case. Let us put forward the case for the prosecution as convincingly as we can, so that our victory (also hypothetical !) may be. the more gratifying. Perhaps you regard the public craze for detective stories as but another example of the rabid delight in sensationalism which is said to be characteristic of our age. Or you may be slightly more magnaminous, and descry in it the lesser of two unfortunate evils—an escape from fiction's obsession in sex problems. Again you may favour a more positive criticism, and regard the detective story as a tonic for jaded nerves, or a means for dispelling the tediousness of a railway journey.

> " And the Devil murmurs behind the leaves, ' It's pretty, but is it Art ? ' "

The question is one that is not often asked. Our Muse is seldom taken seriously. A curious fact this, for levity even in her ribald moments does not show criticism the door. And further we welcome penetrative disquisitions on Nonsense, and applaud when our attention is drawn to its poetry and its philosophy. Yet what is the detective story if not a grown-up nonsense rather proud of its education and its logic ?

Of those who have asked the question, Is it Art ? the majority have seconded the Devil's implication. Is it because they regard Art as the preserve of the intelligentsia ? To maintain dogmatically, as has been maintained, that the detective novel is bad art (and that means not art at all) and is for that reason popular, or even *vice versa*, savours too much of a snobbish sophistication. Popular taste is not necessarily commonplace, nor is a discriminating taste necessarily " caviare to the general." Indeed, the very fact that detective stories are subjected to a criterion whereby some are adjudged good and others bad pre-supposes an artistry in them—otherwise there would be no standard. This is no attempt to make out one's geese to be swans. I do not advocate a reading course. I do not regard Sexton Blake as a stepping-stone to Shelley. All art is essentially " monadic." The detective story must be examined on its own merits. It is useless to compare literary genres like triangles in geometry. One does not probe for psychological complexes when one

reads about Edward Lear's Old Man of Cromer,
" who stood on one leg to read Homer."
But we have forgotten that we were to prosecute.

2

One frequently hears it said that the detective story
is not art because it is badly written. The accusation
is almost too stupid to call for a refutation. It is a
false assumption which can be reduced to a syllogistic
fallacy. Besides, it is the best examples of a literary
genre that we weigh in the balance ; and few are going
to maintain that Edgar Allan Poe, Sir Arthur Conan
Doyle, Mr. E. C. Bentley[1] and Mr. G. K. Chesterton
are *bad* writers. The one grain of truth we can abstract
from this charge is the prevalence of badly written
detective stories. Of this sorry fact we are painfully
aware. We need no censorious critic to cast it in our
teeth ; but we may perhaps turn away his wrath by
the soft answer that the detective story has been
hailed as a public necessity, and that this fact has
had its inevitable results. The detective story is not,
as we have urged, popular because it is badly written,
but badly written because it is popular. Art cannot
pretend to adjust the balances of Supply and Demand.
Once this adjustment is called for Art has to pack
her bags. The voracious public will rather have a
badly written detective story than none at all. Hasty
composition and a precipitate printing mark the
desperate attempt on the part of the author and his
publisher to meet the inordinate demand. With the

[1] Of Mr. E. C. Bentley's *Trent's Last Case* Mr. A. C. Ward, in
Twentieth Century Literature, has had the courage to say : " One
at least of the hundreds of detective stories written during the
quarter-century belongs to literature."

author who thus sacrifices his pen to his pocket we cannot argue. We can only remark the divergence of his standards and values from our own (when we can afford to be dogmatically impartial) and express the pious hope that he may not be too thick-skinned to suffer some pricks of conscience. But even allowing the publishers to be " business men " in the first place, we have some justification for the complaint that most of them treat our Muse with too scant a respect. The compositor of even the most reputable firms must sometimes nod ; the proof reader too must sometimes take a holiday ; and the Olympian reader cannot always stretch the bow of Correction. But one often wishes they would not invariably regard the detective story as the lawful occasion for their constitutional forty-winks. Exeunt accordingly Grammar and Syntax. Enter in their stead Solecisms, Mis-spellings and Inconsistencies. For such sins are the publishers guilty and the public innocently responsible.

I do not, however, wish to dwell on this unpleasant chaos, but rather to draw your attention to a kindred result of slovenly writing which concerns the matter rather than the form of the detective story. I refer to the untold clichés, the jargonistic tags, the lazy habit of describing events in ever recurring phrases— Q's nightmare. Fortunately the bark, as it were, of these clichés is worse than their bite, for they do not usually affect the general trend of the narrative, but only pin the action down to a hackneyed treatment in insignificant details.

It is naturally in the less dignified detective stories that these clichés are rife. If we can afford to be lenient, we can reflect that it is really rather an amusing topsy-turvydom that prevails although arising from so vulgar a cause. The Courts of Law have a " Trial by Jury" atmosphere about them. Inside their "solemn portals" detectives " create sensations " with a charitable regularity. Not only do they burst into the Old Bailey on the last day of the trial with an imperious, " Stop this trial " (just like a John Bull poster), but, what is more, this is just the interruption which our lordships seem to have been waiting for all through the dragging hours. The black cap is put away and the solemnity of the Law is thawed into a Micawberish geniality. " You're all wrong," says the detective, " and your theories are going to tumble down like a pack of cards." " Don't mention it," says the judge, " I know you're right. Only I'm getting rather old now, so butter me up at the end— the public likes it." The trial ends with an orgy of handshakes. Outside the courts there is always pandemonium—but in every case it is an articulate pandemonium. Newsboys have apparently studied elocution by correspondence courses. Their " breathless shouts " rise silver clear above " the roar and din " of the traffic. Nor do they stop there. Their winged words must float up from the turmoil of the thorough-fare through the open windows to plague some character who paces the room in an agony of nervous tension.

Fainting at inquests is an unfair dodge. A fainting fit can be real and earnest ; it can also be shammed. It can be caused, again, from a variety of circumstances. Now, at an inquest we are often told that the room is stuffy and the atmosphere is electric. But if anybody faints, " local weather conditions " simply do not occur to us as a natural cause. For example, if we were to read : " The room in which the inquest was held was confined in space. Owing to an intense public interest in the case it was packed to overflowing.

There was no window through which the rays of the sun might filter in to dispel the dusty and drab atmosphere. Five minutes after the proceedings had opened one or two people had fainted, and the business in hand had to be suspended." Well, there's nothing in that. But when we read :—

> " In the hollow stillness that succeeded the coroner's last pronouncement, one could have heard a pin drop. A faint rustle of silk, followed by a dull thud, turned all eyes to the back of the court, where Mrs. X lay a limp heap on the floor in a dead faint."

It is hardly fair.

Criminals as a class are apt to labour under the grave disadvantage of possessing " tapering and sensitive fingers " (so, by the way, are detectives) ; they are also in the habit of laughing " hollowly." But the significance of this latter characteristic I must leave to M. Bergson to explain. Again I am most ready to admit that any girl in a detective story who has not " perfectly manicured nails " has no business there ; but I am not yet quite sure why our attention is always being drawn to this fact. Is there some dark secret to be learnt from chiropody ? And what is the relative significance of perfectly manicured hands when belonging (*a*) to the detective ; (*b*) to the villain, and (*c*) to the girl ?

Again, people seem to lose their senses at the end of chapters. They take a frenzied delight in " finding themselves looking down the barrel of an automatic," as though they had put a penny in the slot and were determined at all costs to see the " racy Paris pictures." In *The Picaroon does Justice*,* the Picaroon and the police inspector spend most of their time at the " Examine Arms."

* By Herman Landon.—E. F. B.

Of the other more prominent clichés I would merely, in passing, draw your attention to such phraseology as " hawk-eyed sleuth," " the guv'nor," " silky smile," " velvet touch," " bark out," " Perhaps, who can tell ? " and ask you to supply the context. Had I included the one word " sinister " in this list, you had had a labour of Hercules. It occurs everywhere, and has even been raised to titular prominence. It is in itself a perfectly good word, boasting a long and distinguished pedigree, but it needs, like us all, a half-day once a week.

3

" An ingenious theory has been advanced that ' the detective story ' as distinct from ' the crime story,' flourishes only in a settled community where the readers' sympathies are on the side of law and order, and not on the side of the criminal who is trying to escape from justice."—LORD HEWART.

Or perhaps you arraign the detective story for its sensationalism and morbidity. With a platonic censoriousness you object to the making of books in which violent actions, murders, abductions and the like are graphically described. It is lowering : it is dangerous—if not to yourself to " the young," that godsend to the theoretical reformer.

Well, let us take our time in shaping an answer. In the first place Shaw was right up to a point when he said in his preface to *Saint Joan* : " Crime, like disease, is not interesting ; it is something to be done away with by general consent, and that is all about it." Crime, however odd it may sound, is *not* the primary interest of the detective story. For one thing it does not take crime seriously. And by this separation from reality the detective story is removed also from the morbid and revolting. A leader that appeared in

the *Morning Post*, entitled " Desperately Wicked,"
adopted a rather one-sided attitude.

> " The fiction which most amused our ancestors was
> a study in rascality ; and before our fiction began, our
> most popular ballads concerned the homicides and
> robberies of Robin Hood. Indeed, if we go far enough
> back, we come to the theft of an apple as the most
> absorbing topic of the Garden of Eden. How then shall
> we explain this eternal interest ? There is high authority
> for saying that the human heart is desperately wicked,
> and it has been suggested that interest is akin to
> admiration. We do not accept the theory ; we merely
> state it as a hypothesis. But certain it is that crime
> has a very much stronger hold upon the mind and
> heart of mankind than most people would care to
> admit."

Applied to the detective story this is a questionable
assertion. If the interest were solely or even largely
an interest in crime, the ethics that form the basis
of the detective story's setting would be pointless. In
the detective story, alone probably of all fiction, moral
standards are not examined or questioned. They are
healthily taken for granted. You remember Stevenson's
phrase, " Novels clarify the lessons of life ? " This is
not strictly didacticism as that word is usually inter-
preted. The novelist is all the time, consciously or not,
making explicit the moral consciousness implicit in us
(praise be !) by his exemplary presentation of a portion
of life.

It is not quite the same with the detective story.
This may seem paradoxical when we consider that the
problem is bound by all the rules of the game to be
solved in order to bring the guilty party to justice.
But this is assumed before we start : the lesson is
already explicit. There is, however, no harm in repetition, and I doubt whether morality has ever had her

case more loyally or more consistently upheld than in this Tweedledum and Tweedledee combat of anarchy and order over her sleeping body. If publishers took it upon them to refund money when the reading public was dissatisfied with their wares, they would have to do so every time when law and order did not come out top-dog in the detective story.

One has to allow that the detective story revels in violent situations which provoke the tenser emotions— the truly " sensational " emotions such as horror, fear, excitement and suspense. Yet there is no real reason why this should give offence. Squeamishness in this instance is caused by a mistaken interpretation of, and a mistaken attitude to what we read. Violence has always been the happy hunting ground of Literature. We have Aristotle to champion the theory of fear as a catharsis. If we regard the question solely as one of æsthetics, it is only when things are pushed to extremes, when the macabre is cultivated as in *Dracula* for the sole sake of being " sensational " and to give us the creeps, that we feel our artistic sense ruffled by the lack of proportion and distortion. But then our point is that in the detective story the sensational elements are only of a secondary importance ; like the patter of a conjurer, pleasant and to some extent necessary, but not of a basic significance. They are ornament. The horror and suspense are only counterfeit. We may be excited, but we are ready to laugh the next moment. There is surely nothing neurotic in that.

Fortunately we have so far had the sense not to attempt to make a science of an artistic recreation. We do not bring to the detective novel an academic scholarship to swell its bulk with annotation. In the detective story, maugre the *Morning Post*, crime as crime does not interest us.

The allegation that the pages of the detective story are peopled with morbid characters can be refuted in precisely the same manner. The recent tendency to make of the detective story a psychological study of criminal " types " and " complexes," though in a sense legitimate, cannot but be distasteful to the true lover of detective fiction. Criminology may mock at the " instinctive criminals of fiction,"[1] but it is a sad state of affairs when fiction has to own defeat and borrow its characters from the sciences.

Latterly the interest in real crime has grown more widespread. Chicago may be to blame for it—or the *Sunday Express*! On every bookstall are stacked *Classic Detective Tales*, *True Stories of Detection*, *The Detective Magazine*, and *Scotland Yard*—the majority of these papers being of American origin. The memoirs of detectives are appearing more frequently in the Press. An anthology of real crime stories, *Murder Most Foul*, has been edited by George A. Birmingham. So seasoned a judge as Canon Hannay will not for a moment admit that this interest is morbid. The sanest people in the world—like Sir Walter Scott and " Christopher North," who read up the Burke and Hare murders with intense interest—are attracted by the subject. There are so many aspects to interest one— the scientific, the psychological, the legal, the historical. But, says Canon Hannay, the real reason why we like crime stories is because of the thrills, " exactly as children like ghost stories."

The detective story must not be regarded as propaganda. It does not advocate the abolition of capital punishment ; it does not even indict the principles

---

[1] Horace Wyndham's *Criminology*.

of circumstantial evidence. If you want propaganda, you go to the theatre to see *To What Red Hell*; if you want a study of abnormal psychology you plough through Theodore Dreiser's *An American Tragedy*. The same axiom holds good here as before. A distasteful subject can be morbid only when it is treated seriously.

4

" I doubt if Scotland Yard has found anything to learn from fiction unless it be an occasional indication of method."
—J. D. BERESFORD.

Let us suppose you are a realist. You find fact stranger than fiction. You read the murder cases in the *News of the World*. You collect the *Famous Trial Series* on your library shelves. For your benefit—as well as the benefit of writers grown stale—ex-detectives write their memoirs. For your delectation Franz Schmidt's *A Hangman's Diary* was resurrected. You condemn the detective story for its unreality. Society, you argue, is never in danger of being destroyed by the arch-criminal. Outside America the secret organisations of a Moriarty or a Clutching Hand are mere hallucinations. Coincidence, which is merely the last refuge of ineptitude (and you have Poe on your side there), is a god of detective fiction. In real life there is not a bundle of clues to pick and choose between. The investigator's problem is to discover if there are any clues at all. Finally, the detective is not a private individual who indulges in detection to save himself like Sherlock Holmes from ennui, but the ever disparaged official of Scotland Yard.

Even if the indictment were unequivocally true, the argument seems to be beside the point. If literature is to be estimated by reference to a standard of realism, we shall have to scrap a large percentage of the most delightful writing. The theory that Art to be Art has to mirror nature is a downright fallacy, if we regard the Platonic Σἴδοπτον as giving a crystal-clear reflection.

Too much is, perhaps, made of the divergence between the detection of Crime in Fact and the detection of Crime in Fiction. You are of course aware, good sir, that Poe's *Mystery of Marie Roget* was the solution of an actual murder in America ; that Sergeant Cuff was taken from the life ; that some of the Sherlock Holmes stories have a basis of fact, and that Mr. Edgar Wallace was invited by the German police to co-operate with them in their investigation of the Düsseldorf Murders.

Now, naturally, there are differences between the actual and the fictitious detection of crime. Let us take it for granted that the private detective of fiction corresponds to the C.I.D. officer in real life. Of the police in detective fiction we shall have a few words to say later on. The writer of detective fiction in the majority of cases starts with his solution and works backwards in his process of detection. This means that his detective works to schedule. The scope of his investigation is limited and his time is limited. He hasn't time to go to see Chelsea on a Saturday afternoon. Everything is speeded up. Fiction, by nature selective, really excels herself here. The detective has to get results, and get them quickly ; he has also to get them in an attractive way. Inspector French in *The Sea Mystery** hits the nail on the head when he says :—

"There is this difference between a novel and real life. In a novel the episodes are selected and the

* By Freeman Wills Crofts.—E. F. B.

reader is told those which are interesting, and which get results. In real life we try perhaps ten or twenty lines which lead nowhere before we strike the lucky one. And in each line we make perhaps hundreds of inquiries, whereas the novel describes one. It's like any other job, you get results by pegging away."

In the novel there is thus little spadework, little drudgery. There is also a fine loophole for intuitive discoveries. If detection in real life were stranger and more exciting than detection in fiction, fiction would give up the struggle. It would be the survival of the more fitting. Now, allowing for this eclecticism, there is not so very great a difference between the two. I am foolish enough to believe that a person who could reason as the fictitious detective does, off-hand and without having his evidence cut and dried for him, could tackle a real crime problem with a fair prospect of success. But he would need the co-operation of the police.

Police methods vary in different countries. Scotland Yard prides itself on its team work. From systematic " combing " to the simplest form of " shadowing," there is no one man's show. The Berlin police relies chiefly on its comprehensive index system. There is, perhaps, more romance in the methods of the Vienna police. It pins its faith to the expert—the scientific ex-specialist and professor. In *Scotland Yard** a murder case is recorded in which the solution was given over the 'phone. The professor who was best fitted to deal with the case happened to be in Switzerland at the time. Nothing daunted the police put a trunk call through and stayed the professor from his ski-ing. Having been informed of the details the professor gave directions for the carrying out of certain experiments with the revolver found near the scene of the crime.

* Perhaps the British periodical *Scotland Yard*?—E. F. B.

The results of these experiments were communicated to the professor, and in due course he 'phoned back his solution.

The overlooking of detail is fatal both in fact and in fiction ; but perhaps again too much is made of detail in the detective novel. In novels detectives are always finding tobacco ash, wisps of fair hair, minute pieces of steel, stray bullets *after* what was supposed to be an exhaustive search had been carried out. It is, moreover, seldom that such incriminating discoveries are made in real life, or if they are less noise is made about them. In this the novel shows a lack of perspective. On the other hand one remembers that now and again such minutiæ as laundry marks have led to the solution (The Trunk Murder).

The methods of the real and of the fictitious detective are—one might say—similar as far as theory goes, but dissimilar in the way that theory is acted upon. The real detective does not suspect every one ; he has often some difficulty in finding any one to suspect. He relies more on witnesses, on stray pieces of information. And here I might give this piece of warning to prospective murderers. It is astonishing to find so many people who can supply pertinent pieces of information after a murder has been committed. Murder will out. There is always a taximan, a landlady or a barmaid to oblige. In fiction people are not so helpful—apparently they think it would be making things too easy for the detective. The real detective again goes to work on the assumption that the murderer has either not been clever enough or has been too clever. The real criminal has the reputation for giving himself away through some little oversight—like Crippen's lapse. In fiction the detective—bless him— relies more on his own cleverness. But the theory, the science of the investigation, is the same—an exhaustive examination of the evidence whether objective or personal and deduction based on this analysis. A problem is after all a real problem whether its background is real or imagined.

The Garage Murder, which ate up so much newspaper space, impressed one very forcibly at the time as possessing many of the ingredients of an orthodox detective story. The body discovered two months after the murder ; the problem of the letters ; the watch ; the hammer ; the flying visits of the detectives to Southampton and elsewhere. Mind you, I am passing over the morbidity of Podmore's actual crime. Photographs of the garage appeared in the daily press, photographs of the hammer, photographs of the detectives at work and at ease. The public used to smile at a detective's methods in fiction. The cartoonist would depict his sleuth creeping along on hands and knees, a measuring rule protruding from his hip pocket. But now we are accustomed to see Mr. Prothero's and Mr. So-and-So's assistants measuring boxes, reconstructing the crime. This to the imaginative detective story fan spells the death of romance. All the detectives appear so uniformly ordinary and efficient. They all wear bowler hats. They are not comic.

Mr. J. D. Beresford in an article on the Garage Case in the *Daily Chronicle* wrote some very good sense on this subject.

" Sherlock Holmes or Hercule Poirot could, I presume, make a very shrewd guess as to how the crime was committed. I could devise a solution myself if I turned my mind to it. But the chances are that if Sir Arthur Conan Doyle, Agatha Christie and Edgar Wallace were all set to formulate a theory from the facts so far published, all three theories would admirably cover the facts, but would be completely different one from another. . . .

" The difference between the two cases is to be found in the melancholy deduction that whereas writers of detective fiction always play the game, life does not. In fiction we could be perfectly certain that these letters would furnish the clue if we had the wit to interpret their meaning. In life, for all we know, they may have nothing whatever to do with essentials."

In fiction the feud between the police and the hero-detective is a long standing one. The rustic constable has always sucked his pencil ; dumbfoundered he has always stood. The sergeant with PROMOTION looming large on his horizon, has always suspected and arrested the presentable young man or ravishing maiden. Never has the inspector been able to conceal his scorn and jealousy for the amateur. His unholy fear of " the arrival of the Yard " has always been the splendid spur to drive him in hot pursuit of the red herrings. The superintendent has always blindly obeyed the dictates of circumstantial evidence. Yet never has he lost his reputation, thanks to the tactful altruism of our hero.

Not that the writer of detective fiction has any quarrel with the police or police methods. But the real police simply fails to fit in with his scheme of things, so he has created a police force of his own imagination. He has adopted the whimsical attitude of being temporarily " agin the government " and bureaucratic organisation. He finds no fun in knocking a bank clerk's bowler for a six, but he covets the policeman's helmet.

Even in sober life the private detective agency has an aura about it that the criminal investigation department lacks. Take the Pinkerton Detective Agency of the U.S.A. Could you think of a more precious name for a detective than Allan Pinkerton ? Or for that matter of a more majestic slogan than " We Never Sleep," or of a more catching trade-mark than the Open Eye ! For more than half a century this business has flourished. The life of the original founder reads like a romance, from his flight from Glasgow to his rescue of Abraham Lincoln. Pinkerton has handed down to Pinkerton, and Gainsboroughs have been recovered by the old firm. The bare mention of a " Pinkerton's man " in a detective story sends a pleasurable thrill through one.

This delectable feud is begotten of art. The solitary figure of the detective battling against desperate odds commands our sympathy, and he can have the halo of romance for a song. The police working as a crew would have to share the spoils, and so the ingenuity of an organisation palls before the intensified brilliance of individuality. Some admirable criticism on this point has been given us by Canon Victor Whitechurch in his *Shot on the Downs*. (Canon Victor Whitechurch, for one, always submits his novels to the police so that the technicalities may be correct.)

" It is rather the fashion in popular crime stories of to-day to set forth the amateur sleuth with his astuteness as the successful rival of a more or less blundering police force and to portray the said police as either being jealous or scornful of the powers of the amateur. . . . As a matter of fact, the police are ever ready to avail themselves of the assistance of the amateur. . . . Also the methods of the police are not so bungled as often as they are imagined to be. The police to-day are a body of educated men.

" But it is far easier for the writer of detective

fiction to take his one particular investigator of the
' lonely furrow ' type than to attempt to portray the
complicated machinery of a force which depends upon
corporate action. . . . The technical police investigation . . . with its elaborate patience and inter-
co-operation would, as a rule, make far less exciting
reading than the often bizarre deductions and con-
sequent hair-raising episodes so usually characteristic
of the brilliant genius who scores his points triumphantly
alone."

It is the old revolt of romance against realism. Here
the wisdom of Mr. G. D. H. and Mrs. Margaret Cole is
to be commended in causing their Superintendent
Wilson to hand in his resignation to the Yard. In the
detective story he travels fastest who travels alone.
Father Ronald Knox's Miles Bredon is attached to an
insurance company—an ingenious compromise. When
the detective is, so to say, a free agent, he gains the
awe-inspiring eclecticism of the connoiseur. He refuses
to " take up " any cases but the most baffling and the
most dangerous. In *The Five Orange Pips*, Holmes,
who is interviewing a client, says :—

> " I beg that you will draw your chair up to the
> fire and favour me with some details as to your case."
> " It is no ordinary one."
> " None of those which come to me are. I am the
> last Court of Appeal."

But, you may object, the detective has frequently
a retinue of skilled experts, photographers, scientists,
Baker Street boys, Tinkers and Nippers. If this betrays
a confidence in organised investigation, why not substitute for them the police and be done with it ? My
answer is that the introduction of a trained staff for
the detective is a lamentable confession of weakness.

It is an unnecessary appendage except in those stories where action is everything and where the detective needs a bodyguard against the onslaught of criminal gangs.

Thorndyke gives us yet another reason for this rivalry in *A Silent Witness* :—

> " The reason that I ask is this : the machinery of the police is adjusted to professional crime—their methods are based on ' information received.' . . . But in cases of obscure, non-professional crime the police are at a disadvantage. The crimal is unknown to them ; there are no confederates from whom to get information ; consequently they have no starting point for their inquiries. They can't create clues."

5

> " A reader beginning a detective story has two methods open to him in following the narrative. He may regard it simply as a tale, and not trouble his head about the solution of the mystery until he reaches it in due course at the final chapter. Or he may treat the book as an exercise in reasoning and pit himself against the author in an attempt to work out the mystery for himself."—J. J. CONNINGTON.

Having surmounted these three chief objections, our business is to get the horse in front of the cart and attempt to describe some of the positive attributes of the detective story. In its simplest form the detective story is a puzzle to be solved, the plot consisting in a logical deduction of the solution from *the existing data*. In this statement of the subject I am not unconscious of the implications of the language I have adopted. For I am insisting that the construction is essentially synthetic and scientific. Perhaps herein lies the detective story's attraction to E. M. Wrong's " highly educated " people, and also the failure of some of the cleverest detective stories when expressed through the media of the stage and the screen. Note that even in my italics I am vague ; I do not say, for example, when the data begin to exist.

The detective story is, then, a problem ; a dramatic problem, a " feather to tickle the intellect." The basic element is rational theorising. In *The Adventure of the Copper Beeches* Sherlock Holmes takes Dr. Watson to task for not confining himself to a bare record of the logical synthesis, " that severe reasoning from cause to effect."

> " If I claim full justice for my art, it is because it is an impersonal thing—a thing beyond myself. Crime is common. Logic is rare. Therefore, it is upon the logic rather than upon the crime that you should dwell. You have degraded what should have been a course of lectures into a series of tales."

The problem itself is of a curious and complex kind. Only at the beginning is it simple and defined. Thereafter it is a chameleon, changing colour as every page is turned. Our difficulties multiply ; the problem is modified, then changed out of all knowing. Whereas we started with the simple question, Who killed So-and-So ? we have now, in addition, to account for an alibi, or—more welcome labour, to find one. Every chapter brings in fresh information. We cannot say at such and such a place in the story, " Now that I have my data, I can sit back in my chair and argue it out as Descartes argued out his philosophical principles."

Suppose we take up for a moment the attitude of the disgruntled reader :—

" You rather presume on your cleverness, Mr.

Author. You may steal a march on me, but is it by fair methods ? You start by giving me a fact—the murder. You set me the problem of finding the murderer, but I must ask no questions. You tell me the victim was found *in articulo mortis* with his left hand firmly grasping the third waistcoat button ; and that of two glasses of beer found on the table one was left unfinished—a fact which proves the murdered man was neither a gentleman, nor a man of taste, as the beer happened to be . . . (well, your own brand, plus commission). In ninety-nine cases out of a hundred these homely touches will have nothing to do with your solution. When I am trying to have a morbid interest in the corpse—its dimensions and attitude— you whisk me off to fresh woods. You introduce me as fast as you can to your *dramatis personæ*—as though I were royalty and had so many handshakes to accomplish in so many seconds. Then you seem to fasten with some injustice on one of this motley crowd. In an insinuating way you ask : ' If he was not drinking beer with the murdered man on the night of the murder, where was he ? ' You seem to forget that there are some people who do not prefer to account for their actions between ten and twelve o'clock of a Friday night.

" Next you set me puzzling my wits why your blessed detective has gone to Paris. You see I'm the actuality of the ' legal myth '—the reasonable man. If your detective goes off to Paris without a word to a soul—even to his accommodating landlady—well, I'm bound to think the worst.

" You set me the problem of finding out the why, the how and the wherefore of this murder. You won't for a minute let me go the resonable way about it. You are as evasive as a Hyde Park orator. You only give me pinches of information, and slake my curiosity by throwing me the golden apples of fresh problems easier of solution, and for that reason more momentarily attractive. Sometimes these are connected with the main issue—but not always. Small wonder then if towards the end you succeed in bamboozling me. But if I had my way. . . ."

And let us suppose the author deigns to reply :—

"But why should you ? In the first place you assume that I am setting *you* a problem. If you choose to identify yourself with my detective, you are responsible for any displeasure you may experience. At the very least, you cannot cavil at his methods or mine. Your diatribe is neither here nor there. I do not tabulate a series of theories (all founded on some fraction of fact) and ask you to place them in a list of popularity and then write you a cheque for £1000. I have my own and very excellent formula for administering the short, sharp shock at the unexpected dénouement. You are being rather stupidly annoyed because you are not cleverer than you are—that is in being able to read my thoughts."

Obviously we can only have sufficient evidence when the problem is solved. The solving of the problem virtually means complete knowledge of its attendant circumstances. But once given that, there is no problem. Yet a little knowledge, though it may be dangerous, is often a very blissful state. We are thrown on our resources, now to hazard a guess, now to use our intuition, now to answer the author back in his own coin. You see, the problem is changing again. We begin to examine the author's technique : and here, as we shall see later, we have the slender aid of the canons of our Muse to restrain the author's diabolical legerdemain. We have now really two problems.

(1) How is the author in the habit of disposing of his problems ?

(2) How can we apply this knowledge to the problem in hand ?

In one sense the problem is thus not a problem at all, but a host of problems depending on knowledge not only proper to the mystery but also extraneous to it. In another sense it is not strictly a problem at all, but a piece of grand bluff. Even although we can spot the villain, we cannot know the steps. There are mercifully, however, degrees of probability which serve as a guide to the solution ; and we do emphatically regard them as a satisfactory substitute. We scrap the intermediate steps and boast we are in at the kill.

6

" I see, Madame, that you have a *roman policier*. You are fond of such things ? "

" They amuse me," Katherine admitted.

" They have a good sale always, so I am told. Now why is that, eh, Mademoiselle ? I ask of you as a student of human nature—Why should that be ? "

" Perhaps they give one the illusion of living an exciting life," she suggested.—AGATHA CHRISTIE—*The Mystery of the Blue Train.*

Let us now turn our attention to the other principal element in the detective story which has been labelled " the sensational element," but which, owing to the base connotation of that term, you may prefer to call the romantic or even the artistic element. Mental gymnastics are not sufficient to warrant the widespread popularity of our genre. Jaded business men or imaginative office boys are not so keen as all that on mind culture. The puzzle can be overdone, and it is fatal to deprive it of its trappings. Thus *The Baffle Book* by Lassiter Wren and Randle McKay, and similar volumes, are only for the distracted host when the guests are proving troublesome. Herein the crime and the data are provided, and one has merely to take a pencil and " furiously to think "—or crib by looking at the end of the book (upside down). One ingenious firm of publishers, putting their shirts on human nature, tried out a scheme whereby they sealed up the latter half of their mystery stories, and undertook to refund the money for the book if the reader returned it to them with the seal intact. Such is the puzzle fever !

But we must have some more primitive attraction, to serve as an antithesis. This we find in the setting, which is painted at times with an imagination so indifferent to fact and possibility that it reduces the total result to a lurid chaos. In this respect the detective story has just outgrown the penny dreadful. Mountains do not divide Sherlock Holmes from Sexton Blake. But where the penny dreadful rushes in, our Muse is well advised to tread warily. Excitement may be had without the wholesale dissipation of anarchy, and romance without its toll of victims. Mr. Chesterton has boldly called the atmosphere of this setting " the poetry of modern life." It is unnecessary to dwell on its familiar effects—the dangers lurking in darkened alleys ; the mystery of a large city at night ; the secrets and the tragedies it harbours ; the perpetual all but annihilation of law and order ; the hero-detective as the saviour of society.

It is merely a recognition of dramatic values. Take first of all the character of the villain. Our writer of detective fiction is naïvely emphatic in his repetition of the fact that his detective's opponent is no " common crook." And so with a gay will he sets out to people the world with Calibans turned geniuses, whom a streak of madness debars from becoming the legislators of the world. It is not so much an attempt to make some begrudging allowance for evil—to which after all he is professionally indebted—that induces our author to depict these arch-fiends as art collectors, musicians and scientists. Rather he is for Art's sake a zealous *advocatus diaboli* ; he is raising evil to an artistic plane.

Mr. F. Wills Crofts in a paragraph in his *Inspector French and the Cheyne Mystery* pours scorn on these tales of the jeopardising of civilisation ; of gunpowder plots ; of stolen plans ; of the discovery of deadly poisons ; of the " Napoleons of crime " sitting in their spiders' webs, spreading out their " vast tentacles "— the while they plan delirious dreams of harnessing world power. But so often do we stumble in the dark on lonely mansions which hold some diabolical secret, so often are we held close prisoners by their desperate denizens, and such relish do we take in our predicament, that we cannot—to be honest with ourselves— welcome Mr. Crofts's attitude. Surely the compelling reason for our delight is a sense of the dramatic, and the higher the stakes played for, the more is it intensified. Should, however, this explanation fail to satisfy the realist, we must be content to submit the criterion of *excitement* as a substitute. Excitement can only be rated by its degree. If the aim of the author is merely to arouse excitement, he is justified in choosing any means to achieve his object.

Similarly with the death of the villain. It is rightly felt bad artistry to pack him off to the gallows. Few

murderers in the detective story are sentenced at the
Old Bailey, and in only one story that I have read
has there been a description of the execution. "Sapper"*
has confessed the difficulty which he experienced in
getting rid of Carl Peterson for good and all. An arrest
as the final event is tame ; a reticent silence, implying
that the Law is " taking its course," is unsatisfactory.
The truth of the matter is that we expect the villian
to make a " good end." He has been responsible for
some share in our entertainment. Let him choose the
manner of his death, and die " like a gentleman."
The films have robbed him of one means of demise—
the motor smash ; and Melodrama dislikes the familiar.
Let us have, then, just a suspicion of the Old Lyceum.
Where is heard the " jingle of the bracelets," there
must there also be the " fetid breath of almonds ! "

After a moment's thought on this two-fold division
of the problem and the setting, I am induced to make
a further division on the same lines, but this time
a division of the public that reads detective stories.
Like all generalisations it is only a half-truth, but here
it is for what it is worth. The average male reader
reads the detective story for the problem, the female
reader for the excitement of the setting. The man
in the street loves a problem. There is always an
excuse to solve it round the corner. Not that he is
too practical of imagination to snap his fingers at
suspense ; but murders on paper do, as a rule, amuse
rather than excite him. His is the enthusiasm of the
cross-word fiend, as it were, spread out a bit.

Not so with Woman. " Is it worth while ? " says
Miss Emancipated, and in her earnestness stays not
for any answer. Is there love ? And we must confess
there is more cupidity than Cupid. Is there fashionable
controversy, religious, social or sexual ? And we are

* In the Bulldog Drummond stories by H. C. McNeile.—E. F. B.

shamed into admitting that the only kind of controversy she will be likely to find will be between an " impossible creature " and a stupid policeman on the properties of red sandstone. Not a triumphant emergence from the inquisition.

Well, we can be superior and blame the inquisition. One can blame Woman's proverbial illogicality, and say she has not the patience to argue out the problem. Personally, I often wonder which attitude is the more enjoyable, that of the active participator or that of the passive spectator—in view of the nature of the problem. As far as my own experience goes that peculiar property of woman, intuition, fails disastrously on the touchstone of detective fiction. Even her guesses are unusually wide of the mark—possibly because the mystery monger is too much of a rationalist to accept the myth !

But the most obvious reason for Woman's indifference to the intellectual fireworks is her delight in the emotional values. To every woman who prefers the problem there are at least four who prefer the shocker. Woman loves to be thrilled and to have her knees banging each against either like one of Mr. Frankau's heroines. The doubting Thomas I would advise to go to a cinema where a mystery film is being screened or to a theatre where a crook drama is being staged, and to listen if he has not the indecency to watch. Perhaps there is some other less stupid reason for these gasps and sudden twitchings. If there is, I congratulate these victims of hysteria, and envy their escorts.

7

" Do you really think that murder went out with peri-
wigs ? " asked Dent ; " or is it your contention that they
are invented by the Press to supply headlines ? "—FRANCES
NOYES HART—*Hide in the Dark.*

It is time in parenthesis to say a few words about
murder. I have been assuming all along that the
proper subject of detection in literature is murder, as
being the consummation of crime ; while all other
forms, theft, blackmail, larceny, arson, abduction and
the like should scarcely come within its province, as
not meriting " the grand manner." This may appear
heresy in view of the paucity of murders in the Sherlock
Holmes tales ; but, it should be remembered, we have
here to deal with just these artistic and dramatic
values to which reference has been made. From an
æsthetic point of view, the theft of a Rajah's diamond
remains a base act, on a par with the pilfering of a
string of Ciro pearls. With murder it is different ;
we are on a higher plane. " The base element," wrote
Schiller of murder, " disappears in the terrible."
Where there is no murder, it almost seems like wasting
the detective's valuable time.

Van Dine is reported in an interview[1] to have said
that he considered " murder " the strongest word in
the English language. No other word was " so dramatic,
so gripping, so compelling." For that reason he uses
it in the title of each of his books !

On the subject of murder it is well to go back to
De Quincey.

---

[1] Mr. Mark Larkin's *The Philosophy of Crime—Photoplay Magazine.*
This further quotation may also be of interest. " Also he (Van
Dine) resorts to another idiosyncrasy in devising his titles. The
proper noun in each title must contain six letters—six, no more,
no less." *The* BENSON *Murder Case ; The* CANARY *Murder Case ;
The* GREENE *Murder Case ; The* BISHOP *Murder Case* (also *The*
SECRET *Murder Case*).

" People," he says, " begin to see that something more goes to the composition of a fine murder than two blockheads to kill and be killed—a knife—a purse —and a dark lane. Design, grouping, light and shade, poetry, sentiment, are now deemed indispensable to attempts of this nature. And again :

" The world in general are very bloody-minded ; and all they want is a copious effusion of blood ; gaudy display is enough for *them*. But the enlightened connoisseur is more refined in his taste."

Here, then, we have a beginning ; and for the rest— *exit in mysterium*. We must have a murder and it must be well done. As enlightened connoisseurs the question, What constitutes a good murder ? must give us pause. Obviously the more artistic a murder, the more artistic in one sense will be the detection of the murderer ; for the artistry of a murder involves to some extent the immunity of the murderer from detection. Now, despite this correspondence of æsthetic values, the principles determining the murder perfect *per se*, and those determining the perfect murder of detective fiction are somewhat different, just as the latter differs, for example, from the ideal press murder.

In his rulings on the " principles " to which the man of sensibility looks in gauging the artistry of a murder, De Quincey gives us three heads, (1) the kind of person murdered ; (2) the place where, and (3) the time when.

(1) As regards the first, he considers that the murdered man should not be a villain, and follows with the attractive corollary that he should not be a public man either. His former argument is this. If the murdered man be a villain it is just possible that he was himself contemplating murder when he was struck down. This robs the murder of all its

pathos. Now the interest of the writer of detective fiction in the morality of the murdered man varies according to his purposes. For example, he may argue thus :—

" I shall be conventionally simple. I shall increase the reader's desire to have justice done by appealing to this preliminary pathos—parent of vengeful wrath. I shall, therefore, stress the unimpeachability of the victim's morals. The trick always works in the magazines."

Or he may argue thus : " A railway journey or a Saturday night are not the most fitting occasions for an indulgence in pathos. My reader is likely to have as little pity for my victim as I have myself—and I have none. Supposing on the contrary I renounce pathos, and make my murdered man a thorough scoundrel, what can I gain in this equation ? Why, I shall simply float on motives. My characters will vie with each other to have the glory attached to them of ridding the world of a pest to society. I can also work out a happy ending, and incidentally collar the film rights."

Or he may argue in yet anohter way : " I shall trade on the old crux of morality and its semblance. I shall bestow the mythical ring of Gyges on the corpse. Thereby I shall cultivate my reader's righteous indignation, while flummoxing him as to the motive. Then, at my own pleasure, I shall turn the tables.

(2) Place where. Most writers have a preference for staging their murders in the library. It is dignified ; it is homely. The corpse sits bolt upright at the desk, or sprawls over the blotting pad. The library incidentally opens on to a verandah. The folding windows are locked. A Virginia creeper climbs up the walls outside. Corpses have occasionally been stowed *sub*

mensa ; but such humour on the part of the murderer can only be regarded as rather coarse. Cupboards form convenient receptacles, and bathrooms, had it not been for the French Revolution, would have had their points. A murder in a railway carriage leaves too much to chance, and the space is abominably confined.

The murder in a detective story should come unexpectedly ; unexpectedly that is to those concerned. It should also be committed in the last place in the world you would expect it to be. Thus, a murder in the grotesque place has additional virtue. It surprises, it amuses, it takes us by storm.

Imagine a murder in a music shop, in Selfridge's bargain basement, in a parish hall, at the Grocers' Exhibition. After all the golf course takes some beating. It is an ideal depository. And what a joy to lay a corpse dead on the pin at the sixteenth. Some noble souls go through life with the fervent desire on their lips that when their day comes they may be taken away after a daisy down the fairway ! Indeed, if the writers of detective fiction consulted the wishes of some of their victims, the golf course would be much more popular even than it is at present as the setting.

(3) As regards time when and other circumstances De Quincey has little to say. " The good sense of the practitioner has usually directed him to night and privacy "—a sentiment with which we are probably in agreement. In this category we must include also the means ; the motive ; the attendant circumstances ; the presence or more likely the absence of witnesses— all the facts material to the unravelling of the plot. Naturally, the means and the motive are the most important. Miss Sayers has given us an attractive

list of the "unexpected means"—"poisoned tooth-
stoppings, shaving brushes inoculated with dread
disease . . . poisoned boiled eggs . . . electrocution
by telephone—hypodermic injections shot from air
guns." But novelty's reign is usually short-lived,
and the day of secret African poisons has passed. Of
the motive it would be safe to premise that it should
be (1) natural, and (2) adequate. It should spring from
the primary and elemental emotions of jealousy, envy,
fear, covetousness and the like, and the murderer
should have some cause however slight for harbouring
these passions. He should not, for example, commit
murder for the fun of it, or from some trivial pique.
Van Dine makes the following catalogue of primary
motives for murder (1) murders for profit ; (2) murders
for jealousy ; (3) murders for revenge ; (4) murders for
ambition ; (5) abnormal sex murders.

Well, we have made some progress. We have decided
to have a murder. And let us have no beating about
the bush, no subsequent disappearance or resuscitation
of the corpse. That would be gross anticlimax. Father
Ronald Knox should really have known better in
Footsteps at the Lock. Further we shall probably agree
with Macbeth—though we disregard his hypothesis—
that

" 'Twere well it were done quickly."

Mr. Bancroft's long and halting proem to the murder
in the book version of *The Ware Case* tends to destroy
our interest in it when it does come. Logically, the
murder is the First Act, and the greatest economy can
be used in the so-called " creation of atmosphere,"
for the reader is already keyed. Whoso considers the
detective story beastly and morbid can put that in

his pipe and smoke it. Notice how Mr. Chesterton goes to work in *The Three Tools of Death* :—

> " But there came out of him a cry which was talked of afterwards as something unnatural and new. It was one of those shouts that are horribly distinct even when we cannot hear what is shouted. The word in the case was ' Murder.' But the engine driver swears he would have pulled up all the same if he had heard only the dreadful and definite accent, and not the word."

The unity of the plot should not be destroyed by a succession of murders. It is repulsive to the " enlightened connoisseur " to have to

> " Look on the tragic loading of this bed."

We may, indeed, grant the criminal a score of murders to his credit ; the more the merrier, provided our evidence for them is mere hearsay. Even in a life of crime distance lends enchantment. But a repetition of murders within the scope of a single plot, as in Mr. Arthur B. Reeve's *The Exploits of Elaine* or Mr. Edgar Wallace's *The Green Archer*, is monotonously episodic. It is, as Mr. Darlington would say : too " bloomin' 'olesale."

8

" What I always want to know," put in Mrs. Donovan, " is how the ideal detective story ought to be written. Should the author put himself in the place of the criminal, determined to commit the crime, yet determined to conceal it, and so work through the plot backwards ? or should he plunge at once into an inexplicable situation or start inventing plausible explanations of it." RONALD KNOX : *Sanctions*.

We have discovered two ingredients in the detective

story—the problem and the setting. We started the
ball rolling by positing the perpetration of a satisfactory
murder. We have now to fill in some of the details.
Three main emotional elements are distinguishable in
the detective story—the elements of excitement, of
bewilderment, and of surprise. Of these the first is
common, but in a variety of degrees, to all fiction.
In the detective story it ought to be at white heat.
The quick development of the plot, the interplay of
the characters, the lurid background, the final solution
of the mystery with the detective's triumphant
Eureka, all contribute to this effect. The element of
bewilderment is caused obviously by the nature of the
problem. We cannot tell at once who the murderer is.
Even if we claim to have intuitional powers, we shall
experience some difficulty in finding a satisfactory
motive for the murderer. This bewilderment of ours,
be it added, is not always appeased and satisfied as
the writer considers it ought to be. As regards the
element of surprise the detective story may claim an
advantage over fiction in general. Fiction, like government schemes, tends to work out according to plan ;
its conclusions are for the most part foreseen because
they are the natural outcome of character and circum-
stance. In the detective story the important characters
are not usually labelled, and the circumstances are
shrouded in mystery, so that the unexpected is always
happening. Unexpected, only in the sense that we have
nothing to inform us of what is likely to happen next.

How is the plot evolved ? Commonsense will tell
us that it is bound to be a painstaking process, a
putting together of a jig-saw puzzle, rather than the
sudden spontaneity of the poet—the sublime unity of
form and matter, and so forth. It is a cold, calculating
business, cruelly selective—for the author has to

choose between a number of roads all leading to the same place and of more or less equal length and gradient. And in this constructive process he has to be ever so circumspect or his edifice will begin to wobble, or—to change the figure—his cat will come tumbling out of the bag. Disparage, if you will, the limitations of his art, his meanderings in the labyrinth of the plot with the Minotaur of the Obvious, Sensationalism and his other enemies awaiting him at every corner.

Mr. John Buchan in *The Three Hostages* has suggested what must strike one as a singularly happy-go-lucky method for plot construction. The author takes a certain number of incongruous subjects—a Jew's harp, let us say for the sake of argument, a potato patch and a steam roller, and he then proceeds to establish a connection between them. A prolific writer of detective fiction naïvely admitted that his inspiration was due to his typewriter. So long as his fingers grasped the pen in the approved style his mind simply failed to function, but as soon as ever his fingers felt the keyboard, inspiration came to him simply oozing thousands of words. I have heard, too, of an author who constructed so mysterious a problem that (when the time came) he could not for the world solve it himself. Generally speaking it seems reasonable to suppose that the average detective story writer must start with one (supposedly) original idea which he proceeds to work up—this idea in eight cases out of ten being concerned with the actual perpetration of the crime. The process of detection will then be built up backwards. This is naturally a point which we shall have to discuss in greater detail in particular instances.

Be that as it may, the solution of the plot consisting virtually in the shifting of the relative position of the

characters to each other in the light of the murder,
it is the author's business to try to screen the criminal
for as long as possible, and thus to contend with the
reader's powers of identification by drawing before
him a continual stream of red herrings. It is his
business, for that is what his public expects of him.
And what delight his public derives from its realisation
now and again that they are red herrings ! And what
self-gratification in the boast, " You can't hoodwink
me!" The author, recognising his public's perspicacity,
can afford to be patronising and to give it some rope
provided only he can deceive it over the final issue.
But to the Red Herrings—specious and alluring—
our writer must pay his court.

Let us take A, B, C, D, as four principal characters
amongst whom our suspicions may be equally divided
after the murder. The commonest procedure is what
is known as double bluff or double-cross. A is made
to attract our suspicions first ; next B and C temporarily
appear as potential criminals ; then D, who has
hitherto been eating his eggs and bacon, and been
behaving in an exemplary fashion, is most foully
incriminated. And when we imagine his guilt is all
but confirmed, back we go to the laughing unsuspected
A. This is a scheme to which most detective story
writers have at some time or another a very strong
leaning. Of course, even with four principals several
variations are possible. A, as often as not the family
lawyer, may caper genteelly in the foreground during
the whole of the action while B, C and D are in turn
made his scapegoats. Suspicion should be fairly
evenly distributed. The more pigs in pokes that the
author carries about with him the more fun for the
reader. But when one or two characters get more
than their proper share of suspicion—well, it becomes

too patently obvious. When we speak of these suspects, it should be borne in mind that they may either be characters who are in a temporary disgrace to suit the author's purpose, or on the other hand those who for all their sheep's clothing do look unconscionably like wolves. So, if the author is as ingenious as Mrs. Agatha Christie, he can play a double game with the reader by establishing a subtle intercommunication between the sheep and the wolves travelling incognito to the forest and the fold.

I must say I have a special liking for those tales where one's field as a reader is to some extent determined and marked down. Supposing the circumstances make it necessary that the murder was committed by one staying in a certain house, one's attention is thus focused on a fixed number of people. This narrowing down of the possibles serves in a curious way to make the puzzle harder. You no longer try to reason on the assumption that anything is possible, but to choose out of a number of possibles the right solution.

It is with certain misgivings that I now proceed to attempt to summarise from the main trend of detective literature the phases of the action of the orthodox plot. The following structure is not intended to be in any way either a necessary or an exemplary one. It is only a typical one, and, from being typical, naturally a successful one.

(1) Murder most foul !

(2) Introduction of the characters. First suspects, these being either (a) the author's red herrings, or (b) those characters whom the reader suspects intuitively.

(3) The Inquest.

(4) Clues and False Trails. The investigation carried

out by the police (or less often by a bombastic amateur) fails.

(5) Impasse.

(6) The detective " takes up the case ; " his novel line of investigation.

(7) New Suspects ; i.e. those characters whom the reader is supposed to conclude that the detective suspects.   In reality, of course, the latter suspects somebody quite different.

(8) Dénouement. The detective's Eureka.

(9) Explanations.

The eleventh hour dénouement is the most satisfying. Mr. E. C. Bentley's *Trent's Last Case* shows with what effect the dénouement may be delayed. An explanation covering thirty or forty pages, either going over old ground or consisting of an archæological research into ancestral crooks and crimes, is intolerable anticlimax.

9

" The rigour of the game."

Criticism is at bottom a statement of personal feelings of appreciation or of censure. But it involves something more, and hereby criticism saves its face. Our feelings must be accounted for, attributed to certain elements in the work criticised. This is nothing else than the realisation of a code of rules to which the work under consideration must in general conform. Now it is a fair submission that the stricter the rules and the more stringently they are enforced, the higher will be the standard of play. If we admit this—as presumably we must—it will not be difficult to show that the detective story has a just claim to be a work of art.

To the methods of treatment in the detective story there seems no limit. The mystery may be left—if solved—yet unfinished, as in Mr. J. S. Fletcher's *The Mysterious Chinaman.* The detective may prove to be the criminal—a fashionable variation at the present time. Again the murder may turn out to be no murder at all, but a hoax. The story may even be told by the criminal, so that as far as the reader is concerned there is no mystery. An infinite number of variations is possible, yet I insist that there is, and must be in the better detective stories, this common adherence to a set of rules.

I do not wish to be saddled with the task of tabulating these rules. For when one embarks on this task, one is immediately aware of the distressing fact that one is merely emphasising a heap of truisms. This is due to the fact that we take up a detective story in a very definite frame of mind. Let me make myself a little clearer. When we read a detective story in which there is a murder, we expect to be told eventually who the murderer was, and how he murdered his victim. We expect that all the details of the evidence which did or did not puzzle us should be explained. We expect also a host of other things—that the murderer shall pay for his crime : that the detective's theory shall be the right one : that there shall be a detective, whatever those who consider *Edwin Drood* a first-class detective novel say to the contrary. And so on and so forth.

To put it in another way, the reader expects the writer to co-operate with him to some extent. This question has been aptly described as an " ethical " one. The average reader has a very definite idea that the author should play the game with him : and he is instantly up in arms if the canons of fairplay are violated. What he means by this is open to doubt. But probably, he means that the author has solved his problem in a way in which it was impossible for him to solve it. The whole process of detection is based on evidence. From the author's point of view the easiest procedure is to give the reader evidence, evidence, and again evidence : for it is easier to deceive where there is a surfeit of it than where there is a scarcity. This also happens to fit in with the reader's way of thinking. But if the detective should calmly pocket a bullet that he found on the carpet without saying a word to a soul, and then calmly proceed to reconstruct the crime from this valuable clue, the irate reader feels bound to claim a penalty. For had he been there he might have found the clue himself. Similarly he feels that to keep the villain under lock and key—a relative from abroad, a rough diamond from the colonies, whose existence has barely been mentioned, then suddenly to bring him to light at the denouement, is a piece of glaring insincerity. To abstain from recording vital evidence is a technical weakness. Vital evidence should be placed in the shop window.

The average reader is so far justified ; but, before allowing him to have it all his own way, we should consider for a moment his *average* attitude of mind in reading a detective story. In the first place he is at liberty to, and invariably does, suspect every character in the book with possibly an exception or two. Allowing for this fact an impartial judge might on occasion describe the irate reader's plea for fair-play as an instance of sour grapes. Then again the reader is possibly familiar with the individual technique of the author he is reading. If he is reading Mr. Edgar Wallace, he probably sees through the attractive veneer of the villain. In Mr. A. E. W. Mason's yarns he is ready *chercher la femme*, and so forth. So you see the detective is handicapped in some ways. He has got to get the better of his creator. He has on occasion to lose his individuality without losing his identity.

It is just this discipline that justifies the consideration of the detective story as an independent genre. For without this restraint it merges into the other types of fiction, such as the adventure story, the spy story, and the picaresque novel, whose structure cannot be so clearly delineated. These other forms may bear at times the very strongest resemblance to the detective story. It can easily be seen that the " hunt " or " chase' theme is very much akin to the trapper-like pursuit of the detective. E. M. Wrong saw a close similarity between Mr. John Buchan's *The Twenty-Nine Steps* and *The Power House* and the orthodox detective story.

Again we may have the tale of the combat-to-the-death between Law and Anarchy, where the forces and objectives of the two camps are openly divulged. We note the same movements as in the sensational detective story : attack, pursuit and capture. Only the hares and the hounds regularly change sides.

Yet another kindred theme is where the Sword of Damocles is held over the hero for the greater part of the book. He learns by chance of an incriminating secret. A letter in the post asks him politely but firmly to mind his own business. He pays no attention to this, but is surprised to find a second warning, this time couched in language more succinct, under his porridge plate. Of course, he is too pig-headed not to disregard this too. Finally comes the threat of immediate annihilation. Then things begin to happen.

As a sop to the adventurous Adam this theme is frequently introduced into more or less orthodox detective stories. Sherlock Holmes, you remember, after staging his comeback, had the very devil of a time with the last of the Moriartyans. Hourly he stalked in the shadow of death. But though the detective is from time to time threatened with death, he has rarely, in the best circles, to run the gauntlet of organised attempts at assassination. Father Brown does not find bombs in his coal scuttle. In nine cases out of ten, Poirot would be shocked if poisoned arrows were shot at him through the skylight. E. M. Wrong thought that the reason for this *motif* is that the criminal should give the detective a run for his money. Rather it is that the criminal should give his reading fans a run for their money, for the sedentary life of the detective is not yet out of fashion.

9

" Our ancestors took a great interest in homicide. . . . But it was sensation, rather than reasoning they sought, and crude sensation is better provided by real crimes than by imaginary."—E. M. WRONG—Introduction to *Tales of Crime and Detection.*

There remains one question which had better be answered before we come to grips with our subject. Really, it is the conclusion of our argument. What are we to regard as the true proportion of reason and sensation ? We shall see that, historically, the pendulum swings fairly evenly in either direction. There have been thrillers pure and simple ; there have also been puzzles, possessing as little sensational action as a novel of Trollope's. There have also been hybrids, unfailingly attractive because of the compromise. But it was our view that the detective story must be first and foremost a problem. The main ingredient must be logic. If there is to be sensation—and we would not for worlds banish it—it should *seem* rather incidental. All the same, there is quite enough excitement in a problem without calling in the aid of death, crape and flying squads. The logical detective story is the finer form because it recognises a technique. The highbrow form wins.

CHAPTER II

THE HISTORY OF THE DETECTIVE STORY

IT would be as tedious as it would be futile to delve into the pages of the *Apocrypha* or *Herodotus* in an attempt to discover the true and authentic origin of the detective story. It is rather the fashion of anthologists of stories of detection to rake up the tales of Susannah, of Rhampsanitus, and of Hercules and Cacus. I take it that their good taste, certainly not the logic of their method, prevents them from hailing Solomon as a kind of patriarchal detective and the Delphic Oracle as a primitive Scotland Yard. But why they refrained from billing Hamlet as a first-class intuitive detective of the continental school is beyond explanation, unless they fought shy of the family scandal.

You see the antecedents of the various *motifs* that are combined in our genre are time old. The puzzle motif is as ancient as the Prophets. The Erinyes theme—revenge relentlessly tracking down the wicked —is even anterior to literature. "The East," Mr. Valentine Williams once wrote, "has countless legends descriptive of the elucidation of mysteries by means of acute observation. In *Zadig*, in the anecdote of the recovery, by means of deduction, of the missing spaniel and the straying horse, Voltaire possibly utilised some of these stories.

"Kindred tales are recited to this day by the public story-tellers in the Cairo bazaars and on the great

Square of the Dead, ringed round by the snowy Atlas crests at Marrakesh, in Morocco. Similar stories existed among the Redskins of North America and Canada, based on their tracking skill."

Ethnologists could doubtless quote you example after example from folk-lore where evil brute force succumbs to wily virtue. Polyphemus always comes out under-dog. But the combination of these and similar themes, their subordination to the discipline of such rules as have already been enumerated, and the repetition of the central idea of the detection of crime by an investigator especially skilled in that pursuit—all this means the creation of a new genre.

If we are going to look for antecedents or family connections to give our Muse some social standing, perhaps it would not be too fanciful to regard the detective story as the modern substitute for the historical novel. The historical novel—sad though it may be to admit it—is already in its senescence ; its virility is spent. Prior to the industrial revolution the imagination was not stretched so taut as it is now, when it is required to contemplate the events of younger centuries. Conditions did not alter so quickly then. Besides the propagation of historical knowledge grows daily more scientific and " documentary," and therefore more matter of fact. The costume pantomime of the motion pictures has also helped to drive the historical novel to a premature dotage.

With the introduction of machinery and the progress of science, a return to the courts of Richelieu or Elizabeth began to seem artificial and vapid. But even with the blessed little niche of literature with which we are concerned modern conditions are not iconoclastic. They offer a splendid background for the creation of a new romance, a romance which is, perhaps, more essentially exciting than the old because it is progressive and prophetic instead of being retrogressive. Jules Verne jumped off the earth and voyaged round the moon. Mr. H. G. Wells stirred up the planets to war. To another group of writers there occurred the thought of the danger that might threaten mankind if the newly harnessed powers of science were subordinated to evil ends. Fortunately, they had a sense of humour and made a joke out of it. The alchemist theme—the philosopher's stone—had put on modern dress.

The detective story has always been up-to-date. It moves with the times, for its background is not altogether devoid of fact. Although the emotional aspects of crime do not change, criminal methods do, and the divorce of fact from fancy would be too strained if complex modern conditions were passed over in preference for a static Erewhon. It strikes one that this elasticity is an important element in keeping the detective story evergreen. The detective story also anticipates before it parodies. And that, too, is droll.

The detective story is not yet a century old. During the years 1840-45 Edgar Allan Poe composed the famous *The Murders in the Rue Morgue, The Purloined Letter*, and *The Mystery of Marie Roget*. America had, in truth, given birth to a new literary genre. Like Athene in the myth, the detective story sprang into being fully armed. But one might have expected that considering its birthplace. The extraordinary thing is that at its very inception, the principles and canons of detective fiction-writing were brilliantly conceived, even with a touch of finality. Let us pause for a moment and attempt to tabulate these canons.

A.—The Characters.

(1) The problems are solved by the hero. An

amateur at the game, he relies successfully on his own methods, which are of course surprisingly original, and overwhelmingly brilliant. In character he is an eccentric recluse.

(2) The stories are related by a hero-worshipping narrator with an inferiority complex, who conveniently draws our attention to the brilliance of his colleague.

(3) The police are unable to solve the problems, thus proving that professionalism is not a congenial subject for art. If somebody must be suspected, then they will suspect the wrong person.

B.—*The Problem.*

(1) *The Murders in the Rue Morgue.* I must ask your leave to quote from Miss Sayers' clever analysis :—

> " Here is, then, a combination of three typical *motifs* : the wrongly suspected man, to whom all the superficial evidence points ; the hermetically sealed death-chamber ; finally, the solution by the unexpected means. . . . In this story also are enunciated for the first time these two great aphorisms of detective science : first, that when you have eliminated all the impossibilities, then, whatever remains, *however* improbable, must be the truth ; and, secondly, that the more *outré* a case may appear, the easier is it to solve."

(2) In *The Purloined Letter* :—

> " We have besides the reiteration, in inverted form, of aphorism No. 2, the method of psychological deduction, and the solution by the formula of the most obvious place."

(3) In *The Mystery of Marie Roget* we have another example of Miss Sayers' aphorism No. 2 in inverted form.

The detective story did not apparently stagger the world. The infant was for twenty years neglected. Poe was too previous for his public. However, Victorian literature was unconsciously preparing the public for its acceptance of the new genre. Sensational literature (one need only mention Dickens and Stevenson) was beginning to enjoy a world-wide popularity. But villainy was still serenely transparent. The criminal had a black moustache and flashing eyes, and was probably called Rashleigh. Uriah Heep had no cast-iron alibis, and Fagin did not favour disguise.

Our scene is now shifted to France where the detective story first put on its long clothes.

In 1866 Gaboriau published his *L'Affaire Lerouge*, which was succeeded shortly afterwards by *Le Dossier 113* (1867), *Le Crime d'Orcival* (1868),* *Monsieur Lecoq* (1869), and a number of more or less melodramatic mysteries. From an historical point of view there are several prominent features in the Gaboriau novels. Their intricacy is one of plot construction rather than of the execution of a mathematically planned crime. To this extent Gaboriau is more human than Poe, but less clever. Again he sought with some success to make his detectives, Monsieur Lecoq and Père Tabaret, living characters. He evidently saw the artistic possibilities in this innovation. But Gaboriau trod warily and was often parsimonious in the plums he gave to his heroes. As regards detection, the art is somewhat retrogressive, and extraneous events have often as large a share in providing the solution as the efforts of the detective. But the mould is gradually being hammered out.

It was only a year after Gaboriau's *L'Affaire Lerouge* was published that the first English full-length detective story appeared—Wilkie Collins's *The Moonstone*.

* *Le Crime d'Orcival* (1867) preceded *Le Dossier no. 113* (1867)—
E. F. B.

My familiarity with *The Moonstone*, at perhaps rather a precocious age, has endeared it to me, and in my criticism of it *purely as a detective story*, I have attempted to discard hyperbole and risk the taunt of disloyalty. It is indeed hard to sponsor the judgments of Miss Sayers and Mr. Bernard Darwin, that *The Moonstone* is the greatest detective story of all. If we are to consider *The Moonstone* as a detective story, dismissing for the nonce the creeps and the thrills, detection must surely be our first criterion, and the detection in *The Moonstone* is not exhibitional. Sergeant Cuff, the detective, makes the deplorable mistake—the mistake of the Lestrades and the stern police—of suspecting the heroine. That is in the extreme of bad taste. True, he makes some amends for it when he is in lighter vein, smoking his cigar or uttering his pantomimic catchwords. But with Sergeant Cuff it is roses, roses all the way : that is his title to immortality. The paradox has been born : the detective with a sensibility greater than his sense. Character begins to rear its head. With Sergeant Cuff one is tempted to associate Mr. Jeffery Farnol's Jasper Shrigg—the Bond Street runner on whom the mantle of Sam Weller has partly fallen. But the stage is not yet set for comedy.

The following paragraph from an article by Mr. Bernard Darwin in *John O'London's Weekly* will please the realist :

> " Incidentally it is interesting to know that some of the sergeant's theories were founded on those of a real live detective. In 1860 there befell the mysterious murder at Road Hill House, for which, five years later, Constance Kent was, on her own confession, sentenced to death. Inspector Whicher, who investigated the murder, always believed Constance to have done it, founding his belief largely on a matter of a missing

night-gown and a washing-book. His theories were laughed to scorn and he retired a disappointed man ; yet it appeared later that he had been right in every particular. Eight years after the Road Murder, Wilkie Collins appropriated this incident of the night-gown and used it most effectively, with Sergeant Cuff for Inspector Whicher and Rosanna Spearman in place of Constance Kent."

Of its class *The Moonstone* must rank as a classic. The themes are still as fresh as ever, and possibly even more popular. The nemesis of the Oriental stone, the shivering sands and all the paraphernalia of the honest thriller have a perennial attraction. It is a curious fact that the Wilkie Collins habit of telling a story by a series of narratives penned by the different characters has not been imitated to any extent by detective story writers. In such a method there are advantages galore.

In France, Gaboriau was succeeded by Fortuné Du Boisgobey. Such novels as *Le Forçat Colonel* (1872), *Le Crime de L'Opéra* (1880), and *Les Mysteres de Nouveau Paris* proved immensely popular. But historically Du Boisgobey did not alter the trend of detective fiction one iota. To this period belong also the works of Miss Anna Katherine Green, a prolific American authoress who is still living. Possibly the most familiar of all her works are *The Leavenworth Case* (1883), which has recently been reprinted, and *The House of the Whispering Pines*. As with Gaboriau and Du Boisgobey there is a preponderance of melodrama.

In 1887 Sherlock Holmes made his first bow in *A Study in Scarlet*.

Two years later came *The Sign of Four*, which shows a marked improvement in Sir Arthur Conan Doyle's plot technique. In the early nineties, 1891-93, the short Sherlock Holmes' tales began their long and only recently curtailed sequence in the *Strand Magazine*. The *Adventures* and the *Memoirs* were the earliest collections of these short stories. In 1902 appeared his best full-length detective novel, *The Hound of the Baskervilles*. Two years later Sherlock Holmes was rescued by a solicitous public from a premature death at the hands of the arch-fiend Moriarty. The result was a further volume of short stories, *The Return of Sherlock Holmes*. In 1915 *The Valley of Fear* was published ; in 1918 *His Last Bow*, and in 1917 *The Case-Book of Sherlock Holmes*.

Historically Conan Doyle owes a two-fold debt to Poe : the detective relies on analysis, and the puzzle is still the kernel. And secondly, he exploited the theme of " the detective's colleague." In his brilliant creation of Dr. Watson he added a second immortal figure to English fiction. In a sense Sir Arthur borrowed also from Gaboriau and Wilkie Collins. He appreciated the fact that the detective was after all the principal character, and for that reason must have a personality.

It is perhaps true to say that Sergeant Cuff and M. Lecoq interest us most when they are amusing. Sherlock Holmes has never quite lost that touch of the ridiculous which belongs to the caricature : but he has in him the stuff of greatness which his predecessors lacked. He always commands respect and admiration ; he is greater than his parodists. The vogue of the super-sleuth has passed, but the position of the great original has never been shaken.

As regards our two-fold division of the detective story into (1) the intellectual, (2) the sensational, Sir Arthur seemed to show a slight preference for the latter. As a writer, he generally believed in swift action, and curiously enough all his full-length Holmes'

tales are "thrillers," the purely analytical element
being very definitely subsidiary. In the short stories,
however, he seemed to stop at the cross-roads. Murder
had frequently to take a back seat, and robbery,
bogus-impersonations, and blackmail have their
innings.

The success of the Sherlock Holmes tales prompted
Mr. Arthur Morrison to try his hand at the game.
Martin Hewitt, Investigator, appeared in 1894, *The
Chronicles of Martin Hewitt* in 1895, and *The Adventures
of Martin Hewitt* in 1896. The series had a warm
reception from the critics. The *National Observer,* for
example, waxed enthusiastic :—

> "We recommend it to bored persons suffering the
> martyrdom of a family party, to harassed persons
> encompassed about with bills, and to cheerful people
> weary of neurotic problems—feeling sure they will
> thank us."

Mr. Morrison based his stories on the Holmes model.
Hewitt is the great investigator with "well-known
powers," while Brett plays the Dr. Watson. A further
point of similiarity is the absence of fair play. These
stories are sound without being brilliant. Possibly
*The Stanway Cameo Mystery, The Case of the Missing
Hand,* and *The Case of the Lost Foreigner* are the pick
of the bunch.

In the naughty nineties diplomacy downed detection.
Politics and politicians had for some reason or other
found their way into light literature. At one end of the
scale were the aristocratic drawing-rooms of Oscar
Wilde : at the other the Monte Carlo Casinos of William
LeQueux and Mr. E. Phillips Oppenheim. The
devotee of sensationalism was rushed hither and thither

over Europe, to finish up without fail at the Riviera—
that home of lost state documents. He rubbed shoulders
with arch-dukes and dowagers : he fell before the
seductive beauty of the Greta Garbo type. The spy
story—sister of the detective story—came into vogue.
Seton Merriman, a careful craftsman, dispensed in *The
Sowers* and *The Vultures* with the novelette conventionalities, and open-air adventure triumphed over
the hot-house romance.

The Oscar Wilde and *Yellow Book* æstheticism was,
however, reflected to a certain degree in our genre
by the publication in 1895 of M. P. Shiel's *Prince
Zaleski*.

Prince Zaleski lives in splendid solitude attended
only by his Æthiopian servant, Ham. The fantastic
apartments of Dupin and Lecoq have nothing of the
bizzarerie of the Russian Prince's retreat :

> " The room was not a large one, but lofty. Even in
> the semi-darkness of the very faint greenish lustre
> radiated from an open censer-like *lampas* of fretted
> gold in the centre of the domed encased roof, a certain
> incongruity of barbaric gorgeousness in the furnishing
> filled one with amazement."

Midst the fumes of the narcotic *cannabis sativae*,
Prince Zaleski is discovered with gemmed chibouque,
an old vellum print of Anacreon in his hands. Shiel
brings him three problems to solve—*The Race of
Orven*, *The Stone of the Edmundsbury Monks*, and *S.S.*
The first two mysteries the Prince clears up without
stirring from his couch. (Telegrams are, of course,
sent to prevent a miscarriage of justice.) In *S.S.* the
Prince has to take a trip to England, and his short
absence almost breaks Ham's heart.

These stories, as Miss Sayers has shown, are examples

of the purely intellectual detective story. Naturally this calls for an effort of concentration. But the Prince is well equipped.

> " He seemed to me—I say it deliberately and with forethought—to possess the unparalleled power not merely of disentangling in retrospect but of unravelling in prospect, and I have known him to relate *coming* events with unimaginable minuteness of precision. He was nothing if not superlative ; his diatribes now culminating in a very *extravaganza* of hyperbole— now sailing with loose wing through the downy, witched, Dutch cloud-heaps of some quaintest tra-montane. Nephelococcugia of thought—now laying down law of the Medes for the actual world of to-day —had ofttime the strange effect of bringing back to my mind the very singular old Epic epithet, ἠνεμόεγ —airy—as applied to human thought."

In addition to his more conspicuous powers of reasoning, the Prince had also a " fineness of intuition." And he certainly enjoyed the sound of his own voice, for he would hang up the action for page after page by delivering homilies on subjects of social philosophy.

These three tales are grotesque in the extreme. The first is a case of inherited mania and suicide, and the Prince is able to establish the innocence of a condemned woman by proving that she had stabbed a corpse and not a living body. The second is a story of the attempts to recover a jewel in the Moonstone vein. *S.S.* (or *The Society of Sparta*) is the most fantastic of the trio. It tells of the efforts of a secret brotherhood to circumvent society's pampering of its weakest, disease-ridden members. Upholding the old Spartan method of eugenics—the exposure of the infants—they waged war against all *mariages-de-convenance*. The Prince solves a capital cipher, disappears mysteriously, and returns as only detectives know how to return. A gesture, and "the activities of the brotherhood are over ! "

Just before the opening of the twentieth century the scientific detective story was born. Mrs. L. T. Meade, the schoolgirl's novelist, in collaboration with Mr. Robert Eustace, sought in collections of short stories such as *The Sanctuary Club*, " to explain by the application of science phenomena attributed to spiritual agencies." Thus most of Bell's cases comprised the laying of ghosts, and it is hardly necessary to add that he discovered a deal of machinery in such supposedly haunted rooms as *The Circular Chamber*.* *The Felwyn Tunnel* is possibly the star story of the collection. Here the deaths of two railwaymen are caused, not, as is supposed, by any human agency, but by Nature in her deadliest mood. Here in very truth we have the prelude to Thorndyke's lectures :—

> "Why, this is a natural escape of choke damp, carbonic acid gas—the deadliest gas imaginable, because it gives no warning of its presence, and it has no smell. . . . An escape of carbonic acid gas is not an uncommon phenomenon in volcanic districts. . . . It has sometimes been known to follow earthquake shocks, when there is a profound disturbance of the deep strata. It is an extremely heavy gas, and would lie at the bottom of a cutting like water."

In *A Handful of Ashes* there is an even closer parallel. From the ashes in a cinerary urn proof positive is reached that the dead man was poisoned. " Whatever salt of uranium was administered, we shall now from the ashes doubtless find it in the form of Oxide U_3O_8 " —which is precisely what they do proceed to find. We shall see later that Dr. Austin Freeman had a weakness for " cremation cases."

* The supernatural aspects are greatly overstated.—E. F. B.

In 1900 the Baroness Orczy's " Old Man in the Corner " first started to unravel " the thread of his discourse," and the ball was temporarily set rolling in another direction, for here the apparent insignificance of a bath-bun-and-glass-of-milk-please detective had triumphed over the staggering greatness of successive villains. The way is made straight for Mr. Chesterton's Father Brown and Mr. Ernest Bramah's Max Carrados.

For the past few years the thriller had been enjoying a vogue. Guy Boothby's Dr. Nikola* had satisfied sensation seekers, and stories like Richard Marsh's *The Death Whistle* were avidly devoured. However, the great bulk of this literature did not belong strictly speaking to our genre. And despite the antics of Dick Donovan there was a somewhat unproductive interval.

The years 1907-11 brought into the field three detectives of the first water. In 1907 Dr. Austin Freeman produced Thorndyke's first case, *The Red Thumb Mark* ; in 1910 Mr. A. E. W. Mason's Hanaud solved the murder problem *At the Villa Rose* ; and the next year Mr. Chesterton launched out into our genre in *The Innocence of Father Brown*. In the history of the detective story the works of these three writers are of some significance ; a significance which is possibly enhanced by the fact that of the triumvirate the two last named were already established authors and had evidently something up their sleeves in making this venture.

Dr. Austin Freeman concerned himself more conscientiously than any of his predecessors with the scientific process of detection ; and certain minutiæ in the data which had been ignored up till then assumed a new significance. Concrete evidence was having its

---

* *A Bid for Fortune, Doctor Nikola, Doctor Nikola's Experiment, Farewell Nikola.*—E. F. B.

day. Mr. Mason's Hanaud is the first great intuitionalist.
Hanaud soon had a colleague in Mr. Chesterton's
Father Brown. Mr. Chesterton recreated the fantastic
atmosphere of Prince Zaleski. But he wisely dis-
countenanced elaboration, and substituted the leaven
of the Chestertonian paradox.

During the same period two important contributions
were made by France—*Le Mystère de la Chambre Jaune*
by Gaston Leroux, in which the police detective
turned out to be the criminal, and the *Arsène Lupin*
tales of M. Maurice Leblanc, which contained an
amusing parody on the Sherlock Holmes-Watson
cliché. In 1913 Mr. E. C. Bentley's *Trent's Last Case*
was the first successful introduction of the love element
into the detective story.

The war period was the detective story's nadir.
The spy story was naturally given first place. An
exception, however, was the American, Arthur B.
Reeve's *The Exploits of Elaine* and its sequels. Even
the old hands at the game found the odds overwhelmingly against them. Owing to the deluge and welter
of blood the murder theme was out of joint, and its
pathetic fallacy was a mockery. People's nerves were
too much set on edge to regard killing in any shape or
form as a subject for recreation. This is perhaps over-
statement, but it goes some way to account for the facts.

The reaction came shortly after the war when
humour was, so to speak, on safer ground. The fact
that the post-war popularity of the detective story
coincided with a world-wide crime wave, was probably
fortuitous. The old brigade joyfully found they had
to look to their laurels. Sherlock Holmes had yet to
sing his swan song. Father Brown and Hanaud were
still in their prime, and Arsène Lupin could not rest
in peace. But a new generation had arisen. Mrs.

Agatha Christie's Hercule Poirot might carry on the tradition of Hanaud, but Mr. Wills Crofts was now to give realism its day. Authentically, a new style was abroad. The "holiday spirit" permeated the underworld and the annals of crime. By this I mean not only that the detective story was written in a lighter vein as an August companion, but also that the characters of the detective story began to treat the murder just as light-heartedly as the reader, and their desire to solve the mystery did not arise from righteous indignation so much as from the cross-word complex. You have only to turn to Mr. A. A. Milne's *The Red House Mystery*, to the works of Mr. G. D. H. and Mrs. Margaret Cole, or to those of Father Ronald Knox. Georgian sophistication has latterly held the stage. The poseur, the dilettante, the Philo Vance of Van Dine or the Lord Peter Wimsey of Miss Sayers began to usurp the prominence of the Wodehouse type of sleuth.

If I were to summarise the main tendencies of this post-war detective story, I would emphasise the popularity of two themes. The first of these I shall call "the Alibi theme." Before the vogue of the "unassailable alibi," if a person in a detective story had an alibi at all, he was *ipso facto* regarded as innocent. The great chance came when Mr. Wills Crofts took advantage of this attitude ; henceforward, the alibi had to be tested by every conceivable line of inquiry. The actual testing of the alibi came to be almost commensurate with the plot. Of course, the "unassailable alibi" might break down through (1) substitution, (2) supposed death and similar contingencies. Therein lay the author's scope. The alibi theme has meant the triumph of the red herrings.

The other theme which is only now passing out of

fashion was the return to " the most unlikely person."
Mr. Edgar Wallace is the chief priest of this revived
cult. Certainly considerable time was allowed to slip
by before the brilliant idea of Gaston Leroux was
imitated. The police detective, as opposed to the hero-
detective, becomes the villain again (v. *The Ringer,
The Crimson Circle, The Bat, Traffic*, etc.). Sometimes
this villain-detective appears in disguise ; but usually
he has bamboozled the administrative heads of the
C.I.D. into promoting him on their staff. (This was
before the reorganisation of Scotland Yard !)

Mass production makes it impossible to give anything like a comprehensive survey. All the schools
were fully represented. Perhaps I shall be pardoned
for choosing at this stage the easiest course—that of
enumerating some of the foremost representatives.
Such a list is not meant to be complete, and omission
will therefore not necessarily signify either negligence
or an error of judgement. In the " rational school "
we have such writers as Mr. Wills Crofts, Miss Sayers,
Canon Whitechurch, Mr. Ernest Bramah and Father
Ronald Knox. Perhaps the last named is the cleverest
and nimblest ; but in his novels there is a depressing
deficiency of action. " Intuitional " detection is
favoured by Mrs. Agatha Christie, Mr. H. C. Bailey
and Mr. Philip Macdonald. ' Lynn Brock ' has stepped
into the shoes of Mr. Bentley and resurrected the
character novel. Of the sensational School, Mr.
Edgar Wallace is by international reputation " the
prince of thrillers." For the purveyance of sensation
he has, however, a very able executive in Mr. Gerald
Fairlie, the Rev. John Ferguson, Mr. John Rhode, Mr.
Leonard Gribble, and Mr. Francis D. Grierson.

The more recent " psychological " method is possibly
an improvement on the " intuitional " ; for it at least

approximates to a science. And latterly, the most successful detective fiction has belonged in whole or in part to this category. Van Dine, the American, is at once its ablest and most amusing exponent. " You deny even the remote possibility of a common thief having murdered the girl ? " his detective, Philo Vance, was once asked. And his reply was, " If a common thief did it, then there's no science of psychology, there are no philosophic truths, and there are no laws of art."

Another innovation has been the presentation of the detective story in the form of a report of a murder trial, as in *The Bellamy Trial*. At the present moment the development of the detective story in this country is along lines now rather stereotyped. Stunting has been somewhat overdone, and as a reaction there is a tendency to introduce snapshot character study, sentimental propaganda, or the more attractive social comedy and satire.

CHAPTER III

EDGAR ALLAN POE

Indeed take it all round, *The Murders in the Rue Morgue*
constitutes in itself almost a complete manual of detective
theory and practice.—DOROTHY SAYERS — Introduction to
Great Short Stories of Detection, Mystery and Horror.

Poe's detective story begins with a few paragraphs of
analysis that set the key for the rest, somewhere in the
immaterial regions of geometry.—ARTHUR RANSOME—*Edgar
Allan Poe, A Critical Study.*

POE'S reputation as a detective novelist rests on his
famous Dupin trilogy, *The Murders in the Rue Morgue,
The Purloined Letter,* and *The Mystery of Marie Roget.
The Murders in the Rue Morgue* won immediate
attention and popularity. In 1846 it was adapted and
translated by two French writers. The two parties
concerned contested the copyright, and the ensuing
litigation brought Poe's name into prominence. It was
thus that Baudelaire came to read Poe and in a letter
to Armand Fraisse he wrote :—

> En 1846 ou 1847, j'eus connaissance de quelques
> fragments d'Edgar Poe ; j'approuvai une commotion
> singulière.

It is a lamentable confession to have to make that
in England Poe's reputation has been somewhat ad-
ventitious. The anthologists have done their best ;
but a *tour de force* of analysis is apt to leave the average
reader cold. Yet Dupin was the parent of Sherlock
Holmes, and the " narrator " the prototype of Dr.

75

Watson. There is certainly good reason for experiencing *une commotion singulière*.

Poe is notoriously a moodish writer. Any one at all conversant with the perfection to which he has wrought in the other *Tales of Mystery and Imagination* the themes of horror and suspense, might well expect to find in his detective stories more than a penchant towards sensationalism—a study, for example, of the psychological vortex of the murderer's emotions after the manner of his own short story, *The Telltale Heart*, or of Stevenson's *Markheim*. He is, as a French critic has called him, "*un ecrivain des nerfs.*" What is the predominant mood of the Dupin trilogy? Mr. Ransome has well expressed it : "The same faculty that made possible the lyrical excellence of his best works, and gave his critical articles their most valuable paragraphs . . . urged him to the solution of cryptograms and the study of handwriting ; and, turning from the solution of puzzles to their manufacture, set him to the composition of acrostic sonnets and to the invention of tales of analysis in which it becomes the material as well as the tool of art, the excitement of reasoning being substituted for that of love or terror." The theme of horror is by no means absent. Your attention has only to be drawn to the description of the tragedy in *The Murders in the Rue Morgue*. Likewise suspense broods over the river scenes in *The Mystery of Marie Roget*. But these emotional themes are subordinated both formally and materially to the strict and rigid motif of analysis. The detective story, from the very first, has been primarily the solution of a problem.

The detective story, following Nature, was born short. These four tales run on an average to about forty pages. It would scarcely be irrelevant to inter-

polate at this point a few words on the relative merits
of the short and the full-length detective story. The
curtailment of the plot in the one, or—if you like—
the expansion of it in the other, means rather more
than a formal difference. Miss Sayers prefers the full-
length novel. Mr Chesterton in *Generally Speaking*
champions the short, and advances this objection
against the former :—

> " The chief difficulty is that the detective story is
> after all a drama of men's false characters rather than
> their real character. The author cannot tell us until
> the last chapter any of the interesting things about
> the most interesting people."

Yet a little knowledge, although dangerous, invariably whets the appetite of inquisitiveness. And
that is something. This question I would, however,
be loath to leave to so uncertain a criterion as that
of personal taste. Let us proceed to examine the
respective wares of Mr. Short and Mr. Long.

The author of the short detective story, with no
elbow room to spare, must devote his attention to the
working out of a single idea, such as an original murder,
a clever impersonation, or a deceitful alibi. And he
must be pretty slick in putting his detective on to the
right clue. His detective—let alone the reader—will
have little or no time to waste in harbouring mares'
nests. Thus the short story has always had a sneaking
regard for the unities. The detective takes a morning
train to the scene of the crime, solves his problem and
arrests the villain just in time to catch the last train
home, thus charitably enabling the author to squeeze
the story into the stipulated number of thousand
words. Believing, as we do, that the criminal should
be one of the principal *dramatis personæ*, we find that

it will be practically impossible for the author to screen his villain—legitimately that is—without indulging in some " double-crossing " backstage. He may introduce the reader to a number of characters, but that takes up valuable time. Probably he will decide to sacrifice his red herrings. Abstracting the human interest he will concentrate on mystery mongering. The author of the full-length story on the other hand has time and leisure to play with the red herrings, the opportunity to introduce not one but several of these " startlingly original " ideas. His chief difficulty is to keep the interest uniformly tense.

The Murders in the Rue Morgue

The Murders in the Rue Morgue, the first (and also the best) of Poe's detective tales, repays a careful analysis. Amidst cries of terror and agony, amidst a scene of the utmost confusion, the bodies of a mother and her daughter are found terribly mutilated. Common sense points to murder, but receives a check when the evidence suggests that the murderer could not have left the room in which the crime was committed. The problem becomes more complex still when the consideration of motive is examined. The police investigation of the case establishes these several conclusions :—

(1) The mother and daughter have been foully done to death.

(2) The evidence is peculiarly contradictory. The personal evidence of the neighbours confirms the murder theory. The objective evidence (the disposition of the room, etc.) seems to show that murder was an impossibility, as the murderer could not have left the room.

(3) There is a complete absence of motive.

Dupin now tackles the problem. Having exhausted the official evidence supplied by the *Gazette des Tribunaux* and the statements of the various witnesses, he hastens with his friend to the scene of the crime. He examines in the approved style not only the house, but the whole neighbourhood with a " minuteness of attention." This means all-fours and the magnifying glass. " I " is hopelessly at sea—perhaps not without cause. The champions of the fairplay method will point out that in his reconstruction of the crime Dupin relied on some pieces of evidence which he had discovered in this mysterious investigation—the evidence, for example, afforded by the window nail and the finding of the ribbon at the foot of the lightning board. This objection is certainly justified.

Dupin returns home. Now starts his analysis. He sifts out the vital evidence. He changes the viewpoint from the egress to the ingress. He reconstructs the crime. What would be the actions of the murderer ? Then having built his structure, he abandons this line of thought and turns to the question of motive. There can, he argues, be *no* motive after all. Finally he returns to the medical evidence. His solution is complete. Cuvier's history is taken from the shelf. Then we have a breath of excitement. Pistols are cocked in the best Sherlock Holmes vein. The sailor arrives only to confirm Dupin's deduction, and to explain everything. But there is no shooting.

Perhaps it is worth while to catalogue those features in this story which can boast a literary descent.

(1) The success of the unexpected means.

(2) The seeming absence of motive becomes, contrary to expectation, not the presence of some looked-for motive, but the actual absence of motive.

(3) The inability of the police to arrive at the real solution was due to their innocent refusal to observe their data, and hence

(4) The importance of detail.

(5) The apparently " hermetically sealed chamber."

The *outré* theme as such is entirely successful. We must beware of criticising Poe *sub specie æternitatis* or rather *modernitatis*. Dupin had not at his command the elaborate science of finger-prints. There was no telephone at his elbow ; no camera to portray the disposition of the corpses. Orang-outangs, you must remember, had not yet come into vogue. Years later they were destined to become in innumerable thrillers a popular means of a sticky death. Fiendish madmen began to cultivate them for their evil ends. But the apes knew better than to practise their " windmill arm " exercises and " death grasps " upon the hero or heroine. They have been really rather partial to poetic justice in the way they have rebelled against the tyranny of the lash. One of Mr. Edgar Wallace's apes actually donned livery and lit the cigars of his master's guests after dinner—a novel solution to the domestic problem. But the Tarzan series mercifully drove the pithecanthropoid theme out of literature.

The Purloined Letter

If you are at all in the habit of reading advertisements, you will remember that some time ago the advertisers of a popular brand of cigarettes devoted a campaign to the preaching of the paradoxical sales message : " Recognise the obvious." The " copy " in each advertisment consisted of a fable followed by this moral. It is gratifying to remember that twice the fable was culled from the pages of detective fiction.

There was Poe's *The Purloined Letter*, and there was Mr. Chesterton's *The Invisible Man*.

The theme of *The Purloined Letter* is a simple one. A villainous politician in the best William Le Queux manner has unlawfully gained possession of a letter which compromises the honour of a charming Parisienne. Already the victim of blackmail she has gone to the police with prayers and entreaties to recover the incriminating document. But alas their gallantry exceeded their ability. They have searched high and low, cut open chairs, even hired undesirables to waylay the dastardly minister on the off-chance that he might have the letter on his person. Foiled in every attempt the police bethink themselves of Dupin. Will he solve the mystery, find the letter and pocket 50,000 francs ? But of course !

Dupin's solution is this time psychological. He argues from the assumption that the minister will resort to the expedient of not attempting to conceal the letter at all. Gauging to a nicety the police's ingenuity in hunting in every nook and cranny, the latter will be bound to stick the letter in guilty obtrusion before their very noses. The police obsessed with the pageantry of the furniture leaves the rack behind ! Dupin suspecting just such a ruse, goes disguised to the minister's room, spots the letter at once, and by a trick similar to that practised by Sherlock Holmes in *The Reigate Squires* and on other occasions, succeeds in recovering the letter.

The variations of the " lost spectacles " theme from Plato's *Republic* to the present day always coax a smile. In *The Purloined Letter* the gamble just fails to come off. The paradox strains our notions of probability. It is almost inconceivable that " G " with all his thoroughness could have overlooked the rack. It would necessarily have been one of the first objects of his scrutiny. In a systematic search the investigator pays no attention when his intuition whispers " hot " or " cold."

But Poe's aphorism contained in the minister's dexterous argument, and also in Dupin's recognition of it, is all the more apposite as it defines the relationship between the person who sets the problem, and the one who has to solve it—between the writer and the reader of detective fiction. " And the identification of the reasoner's intellect with that of his opponent depends, if I understand you aright, upon the accuracy with which the opponent's intellect is admeasured." This applies with equal appropriateness to the detective story writer and to his public. Indeed, it is a necessary step for the author to prejudge the probable re-actions of his audience. Thus, an author might choose to make the most obvious person the murderer from the consideration that his public, expecting subtlety, will cold shoulder the obvious.

Note that our author knows nothing of Art for Art's sake ; he writes definitely to his public. And this enables him to laugh at his own joke.

The Mystery of Marie Roget

To the realist the chief interest of this tale is derived from its basis of fact. Dupin's solution was Poe's solution of a contemporary murder case. Poe, handicapped by his conscience and thus debarred from altering his data to suit his pen, survived the detective novelist's trial by ordeal. " The disappearance," writes Miss Sayers, " was a genuine one, its actual heroine being one Mary Cecilia Rogers, and the actual place New York. The newspaper cuttings were also *mutatis* *mutandis* genuine. The paper which published Poe's article dared not publish his conclusion. Years later, however, the general lines of his argument were shown by the confession of the parties involved to have been perfectly correct. Poe may, therefore, be ranked among the small band of mystery writers who have put their skill in deduction to the acid test of a problem which they had not in the first place invented."*

To the reader accustomed to the racy action of an Edgar Wallace novel *The Mystery of Marie Roget* will probably seem dull and pretentious. There is no action in it. It is a piece of pure analysis from first to last. But as such and within these limits it is undoubtedly a masterpiece. I do not intend to describe at any length Dupin's method of attacking this problem. It is the analytical method of *The Murders in the Rue Morgue* applied to a more intricate and difficult puzzle ; more difficult seemingly because it is not outré but ordinary. The data concerning the disappearance of Marie Roget are presented to us in the form of press accounts, corresponding to the affidavits and depositions of the witnesses in *The Murders in the Rue Morgue*. Dupin does not this time visit the scene of the crime. His solution is arrived at purely by an analysis of the rival newspaper theories. Dupin picks up *L'Etoile*, *Le Commercial* and *Le Soleil*, reads their suggested solutions, tears their arguments to pieces ; and by an analysis of the results of this process, with ever an eye to the non-controversial data, he arrives at the only rational solution—or more strictly speaking the " apparently slight clue," for censorship forbade the formal conclusion.

Never in the history of the detective story has there been a more telling example of the fairplay method. The reader might himself have applied the principle

* Miss Sayers is wrong on two counts. There was no question of not daring to publish, and the murder of Mary Rogers was never solved.—E. F. B.

of Archimedes, might himself have questioned that
phrase in *Le Soleil* about the petticoat—" looked like
strips torn off." Another reason why this story is so
successful is the rather unexpected application of
physics and science. In *The Murders in the Rue Morgue*
Dupin is the proverbial Sherlock Holmes with the
magnifying glass. In *The Purloined Letter* he resembles
the intuitionalist Father Brown. In *The Mystery of
Marie Roget* he is most definitely the prototype of
Dr. Thorndyke.

" ' Is he (the editor of *Le Soleil*) aware,' asked Dupin,
' of the nature of this mildew ? Is he to be told that
it is one of many classes of fungus, of which the most
ordinary feature is its upspringing and decadence
within twenty-four hours ? ' " That is pure Thorndyke.

I should like in passing to draw your attention to the
rather tentative introduction of humour. This humour
is of the donnish sort, rather heavy and rather forced.
There are the remarks on the engrossing subject of
THE CRIMINAL CLASSES AND POCKET HANDKERCHIEFS
(it looks better as a headline). There is also this
delicious *reductio ad absurdum* :—

" And furthermore it is exceedingly improbable,"
continues our journal, " that any villains who had
committed such a murder as is here supposed would
have thrown the body in without weight to sink it,
when such a precaution could easily have been taken."

" Observe, here, the laughable confusion of thought.
No one—not even *L'Etoile*—disputes the murder committed on the *body found*. . . . It is our reasoner's
object merely to show that this body is not Marie's.
He wishes to prove that Marie is not assassinated—not
that the corpse was not. Yet his observation proves
only the latter point. Here is a corpse without weight
attached. Murderers, casting it in, would not have

failed to attach a weight. Therefore, it *was not thrown* in by murderers."

Structurally the three Dupin stories are dissimilar. In all of them the problem is the thing. Now it is obvious that the answer to the question presented may be given at various stages in the story. Hence it is unnecessary to keep the answer to the last page, although that is broadly speaking perhaps the most common procedure. This is certainly what Poe does in *The Mystery of Marie Roget*. The problem is first stated, and is followed by the evidence and a series of irrational theories. By refutation Dupin arrives at his own solution. In *The Murders in the Rue Morgue* another very familiar variation in plot structure is employed. The sequence is as follows : evidence, experiment, solution, explanation. In *The Purloined Letter* we have a repetition of this latter treatment except for the fact that the experiment—the finding of the letter—is the solution.

One has to admit reluctantly, however, that there is a certain lack of finesse in these tales. There is a cold mutton taste about their climax. We prefer action's relish. Moreover, although it is child's play to make the threefold division of statement, theory, solution, there is a tendency for these divisions to overlap. One might well hesitate if asked to state the precise points at which the dénouement begins and ends. This means but one thing. There is little rhythm in the movements. The strophes of excitement, suspense and suspicion are not answered by corresponding antistrophes. The Red Herrings have not arrived.

Although Dupin came to be a household word with the emissaries of the Parisian prefect, he has not been so successful with the world at large, or even with the more limited circle of detective story fans. Perhaps it

is a pity—for Poe might easily have made Dupin one
of the great characters in fiction. Perhaps again it is
a blessing, for the notoriety of Dupin might have
meant the obscurity of Sherlock Holmes. Dupin has
some of the characteristics of the old-style detective.
When we first meet him he is poor, but naturally " of
illustrious parentage." He is also young and romantic.
As to his personal appearance, we are told he was
short-sighted and favoured green spectacles, which as
an inventory of physiognomical features is not very
much to be going on with. He was widely read and
prowled about Montmartre libraries. At one period he
had been guilty of a " certain doggerel," a phrase
which suggests to the modern reader that he composed
limericks. He was a heavy smoker, and, like all good
detectives, preferred to smoke in silence. His habits
were eccentric in the extreme. He would keep his
room for a month without stirring or admitting a
visitor. What he did " when the fit was on him "
heaven only knows ! The narrator shirks it and says
vaguely : " he was engaged on researches "—elegant
innuendo ! Yet his nocturnal rambles suggest a double
life.

This is as much as I can make of Dupin's character.
Perhaps it has been time wasted for the simple reason
that Dupin has no character. He is the personification
of analysis, the mouthpiece of the logical activity.
Poe thought it sufficient to label him an eccentric and
a recluse. As we might expect this fails to make
Dupin human. An hour in his company and we
should either be fast asleep or questioning his sanity.
So inhuman in art is transcendental reason. Poe is
really guilty of committing a breach of artistry. Now,
we started with the submission that the detective story
is primarily the solution of a problem. Unless it is

to resemble a proposition in Euclid or a puzzle of
H. E. Dudeney's, there must be some *human* interest,
some *real* character apart from the pawns and the
supers. Naturally we turn to the detective, the
legitimate apex of the character structure. He is after
all the protagonist, and we have paid to see *him* act.
But here there is a difficulty, and a very real one.
How is the author to make us interested in one who
is merely the spokesman of rational analysis and
deduction ? Poe shirked the difficulty ; he let his
analysis remain analysis, although he labelled it Dupin.

" The abstract," says Mr. Arthur Ransome, " can
never be the material of art." In these four tales there
is an almost complete abstraction of human interest.
The characters one and all remain vague and un-
recognised. It is due to just this shortcoming that
we note the absence of what we have come to regard
as one of the most important items in the detective
story—the inculcation of suspicion in the wrong
quarter, and the corresponding allaying of it in the
right. Poe does not give us any one to suspect. The
police may arrest Adolphe le Bon, but the reader never
even suspects him for a moment ; nor, which is equally
important, does Poe intend the reader to suspect him.
The red herrings are buried in the dust of depositions.
Worlds were to be gained by sacrificing this formal
objectivism ; by substituting for the black and white
of oral and written evidence the living characters of
the barber, or the innkeeper, or the tobacconist. Thus,
in *The Murders in the Rue Morgue* the witnesses would
become in modern dress either suspects or incredibly
willing allies of the detectives. The theories of the
Press in *The Mystery of Marie Roget* would become the
theories of rival investigators, principally of the
Parisian police, or again the successive theories of

Dupin himself if he were to worry out a problem
something after the manner of Inspector French.

A word now about the narrator, the " I " of these
stories. As to his character there is a touch of the
Thucydidean silence—the negation of ego. His
personality, if he has one, is never obtruded. He has
not the courage or perhaps the wits to theorise off
his own bat. He sits back in his chair—after collecting,
like an office boy, the newspaper cuttings and affidavits
—and still he gazes at Dupin and still his wonder
grows.

A certain congeniality of temperament had brought
these two together and cemented this fantastic
friendship. This is Poe's formal explanation. We have
another notion. The technical requirements of the
genre called for the existence of one as unlike the
detective as possible in temperament and everything
else. Boswell writes his notes ; the reporter interviews
the great man. Poe's narrator is of course the father of
Dr. Watson, and it will be time to discuss this relationship of opposites when we come to the more illustrious
son. At this stage, however, it may be historically
interesting to note some of the original family idiosyncrasies.

> " We were strolling one night down a long, dirty
> street, in the vicinity of the Palais Royal. Being both
> apparently occupied with thought, neither of us had
> spoken a syllable for fifteen minutes at least. All at
> once Dupin broke forth with these words :—
> " ' He is a very little fellow, that's true, and would
> do better for the Théâtre des Variétés.'
> " ' There can be no doubt of that,' I replied un-
> wittingly, and not at first observing (so much had I
> been absorbed in reflection) the extraordinary manner
> in which the speaker had chimed in with my medita-
> tions. In an instant afterwards I recollected myself,

and my astonishment was profound. ' Dupin,' said I, gravely, ' this is beyond my comprehension. Tell me, for heaven's sake.' I exclaimed, ' the method—if method there is—by which you have been enabled to fathom my soul in this matter.' "

The police cuts a sorry figure on its first appearance. It is perhaps an open question whether in his presentation of the Parisian prefect and his associates Poe was actually drawing from the life. His successors, and notably the French school, followed directly in this tradition. The *roman policier* seldom, if ever, amounted to a panegyric of police methods as such, although it might boast the triumphs of an individual representative of the system like Gaboriau's Lecoq. It is usually taken for granted that the tradition was in a sense "accidental." But authors of detective fiction soon discovered that besides being humorous, the caricature carried with it certain technical advantages, which were too valuable a cargo to be dropped overboard. But was this discovery in itself " accidental " ? On reading the historical accounts[1] of the French police system one finds that the gulf between fact and fiction was not nearly so vast as one might suppose. In the early nineteenth century there was naturally no large and organised body, no up-to-date criminal investigation department, no chemical laboratories at Lyons to encourage specialisation in scientific criminology. The reins of authority were in the hands of the prefect, a much more important official than one would suspect from Poe's portrait. He has been called " the brain and strength of Paris." He was responsible for the supervision of morals, games, theatres and roads. He controlled the delivery of

[1] V. Pierre Guitet-Vauquelin, The French Police System. *Police Journal*, January, 1929.

passports, the collection of taxes, the circulation of
supplies. Endued with such power, the prefect might
prove either a conscientious administrator, or an
unscrupulous tyrant. A most interesting feature of
his régime was the practice of having secret assistants
on his staff, these being drawn not infrequently from
the criminal classes. In other words the odds were
fairly even that the ordinary detective of the day
was an ex-convict, an anomaly which will help us to
explain one of the main characteristics of French
detective fiction.

Vidocq is the classic example—Vidocq who is the
Jean Val Jean of *Les Miserables,* and about whom Mr.
Ashton Wolfe in *The Clue of the Devil's Footprint* has
woven a slightly specious romance. Here is a summary
of his history. At sixteen perpetrated his first theft ;
became an acrobat ; joined the French army only to
desert ; joined the Austrian army only to desert again ;
joined the Belgian army ; was wrongly sentenced for
forgery and condemned to eight years' hard labour ;
escaped and offered himself as an informer to the
Chief of Police. In course of time his success proved
too much for him, for he staged burglaries in order to
obtain the credit for some brilliant coup. This led to
his resignation. He died in poverty.

Thus to the novelist the police became both an easy
and an attractive target. Owing to actual malpractice
the caricature grew satirical. The dualism, moreover,
of the villain and the detective became fashionable.
Hence Arsène Lupin; hence the Fantomas tales.
Note, too, the amusing and effective argument at the
novelist's elbow. " The clever detectives are the old
rascals, the experienced ones the time-servers ; the
virtuous policemen and detectives—bah, they are the
stupid ones."

Although Lupin boasts the friendship of the prefect, he has little admiration for him and yawns when he theorises. To him the police are muddle-headed. Capable enough to solve everyday problems, they throw up the sponge when confronted by a real problem. Conceit is writ large on them ; and they are stamped with vanity and veniality.

The Gold Bug

It is surprising to find *The Gold Bug* described as " the best detective story ever written." With all due deference to the encomiasts, it is a debatable point whether it is a detective story at all. The kernel of the theme is merely the solution of a cipher, and, moreover, an elementary cipher which the veriest tiro in cryptography would have little difficulty in solving. No geometrical figures even are necessary. In *Inspector French's Greatest Case,* French tackled the more difficult form of " dictionary " cipher all in his day's work—as a piece of routine. Mark you, Legrand's discovery of the reaction of the parchment to heat and his subsequent deductions would be a feather in any detective's cap. But deduction is not the whole of detection. Consider also these further points. There is no problem of our standard variety. There is no detective, or, if Legrand is allowed to pass for the detective, it is an unpardonable breach of etiquette for the detective to set his own problem. Finally, the canon of fairplay is violated from the start.

Far better to regard *The Gold Bug* as a tale of hidden treasure with a slightly highbrow treatment. Our Muse frowns on the crossbones of Captain Kidd and the hysterics of a " movie " negro servant.

CHAPTER IV

THE FRENCH DETECTIVE STORY

I

" THEY are books that may be safely left lying about
where the ladies of the family can pick them up and
read them. The interest they create is happily not of
the vicious sort at all."

The above notice from a nineteenth century review
holds good in the main of French detective fiction.
Paterfamilias can feel reassured when he espies the
children devouring the pages of Gaston Leroux or of
M. Maurice Leblanc, instead of slinking off with a
yellow paper volume of Guy de Maupassant secured
from the top shelf of his bookcase. The English detective
story observes and preaches a rigid code of morals ;
the French, *mutatis mutandis*, does the same. There
could not but be a difference owing to the conflicting
views of society in the two countries. Take one rather
obvious example. In the earlier English detective
story if a man kept a mistress he was *prima facie*
the criminal (or if that is an exaggeration, he was
certainly a suspect). In the French it was the other
way round, which makes the problem a shade harder
for us to solve. Once these " irregularities " are taken
for granted, there is nothing to assault our squeamishness ; nothing revolting, nothing " unmentionable "
unduly stressed. The confirmed reader of our own
flapper-press would find nothing in them.

If national characteristics are taken into account,

then the French detective story should be pre-eminently rational. And that is just what it is not. The French detective story is apt to be sensational, and to follow in the path of Eugène Sue's *Les Mystères de Paris*. An explanation of this might, it is true, be found in the unfailing attraction the *crime passionel* has for the Gallic temperament ; and we shall have to leave it at that. There are, on the other hand, two points in which the French school is more rational than our own. Whereas it is quite possible to name a number of English detective stories in which the police does not figure, so unreasonable a state of affairs in the French *roman policier* is almost unknown. Secondly, the French detective story carries the joke a step farther ; and the step, although a perfectly logical one, has never found favour with the Englishman. This is the dualism, or the identification of the arch-criminal with the super-detective. In the last chapter we suggested the reason for this was an historical one. But the persistence of this fashion suggests that the French school believes in fooling to the top of their bent.

The French detective novel is a year older than the English ; but compared with the latter its growth has been terribly stunted. Indeed, in the whole history of French detective fiction, there are only four giants—Émile Gaboriau, Fortuné Du Boisgobey, Gaston Leroux and M. Maurice Leblanc. Of this band Gaboriau is historically the most important.

2

ÉMILE GABORIAU

Émile Gaboriau was born at Saujon in Charente Inférieure in 1835.* The son of a notary, he enlisted in

* Gaboriau was born in 1832.—E. F. B.

a cavalry regiment. Later he was attracted to Paris, and was employed in a carriage factory. Writing, however, appealed to him as a more congenial occupation, and he contributed to the less known Parisian papers " stories of military and fashionable life " (*Encyclopædia Americana*). He also won some recognition as a humorist, and fortunately this sense of humour never deserted him. In 1866 *L'Affaire Lerouge* was published in *Le Pays*, and Gaboriau awoke one fine morning to find himself famous. The elaborate detective story immediately became the rage. Gaboriau was not slow to follow up his success, and from 1867 to 1870 he wrote several more detective novels including *Le Dossier* 113 (1867), *Le Crime d'Orcival* (1868), *Monsieur Lecoq* (1869), *Les Esclaves de Paris* (1869). He died in 1873 at the early age of thirty-eight.

Until recently Gaboriau had fallen on evil days. He was once regarded as second only to Sir Arthur Conan Doyle, and his detective, Lecoq, was as famous as Sherlock Holmes. After a time the Victorians seemed to forget him, and the younger generation knew him only as a name. (In France, I am told, only two of Gaboriau's novels are at present in print—*Le Crime d'Orcival* and *L'Argent des Autres*.) Then Mr. Arnold Bennett came to the rescue. On several occasions in 1928 he gave to Gaboriau " the powerful publicity " of a double column in the *Evening Standard*. It is said that Mr. Bennett's eloquence will sell any book, and publishers were not slow to profit from this gratuitous propaganda. A translation of *Le Crime d'Orcival* (*The Mystery of Orcival*) soon appeared, to be followed shortly afterwards by one of *L'Affaire Lerouge* (*The Widow Lerouge*). A translation of *Le Dossier* 113 (*The Blackmailers*) is also easily procurable in an English translation, so that it would seem that what is true of the prophet is also true, in this instance, of the detective novelist.* "The Great Gaboriau Revival" is under way. This was bound to come independently of Mr. Bennett's influence. There is a growing habit amongst publishers of reprinting earlier examples of the genre—an act of grace which confers on the detective story a definite literary status. Presumably it will be Du Boisgobey's turn next.

In *L'Affaire Lerouge* the amateur detective, Père Tabaret, describes how he was left a rich man at the early age of forty-five through the unwise thrift of his father. Casting about for a hobby to escape an oppressive boredom, he became a bibliomaniac of a then unusual kind. He grew fascinated with police and criminal lore. The passage which follows is so full of interest owing to the fragment of obviously genuine autobiography, that I feel obliged to quote at length :—

". . . I read all the books I bought, and mine is an unique collection. It consists of all the works I could find, far or near, that told anything about the police. Memoirs, reports, discourses, letters—all were delightful to me ; and I devoured them as Don Quixote did the books of chivalry.

" Reading these adventures so exciting and so real I became little by little attracted towards this mysterious power, which, from the obscurity of the Rue Jerusalem, watches over and protects society from fraud and violence—that unseen hand that lifts the most impervious veil ; that invisible eye that sees through every plot ; that unknown intelligence that divines even the secrets of men's hearts, knows to a grain weight the worth of women's reputation, and the price of men's integrity ; that universal confidant who keeps in her secret record the most terrible as well as the most shameful confessions !

" In reading the memoirs of celebrated police agents (more attractive matter to me than any novels) I

* The translations of Gaboriau date from the 1880's and have nothing to do with Mr. Bennett. *The Blackmailers* is an abridgment and is not recommended.—E. F. B.

became inspired by an enthusiastic admiration for these men, so untiring in pursuit, so fertile in expedient, who follow crime to its stronghold as relentlessly as the savages of Cooper pursue their enemies in the depths of the American forest. The desire seized me to become a wheel in this machine—a small assistance in the punishment of crime and the triumph of innocence. I have tried ; and I am proud to say, monsieur, I find I have not mistaken my vocation.'

" Then this employment pleases you ? "

" I owe to it, monsieur, my liveliest moments. No more boredom. . . . I shrug my shoulders when I see a foolish fellow pay twenty-five francs for the right of hunting a hare ! What a prize ! Give me the hunting of a man ! *That* calls the faculties into play, and the victory is not inglorious ! The game in my sport is worth the hunter. He has against him intelligence, force, and cunning. The arms are nearly equal. Ah, if people knew the excitement of these parties of hide-and-seek which are played between the criminal and the detective, everybody would be wanting employment at the bureau of secret police. The misfortune is, that the art is being lost because fine crimes are rare."

Gaboriau, experimentalist that he was, had quite a definite opinion of what the detective story ought to be. " The inquest of a crime," he makes Lecoq say, in *Le Crime d'Orcival*, " is nothing more nor less than the solution of a problem. Given the crime, proved, patent, you commence by seeking out all the circumstances, whether serious or superficial ; the details and the particulars. When these have been carefully gathered, you classify them, and put them in their order and date. You thus know the victim, the crime and the circumstances ; it remains to find the third term of the problem, that is X, the unknown quantity —the guilty party. The task is a difficult one, but not so difficult as is first imagined."

Gaboriau's novels do not, however, quite satisfy our own notions. They are not so much detective stories, as stories in which a detective has helped, but only helped, to unravel an entangled skein of events. A prolonged course of reading may have prejudiced us against Gaboriau, in much the same way as reading a sequel before the original is apt to spoil the latter. The scheme of the Gaboriau novel is as follows. A murder is committed. Certain conclusions, sometimes obviously false ones, are reached by the investigators. The criminal is usually inexperienced and leaves behind him a number of clues. He is apt to lose his head, and make things easier for the detective. He pours vinegar, for example, into five wine glasses in his attempt to put the police off his track. In all probability an innocent man will be arrested. So much for the Prologue and the First Act. Thereafter the plot begins to unwind itself. Either from evidence given by interested parties, or from admissions and confessions extorted in the courts, or from the subsequent conduct of the characters, or again from an objective narrative of events, the mystery is gradually cleared up. There is no grand dénouement. The reader having read only half the book can name the guilty person. The problem is not protracted enough ; and even from a grossly material point of view the detection occupies only a fraction of the whole.

Nevertheless, Gaboriau does not seem to have made up his mind as to what constituted the *ideal* construction. Experience, in a way, handicapped him ; for, knowing that court proceedings bulk largely in the history of any criminal case, he felt obliged to retain the proportion. Gaboriau's court scenes are delicious entertainment. In a few bold strokes he paints the examining magistrate, the prisoner, the detective all agog with excitement. He packs his novels with axioms of criminal procedure, and that type of psychology which betokens the witty precisian.

Gaboriau leant towards realism in another particular, chiefly in his later novels. He seems to have formed a preference for a more concrete type of investigation. What is said of Lecoq in *Monsieur Lecoq* is equally true of Gaboriau himself :—

> "He next had recourse to a mode of investigation which is generally the last resort of the police, but which is generally successful, because it is so sensible and simple.
> "He determined to examine all the books in which the law compels the proprietors of hotels and lodging houses to keep a record of their guests.
> "Rising long before daybreak and going to bed late at night, he spent all his time in visiting the hotels, furnished houses and lodgings in Paris."

Here is Inspector French's prototype.

This is one instance which shows that Gaboriau latterly tended to make his stories *romans policiers* pure and simple—chronicles of the police methods adopted to catch a known criminal.

Historically, Gaboriau is one of the pioneers. He was the father of the detective novel as opposed to the detective story. He made the way straight for Sir Arthur Conan Doyle. He was a master in the art of story telling. Mr. Arnold Bennett's description of *L'Affaire Lerouge,* "the narrative sweeps you swiftly and irresistibly along," is equally true of his other novels. Where Gaboriau improved on Poe was in his heightening of the interest and in the intensification of the human appeal. Gaboriau took no half measures. He decided in the first place to make the problem such that it would give rein to the emotions. Secondly, he gave the detective a personality.

(1) *The Problem.*—All Gaboriau's problems arise from family scandals and intrigues. A blot on the escutcheon and there was no saying to what crime it might not lead. Gaboriau saw that there is no secret so well kept as a family secret. Complication of the plot would be easier when the origin of the mystery might take one years back.

(2) *The Detective.*—Gaboriau gave us two detectives, Père Tabaret and Lecoq. As far as reputation goes the pupil has quite eclipsed his master. Lecoq was certainly Gaboriau's favourite. His appearance is more frequent, and we are allowed to witness the development of his powers. Père Tabaret is a type of detective very much in the contemporary fashion. He took up detection, as we saw, to dispel his boredom. (There is a no more discontented class of people than the dilettante detectives, even at the present moment when unemployment and an aristocratic scorn for the dole would constitute a more cogent reason for adopting the pursuit.) Tabaret is an amateur at the game, the magnet from time to time of the professionals' ridicule. He is also an amateur in the less flattering sense. Always liable to make mistakes, he was once actually responsible for the execution of an innocent man. He is as eccentric as Dupin, and his garrulous landlady has not got a dog's chance. His eccentricity gives comic relief, " but unlike Holmes's does not give an impression of latent genius." Thus in *L'Affaire Lerouge* :

> " He remained there about half an hour ; then came out running, then re-entered and came out again ; again re-entered, and again re-appeared almost immediately. Daburon could not help comparing him to a pointer on the scent. . . . All the

while he talked loudly and with much gesticulation, apostrophising himself scolding himself, uttering little cries of triumph or self-encouragement. . . . He wanted this or the other thing. He demanded paper and pencil. Then he wanted a spade ; and finally he cried out for plaster of Paris and a bottle of oil. . . .

"He is on the road," replied the sergeant, "lying flat in the mud."

In his use of paradox he is almost as doctrinaire as Father Brown.

Lecoq is often mentioned in the same breath as Dupin and Sherlock Holmes. He is an amusing character ; *that* needs no stressing. But it must occur to one that perhaps after all his name is just a shade greater than his deserts. His is borrowed plumage. The Lecoq method is Tabaret's. In *L'Affaire Lerouge* Tabaret says : " Given a crime, with all the circumstances and details, I construct piece by piece a plan of accusation, which I do not warrant until it is entire and perfect. If a man is found to whom this plan applies exactly in every particular, the author of the crime is found. . . ."

" The object," says Lecoq in *Le Crime d'Orcival*, " is to find a man whose guilt explains all the circumstances, all the details found—all, understand me. Find such a man, and it is probable—and in nine cases out of ten, the probability becomes a reality—that you hold the perpetrator of the crime."

(Not so nowadays, not the criminal, but the principal suspect.)

Lecoq joined the Sûreté to save himself from a life of crime. As an astronomer's drudge he began to " perpetrate in fancy the most abominable crimes." One of these schemes he divulged to his patron, who promptly fired him with a fortune-teller's blessing—

to the effect that either he would be a famous thief
or a great detective.

Had he not come to this laudable decision, Lecoq
might have out-Lupined Lupin. He is usually pictured
as a young detective. Continental laxity allowed him
to choose a mistress from the demi-monde. We see
him now as the raw tiro picking up crumbs from his
mentor ; now as " M. Lecoq of the Sûreté " who has
found his feet ; now as an almost legendary figure
who can masquerade as a M. Verduret throughout a
case. Round Lecoq are beginning to gather the
detective's recognised paraphernalia. He has a wardrobe
of disguises, a chamber of horrors as his living-room.

> " The whole of one side of the wall was taken up
> with a long rack, where hung the strangest and most
> incongruous suits of clothes. There were costumes
> belonging to all grades of society . . . a toilet-table,
> covered with powders, essences and paints, stood
> between the fireplace and the window. On the other
> side of the room was a bookcase full of scientific works,
> especially of medicines and chemistry. The most
> singular piece of furniture in the apartment, however,
> was a large ball, shaped like a lozenge, in black velvet,
> suspended behind the looking-glass. A quantity of
> pins were stuck in this ball . . . The ball was meant
> to recall to him perpetually the people of whom he
> was in pursuit."

As for personal appearance and manner it is generally
held that the detective never betrays his calling. The
detectives with whom I have had the privilege to come
in contact—in a social sort of way—really did impress
me as having mistaken their *metier*. This is, to be sure,
their guile. But what do the psychologists make of
it with their talk of the square bovine face ? Lecoq
was never taken for a detective. He was a man of
many faces, a perfect Lon Chaney.

Gaboriau's murders and robberies are not the meticulously planned affairs with which we are now familiar. Smith Minor would turn up his nose at them. Père Tabaret himself complained that criminals were not what they used to be. "Blunderers as well as cowards," he styled them. And if they did not leave behind them their visiting-cards, they left quite enough evidence to be going on with.

Gaboriau's legacy is for all that a rich one. Many of his tricks and ruses have now become clichés. Of his maxims possibly the following are the most interesting. Subsequent history has certainly approved their effectiveness.

Identity.—Questions of personal identity are among the most difficult and delicate that the detective has to probe.

> "Railroads, photography, and telegraphic communication have multiplied the means of investigation in vain. Every day it happens that malefactors succeed in deceiving the judge in regard to their true personality, and thus escape the consequences of their former crimes.
> "This is so frequently the case that a witty attorney-general once laughingly remarked—and, perhaps, he was only half in jest : ' This uncertainty in regard to identity will cease only on the day when the law prescribes that a number shall be branded upon the shoulder of every child whose birth is reported to the mayor.' " (*Monsieur Lecoq.*)

Alibi.—(*a*) Beware and mark down for slaughter the man who gaily produces a perfect, unassailable alibi.

> "He will present you with a magnificent alibi, an alibi that cannot be gainsaid. . . . The only means of securing conviction is to surprise the miscreant by a

rapidity against which it is impossible he can be
on guard." (*L'Affaire Lerouge.*)

(*b*) The converse holds good. The man without an
alibi is *ipso facto* innocent, as no criminal would throw
up the sponge like this. When a character in a detective
story refuses to account for his movements, it means
one thing—that he has an alibi, but cannot for the
good of the plot reveal it.

> "'Not an *alibi*, nothing?' murmured the old
> fellow. 'No explanations? The idea! It is in-
> conceivable. Not an alibi? We must be mistaken;
> he is certainly not the criminal.'" (*L'Affaire Lerouge.*)

Many of Gaboriau's stratagems are now hackneyed.
Time stops whenever a murder is committed. The
clock never escapes, and the deceitful hands play the
deuce with one's calculations. Thus in *Le Crime
d'Orcival* we read :—

> "'But see here,' said M. Plantat, 'it was the odd
> hour marked by that clock that struck me. The hands
> point to twenty minutes past three; yet we know
> that the Countess was fully dressed, when she was
> struck. Was she up taking tea at three in the morning?
> It's hardly probable.'
> "'I too was struck by that,' returned Lecoq, 'and
> that's why I said, "not so stupid!" Well, let's see.'
> "He lifted the clock with great care and replaced
> it on the mantel—— The hands continued to point
> to twenty past three.
> "'Twenty past three,' muttered he while slipping a
> little wedge under the stand. 'People don't take tea
> at that hour. Still less common is it that people are
> murdered at daylight.'
> "He opened the clock-case with some difficulty and
> pushed the longer hand to the figure of half-past three.
> "The clock struck eleven.

"'Good,' cried M. Lecoq triumphantly, 'that is the truth.'"

Furniture again, according to so convincing an authority as Du Boisgobey, has a " physiognomy." An escritoire and overturned chairs are never absent from the scene of the crime. We note too the never failing presence of a confusing number of wine glasses or coffee cups— seldom of plates, forks or spoons. Tobacco in some form or another of disintegration is another necessary stage property. Gaboriau makes one of his careless criminals leave behind him the end of a Trabucos cigar. Then there is the undergraduate's trick of rumpling the bed clothes to make the bed appear to have been slept in. But one rumples in vain if only the bolster is removed. " A bed is one of those terrible witnesses which never misguide." Footprints are always being discovered ; but at this stage they are used to trace movements, rather than for identification purposes. Lecoq once has recourse to a regular Austin Freeman expedient when he preserves the footprints in the melting snow by means of his plaster casts. Whether it is a piece of symbolism or realism, a murder is inevitably accompanied by a heavy fall of rain. Generally speaking the detection is of the familiar Sherlock Holmes variety —keen observation coupled with rapid inference. A leap of more than two yards to avoid a flower bed is assumed to prove that the man " was active and, therefore, young."

It was Gaboriau's idea to present the reader with a sketch plan of the scene of the crime. The idea is in itself a sound one ; a picture may brighten a narrative as a graph may give life to tables of figures. But an excessive use of it has converted it into a mixed blessing. It is apt, as Mr. E. V. Knox has stated, to get on one's nerves. Gaboriau uses it properly and does not force the conscientious reader to turn back to it nor annoy the unconscientious by continual and unnecessary reference. The most attractive form of plan is where we have a picture of the room in which the murder was committed with the chairs and table all neatly drawn to scale and an X for the corpse. The day may possibly come when photographs will be used to make up for any deficiency in the reader's imagination. In the *Strand* Xmas Number, 1929, the solution of H. E. Dudeney's *Can you solve the Brookman's Mystery?* was to be found in half a dozen photographs.

L'Affaire Lerouge and *Le Crime d'Orcival* are undoubtedly Gaboriau's best novels. Of the rest the best that can be said of *Le Dossier No.* 113 is that it would make an excellent film ; of *Monsieur Lecoq* that the first part, *L'Enquête*, falls under the less attractive category of a pure *roman policier*, while the second, *L'Honneur du Nom*, is rather tedious family history. The majority are nothing more or less than emotional blood and thunder novels like *The Catastrophe* and *The Champdoce Mystery.**

L'Affaire Lerouge

The Plot.—The Count de Commarin had the very bad taste to have two sons born to him at the same time ; one by his lawful unloved wife, the other by his much loved mistress. *An Arabian Night's* plot was formed by his mistress to substitute the children, so that the supposititious child might eventually become a peer of the realm. The plot, which implicated several people, miscarried. Years later the illegitimate son became a hard-working advocate (in the daytime).

* Most authorities would not agree with the categorizations here. —E. F. B.

After office hours he amused himself with so expensive a mistress that ruin was beginning to threaten him. Faced with this predicament, he plotted to claim legitimate descent from the Count and oust his half-brother from the lap of luxury. To do this he had to silence those whose knowledge would hinder the execution of his plan. The nurse—the " Widow " Lerouge—had to go. (The husband who was also " in at " the attempted substitution unexpectedly turned up later on.) His mother, too, who saw what her son was after, had likewise to be silenced. A convincing alibi ; the " framing " of the legitimate son, and the trick was done.

There was, however, a coincidence. The true heir had a " date " with his girl at the hour of the murder, and to save her honour in the good old-fashioned way he had to observe a strong silence and forgo his alibi. This is a well-known cliché now ; and romanticism rightly holds a girl's " honour " over a man's life. The girl comes up to expectations with a " Why talk of propriety ? " (Why, indeed ?) and tells her convincing story to the magistrate. He, as it happens, is also in love with this girl and that makes things awkward. However, the death of Noel's mother throws light on some important facts, and Tabaret, having found out from the " widow's " husband that the substitution never took place, applies his formula and discovers Noel's guilt.

L'Affaire Lerouge is a good example of the unlikely person *motif* in its first infancy. The assassin is a close friend of the detective and lives in the same house. But all the same we are very soon convinced of Noel's guilt. We suspected the worst when Juliette the vamp appeared on the scene. America has thus far educated us. This spoils the plot for us, although the incident of the examining magistrate's passion might give us pause for a moment to reconsider things.

> " The scene of the discovery of the crime," said Mr. Arnold Bennett in the *Evening Standard*, " and the first activities of the amateur detective are brilliantly presented. All the detective parts are indeed excellent. But in the scheme of the book, they are not more important than the human drama ; nor are they developed at such length as the human drama. Take away the entire business of detection and the book remains a good, sound, old-fashioned emotional novel. Gaboriau was a novelist, not merely a clever amateur detective."

Mr. Bennett implies that in the detective story detection should be subordinate to the human drama. He does not take into account the fact that the two should be mutually dependent on each other : and that what we look for first in a detective story is surely detection. The weakness, not the strength, of *L'Affaire Lerouge* lies in just this separation. This human drama did not really need a detective at all.

Le Crime d'Orcival

Le Crime d'Orcival is a better detective story than *L'Affaire Lerouge,* although the general arrangement of the structure is not so neat. The plot is a simple one, and the murder is a *crime passionel.* Owing to his debts Hector de Tremorel—one of the bright young people of his day—determines to commit suicide and turns a deaf ear to the tragic appeal of his mistress, Jenny. When on the point of blowing his brains out; Sauvresy, an old friend, providentially stays his hand, takes him home and makes a fuss of him. Trading on his friend's good nature, Hector reverts to his old tricks, and encourages the sex-starved wife of Sauvresy, Berthe (the name had probably something to do with the sex-starvation !). Sauvresy at this time is keen to make a match for Hector and shoves him into the arms of Laurence Courtois, the daughter of the Mayor. Big Bertha, however, wanted Hector so much that she determined to rid herself of Sauvresy : so she and Hector proceeded to poison Sauvresy slowly but surely. Sauvresy got wind of the conspiracy before he died, and as a revenge forced Berthe and Hector to marry within a certain time unless they wished to be tried for his murder. (He had given a M. Plantat a document which set out the facts and which was to be opened if the marriage did not take place.) But Hector, in turn, wanted Laurence so badly that he murdered Berthe, and making it appear that he also had met a similar fate disappeared with Laurence.

The flaw in the construction is that Lecoq's solution comes too soon. When we have read roughly a third of the story, we know that Hector is the murderer. All that is needed to confirm Lecoq's theory is the bone-setter's suicide and M. Plantat's story. (Curiosity had got the better of him and he had devoured the contents of Sauvresy's incriminating document.) It remains for Lecoq to trap the criminal.

The detection is much brighter than in *L'Affaire Lerouge*. It is no longer tentative guesswork, possibly because Hector was a clumsy criminal. Certainly Lecoq is in his best form.

3

FORTUNÉ DU BOISGOBEY

Gaboriau's successor was Fortuné du Boisgobey. Born at Granville in Normandy in 1824, Du Boisgobey served as an army paymaster in Algeria (1844-48). In 1868 he contributed a story, *Deux Comédiens*, to *Le Petit Journal*, and thereafter occupied himself in producing a large number of sensational police stories. Of these *Le Crime de L'Opéra* (1880 : English translation, 1886) is possibly the best known. Others which gained some reputation at the time were *L'homme sans Nom* (1872), *Le Forçat Colonel* (1872), and *Les Mystères de Nouveau Paris*. He died in 1891.

Du Boisgobey for a time became an immensely popular writer. In England the sixpenny translations of *Du Boisgobey's Sensational Novels* had printings of twenty-five thousand. At the moment every title is out of print : but in France *Le Crime de L'Opéra* is included in a popular series. It is a serious handicap to our appreciation of Du Boisgobey to have to rely on the older editions, as both the typography and the translation are alike execrable. The translator was a curious fellow. " Deteriously " finds great favour with him. " Serpent," " animal," are the choice morsels of his invective. He grows sententious when he is with the ladies—" fine toilets will fittingly become her." His rhetoric is of the Elephant and Castle variety.

> " ' What ! another ! ' he exclaimed, starting back with surprise. He had just seen a bloody corpse lying upon its back with its arms extended."

He is not a dull dog, however, and can append an

amusing footnote when he is in the humour. Thus in
An Omnibus Mystery—

> " When a man has waited at a crossing and after
> vainly signalling to the driver, sees the word ' Full '
> appear in white letters on a blue background he
> rages and no wonder."
> *Footnote.*—" It should be remembered that Paris
> omnibuses are alone in question here. The London
> General Omnibus Company with all its capital has
> never adopted the simple but ingenious contrivance
> by which the Parisians are informed whether an
> omnibus is full or not. We are supposed to be a
> practical people ; but as for omnibuses they order
> these things better in France."

Du Boisgobey had an immense admiration for
Gaboriau's work. Of the detective Lolif in *Le Crime
de L'Opéra* he wrote : " His library was composed of
judicial romances—the works of that talented and
lamented writer, Émile Gaboriau, for instance—and the
memoirs of Canler and Vidocq. He knew the operations of these illustrious detectives by heart, and he
dreamt of equalling even the great Lecoq himself,
but so far he had not had the luck to discover the
great murderer, or even a simple thief ; and this injustice of fate made him melancholy at times." The
greatest compliment he paid Gaboriau was when he
boldly borrowed Lecoq and made him the principal
character of one of his novels—*The Old Age of Lecoq
the Detective*.

Like Gaboriau, Du Boisgobey made use of official
documents—*Le Gazette des Tribunaux*, for example—
to provide him with matter for his plots. Some of
the incidents in *Le Crime de L'Opéra* were based on
the circumstances of the murder of a Maria Fellerath—
" a crime which was perpetrated by means of a dagger

similar to the one described " in the story. He is
likewise a close student of police methods. He never
wearies of describing shadowing, and the simple ruse
of giving a suspect rope by releasing him soon after
the arrest. He is keenly interested in the art of disguise
and in an amusing passage describes the change of
fashion.

> (Formerly) " Even the disguises of detectives were
> pre-arranged, the *mouchard* was bound to imitate a
> classic type of ' elegant gentleman.' A well-arranged
> wig, with whiskers artistically stuck to the cheeks, a
> white cravat, blue coat with gilt buttons and a decora-
> tion, such was the *ne plus ultra* of *camouflage* or dis-
> guisement. But the days when these practices flourish
> have fled, and the modern detective no more resembles
> the *mouchard* of the old régime than the usurers of
> nowadays, with their horses, carriages, and opera
> boxes, resemble the lenders of small amounts who wore
> patched pantaloons and slept in dog kennels in the good
> old times. It has been discovered even in official circles
> that for a spy or a detective to achieve success he must
> in no wise resemble what he really is. It is not enough
> to don a costume ; he must assume the ways of the
> person he wishes to represent. It is absolutely necessary
> to ' get into the old man's skin.'
> " It is easy to understand that, under these con-
> ditions, powder, rouge, false hair, false beard—are of
> very little use."

Le Crime de L'Opéra is in length over four hundred
pages of microscopic type. Du Boisgobey relies on the
same effects as Gaboriau, but he is distressingly
prolix. Intrigues and love affairs give a loophole to
blackmail, and this in turn leads to murder. With
more space at his command he keeps half a dozen of
these " irregular " affairs running at once. This
gives him an advantage over Gaboriau, because he

can keep the secret to himself a little longer owing to the perfectly natural confusion of the reader. But as regards detection he falls sadly behind his master. Coincidence solves the majority of the problems. *An Omnibus Mystery* is simply chock-full of coincidences. Indeed many of Du Boisgobey's novels have, if any, at least so little detection in them that they cannot be included in our genre. It is the more disappointing when an intriguing title like *Who Died Last?* raises our hasty expectations. There is again no method in Du Boisgobey's detection. Detection is undertaken by his characters with the purpose of getting their fiancèes or mistresses out of a mess. They seem to wander rather aimlessly about till they meet some one who can supply them with information. Gradually they accumulate enough evidence in this pleasant way to take the offensive and beard the guilty parties in their dens. A dramatic suicide, and then Du Boisgobey can " spill " his melodramatic rhetoric.

> " Too late ! . . . vanity had guided him through life, vanity had impelled him to seek this fate."
> " She has hurt herself ! " cried Elise.
> " No ; she has killed herself ! " said George Darres, " and in doing so, she has paid the penalty of her crimes ! "

What the police were supposed to be doing for their bread and butter, Du Boisgobey alone knew. They arrest the wrong people ; that is expected of them. But it is also expected of them to examine thoroughly the scenes of the various crimes and cross-examine those who would obviously know something about those implicated. In *Le Crime de L'Opéra* they simply won't do a thing.

As far as the actual perpetration of murder goes,

Du Boisgobey had a fine dramatic sense. The Opera House was a capital setting. The last bus home was equally good. In another story the body of a woman was found in a trunk, and it is just possible that the circumstances of this murder suggested to Mr. Wills Crofts the idea of *The Cask*. Then there was a necklace to which needles steeped in deadly poison were attached. And a bridegroom had the shocking bad luck to be shot at the wedding breakfast.

Le Crime de L'Opéra is the first detective story in which at least half a dozen characters had each a very good reason for committing, or for being supposed to have committed, the murder. The whole mystery might have been dispelled in a chapter or two if a search had been made at the flat, and the fur coat been recovered !

The Old Age of Lecoq the Detective is highly amusing and may be recommended on that score alone. Father Lecoq has settled down to an old age of peaceful retirement. The commission he pocketed from his cases secured that, and enabled him to give his son a good education. A double murder is committed : the police apply for his assistance, but Lecoq is adamant and won't upset himself. So the police call in the English Tolbiac, who is regarded as Lecoq's successor. Lecoq's own son is suddenly accused, tried and condemned ; and old Papa Lecoq has to go into action again, accompanied by the comic Piédouche. The case for the prosecution is naturally based on :

(1) " Planting."
(2) The fact that Louis Lecoq is unable to account for his movements.

It soon becomes patent that Tolbiac is at the bottom of it all, and that an inheritance is his goal. There is a delicious scene where Lecoq disguises himself as an

Indian Nabob and interviews Tolbiac also disguised. Thereafter the story becomes a thriller pure and simple, and Lecoq just manages in the nick of time to save his son from the guillotine. Possibly the most amusing episode is where a detective hides himself in a grandfather clock to observe the actions of a suspect, and gets locked inside for his pains.

4

GASTON LEROUX

Gaston Leroux was for many years a correspondent on the staff of *Le Matin*, and in this capacity he contributed special reports on famous trials. He died in 1927. Leroux's *Le Mystère de la Chambre Jaune* (English translation, 1909—*The Mystery of the Yellow Room*) is, by general consent, the greatest masterpiece of French detective fiction. Mr. Bennett called it " the most dazzlingly brilliant detective story I have ever read," and Mr. George Sims found in it " an entirely new sensation." Leroux adapted *Le Mystère de la Chambre Jaune* for the stage, and the play, which was presented in 1912 at the Ambigu Theatre with Jean Coquelin in the cast, proved a great success.

To Leroux Mr. Edgar Wallace owes a debt untold, for the former made the official detective the villain of the piece. Frédéric Larsan, the famous detective, is none other than the notorious Ballmeyer in disguise—Ballmeyer, a desperate criminal who had time and again escaped from the clutches of the police of two continents—Ballmeyer, the expert at wielding the sheep's bone. To carry off his grand deception

Leroux introduced, perforce, another detective, Rouletabille, a young journalist—the first of the bright young detectives of the Press. Where Leroux triumphs is in his forecast of what the ordinary reader would make of the ensuing rivalry. He knew very well that the reader would want Rouletabille to win the day, but he also expected the reader to entertain at the back of his mind the idea that it would be Larsan, owing to his official experience. One had by this time grown accustomed to the skirmish between the amateur and the professional, and a reversion of the issue would have thus been surprising yet not unexpected.

The plot is brilliantly contrived, and we note the improvement made in the construction by keeping the problem unsolved till the end. For sheer excitement there is no dénouement more hair-raising than the famous trial scene. The problem itself is a pretty one. We start with the hermetically sealed Yellow Room. Cries of " Murder " and " Help, help," rend the air, and the household break in in time to find that an attempt has been made on Mme. Mathilde Stangerson's life. The room being hermetically sealed and the door being bolted, how did the murderer get out ? Here there is no exit up the chimney and no orang-outang. Later, when the Green Man (the name of a character and not of a public house) is murdered, a similar problem is presented. Rouletabille, having convinced himself that it was impossible for any one outside the circle, i.e., those of the household at hand, to commit the crime, turns his attention to those inside it. By a process of elimination he concludes that Larsan must be guilty. But this does not solve the first problem. The solution of the first problem is more difficult possibly because it rests on a coincidence. Larsan assaults Mathilde ; she shoots at him and drives him from the room : then later in the evening she has a nightmare and waking from it utters the cries that rouse the household. That is the central problem. Leroux, of course, has to make Mathilde have a very pressing reason for being secretive : Ballmeyer had married her in America and this causes complications owing to the forthcoming marriage between her and Darzac, the chief suspect. Other suspects are the Green Man and Rance (the *concierges* are regularly arrested in the French detective story and as regularly dismissed). Possibly also the Good Lord's Beast. The crime is a *crime passionel* : but Leroux does not let the question of motive worry us. We have our hands full in trying to cope with the purely physical problem.

There are several points that deserve emphasis :

(1) The fairplay method is observed throughout. It is possible for the reader to arrive at the solution— possible, but not probable. Never in the world ! Particularly interesting in this context is the verbatim report of the magistrate's examination.

(2) Leroux has followed the Dr. Watson convention—a convention rarely to be found in French detective fiction : Rouletabille has his perplexed Sainclair.

(3) The art of incessant innuendo is used for the first time with great effect.

> " Ah ! " said Rouletabille, " I can see the footsteps on the path there, the ground must have been very moist—I'll examine them presently."
>
> " Nonsense," interrupted old Jacques, " the assassin did not go that way."
>
> " Indeed. Well, which way, then ? "
>
> " How do I know ? "

And—

> " I am extremely pleased. I have discovered many things."
> " Moral or material ? "
> " A few moral and one material. Take this one for example."
> . . . And rapidly he drew from his waistcoat pocket a folded piece of paper. . . . In that folded paper there was a blonde hair of a woman !

Other good examples are Rouletabille's interest in Mathilde's coiffure and in M. Fred's walking stick.

The story of *The Mystery of the Yellow Room* was continued in *The Perfume of the Lady in Black*, but, as is the rule with so many solicited sequels, we are harder to please at a second sitting. *The Perfume of the Lady in Black* is vastly inferior to its predecessor ; in fact, it deteriorates into a purely sensational thriller. Ballmeyer-Larsan and Mathilde had a son who turns out to be Rouletabille. Larsan, risen from the dead in the good old serial style, continued his persecution of Mathilde, now Mme. Darzac. He disguises himself as Darzac so that Mathilde has a pretty exciting time of it. Leroux repeats his idea of the hermetically sealed room ; Rouletabille again is forced to look inside " the circle." The problem this time is chiefly to discover whom Larsan is impersonating—which is not so interesting a problem, since the strings of probability are cut. Prince Galitch and Old Bob are too obviously selling their red herrings. The trick of the wardrobe in which the real Darzac was concealed is deftly executed ; but the plot is really an accumulation of the crudest impossibilities. The book is for all that genuinely exciting, and it is curious that it has been allowed to go out of print. Seldom has suspense been so cleverly intensified chapter by chapter.

Gaston Leroux touched the high-water mark of his art in *The Mystery of the Yellow Room*. His other work —so much of it, at least, as falls within the genre— is sensational in the extreme and decidedly not up to standard. There is the Chéri-Bibi saga, for example. *Chéri-Bibi Mystery Man*, *The Floating Prison*, *Chéri-Bibi and Cecily*, etc. Here is one form of the dualism to which we have already referred. Hardigras (*The Son of Three Fathers*, etc.) who plays a game of catch-can with the police, is another familiar type of French fiction. For our purpose it is necessary only to describe a character who combines most of these idiosyncrasies —M. Maurice Leblanc's Arsène Lupin.

M. MAURICE LEBLANC

M. Leblanc was born in Rouen in 1864. In 1919 he was made an officer of the Legion of Honour. He now lives in retirement at Etretat, one of the Lupin centres. According to *Le Matin* M. Leblanc works very slowly and conscientiously, and " he is considered to have done for French literature exactly what Sir Arthur Conan Doyle has done for English." Arsène Lupin, " gentleman cambrioleur," is the most familiar figure of French detective fiction. He has a far greater public than Rouletabille or even Lecoq. He captured the popular fancy as early as 1907, and he is still going strong. Lupin is the apache of romance, but he is credited with a little more intelligence and a little less of the animal than this absurd figure is usually made to have. Lupin's pose is an old one—that of a street urchin with his fingers to his nose. He attacks the conventions, because law in the shape of the policeman is a pompous ass.

Lupin is completely a-moral. He is not a legendary

Robin Hood or Dick Turpin robbing the nasty rich to relieve the honest poor. Nor is he a Raffles stealing from horrid plutocrats to support charity. He burgles because he finds it amusing, because he loves the sport of it just, and for the same reason, as the detectives love to whip out their magnifying glasses.   In part Lupin is a parody of the conventional detective ; and the fact that he was on the other side of the fence *makes* the parody. It is true that Lupin runs with the hare and hunts with the hounds, that it is impossible at times to know in what camp he is serving—whether he is teaching the stupid but zealous Prefecture its business, or is merely being a " smiling," damned villain." (For four years Lupin—as Lenormand, the head of the Paris detective force—" directed operations against himself ! ") Yet Lupin's pose is unsatisfactory. He stops short of murder. Why ? If he appears to blackmail we later see it was a piece of bluff. Why ? When he loses his heart, which is not seldom, he has moments of remorse. Why ? Because Lupin was within an ace of becoming a low criminal. Battery and assault are, of course, not actionable in a detective story. Lupin's wit, his virility, his impudence, his self-confidence are all right up to a point. . . . E. M. Wrong hit the nail on the head when he drew this conclusion :

> " To make a hero of the criminal is to reverse the moral law, which is after all based on common sense, for crime is not in fact generous and open, but mean . . . not even success can make robbery appeal to us as a truly noble career. Is the criminal then to try other crimes than theft ? Blackmail hardly provides a fitting career for a hero, and we are driven back on murder. Now it is possible for murderers to show courage and resource, to be less mean than the pickpocket or forger. But murder to be successful must be selfish. . . ."

Analysed in the cold light of reason, Lupin is not so supremely clever as he himself (or possibly M. Leblanc) imagined. His bag of tricks consists of an infinite capacity for masquerade and impersonation ; an acrobatic agility, and an " iron nerve."

M. Leblanc has two moods—the sensational and the humorous. The nature of the Arsène Lupin joke once considered, it is easy to deduce that he is more successful when he is in lighter vein. In fact, his sensational novels, such as *The Teeth of the Tiger*, *The Hollow Needle* and *The Eight Strokes of the Clock*, are second-rate. Lupin is really out of place in the sensational thriller. Bent on amusement, he stumbles unwittingly upon murder. It is almost as distasteful to Lupin himself as it is to us, for M. Leblanc loves lurid pigments, and his blood-and-thunder is of a crude, almost brutal description.

But it is in the collections of short stories—*The Exploits of Arsène Lupin*, *The Arrest of Arsène Lupin*, *The Seven of Hearts*, etc.—that M. Leblanc scores. Not the least interesting feature of these tales is the burlesque on Sherlock Holmes and Dr. Watson, or Holmlock Shears and Wilson, as he sometimes calls them. The burlesque is all the more interesting as it comes from France. M. Leblanc, it is worth mentioning, had a tremendous admiration for Conan Doyle, and on the latter's death wrote one of the most striking tributes. Holmes and Watson are called in to join issue with Lupin, since the police have proved their incompetence. Naturally Holmes gets the worst of it, but only just. Lupin recognises that he has a redoubtable opponent : so does Holmes, but Dr. Watson is sanguine in his confidence. It is a great joke, and both parties treat it as such and entertain a studied politeness to each other. It is perhaps worth mentioning just those traits in Holmes which appealed to M. Leblanc. Holmes is always caught lighting his pipe. (It was a shocking mistake to make him roll a cigarette on one occasion.) He has lost his epigrammatic skill and adopted the brazen attitude of a super-salesman. In appearance he now resembles a city clerk. He relies on intuitions and cigarette ash.

> " He was a sort of miracle of intuition, of insight, of perspicacity, of shrewdness. It is as though Nature had amused herself by taking the two most extra-ordinary types of detective that fiction had invented, Poe's Dupin and Gaboriau's Lecoq, in order to build up one in her own fashion, more extraordinary yet and more unreal."

Dr. Watson is drawn in a much coarser caricature, and has even to submit to some knock-about. He gets his arm broken for his pains on one lamentable occasion. But the best scene of all is where Holmes and Dr. Watson encounter Lupin and his biographer. After an exchange of greetings Sherlock magnanimously calls for four whiskies and sodas. That is in the grand manner !

CHAPTER V

SHERLOCK HOLMES

" 'You are a benefactor of the human race,' said I."
The Adventure of the Red-Headed League.

EVERY one, from Macaulay's schoolboy to the " every one that matters " of the *Morning Post*, is familiar with the exploits of Sherlock Holmes. Mr. Chesterton regards Sherlock Holmes as the only well-known character of recent fiction. The name is household and has gained the currency of popular conversational usage. No pages of psychological analysis are necessary to obtain the passport of our recognition. The aquiline nose, the curved pipe, the dressing gown, the violin and the hypodermic syringe. What power is this that sways our association of ideas ?

The recently published collections of the short and full-length stories are the two most popular omnibus volumes on the market : and although *A Study in Scarlet* was bought for £25, in his later years Sir Arthur Conan Doyle was paid more for his Sherlock Holmes contributions than any other magazine writer in this country. These stories have been translated into almost every European language, and are available in Japanese and also in some Indian dialects. Their circulation runs into millions.

Their fascination, however, may be evidenced more concretely. A railway engine, whose decrepitude calls for governmental subsidy, puffs in and out of Baker Street Station flaunting the great name. It is no idle story that a party of French schoolboys on a visit to

London demanded to be shown the chambers of their idol before they condescended to be led to the Tower and St. Paul's. Shy, but zealous, foreigners may frequently be caught scanning the houses of Baker Street if haply they may descry a blazoned memorial plate. During 1920 the Turks at Constantinople, according to a correspondent in *The Times*, were convinced that " the great English detective, Sherlock Holmes," was working behind the scenes. Despite Sherlock's philippics against the police, the Chiefs of Scotland Yard have borne him no ill will. John O' London in *Unposted Letters* records an interview he once had with the late Sir Robert Anderson, who was for many years Head of the Criminal Investigation Department, and refers to an article written by him on *Sherlock Holmes as Seen by Scotland Yard*. Sir Robert Anderson attributed the popularity of the Sherlock Holmes tales to the moral underlying them—the value of observation—and to the success of Sherlock as a character. Of particular interest is his description of the difference between detection in fiction and detection in real life.

> " The inventor of a detective story makes both the lock and the key, whereas Scotland Yard is limited to the finding of the key to the lock."

On the other hand Sir Basil Thomson, a former chief of the Special Department, was not so magnanimous:—

> " I have often asked myself, when I have had a particularly difficult problem to solve, what Sherlock Holmes would have done in such a case. I imagine him, for instance, examining with his piercing gaze a bit of mud on a gate—the only clue to a crime.
> " I see him go to a cupboard where he keeps samples of the mud of every street in London. He scrutinises

each sample intently, and ponders for the space of a few seconds. Presently he turns to Dr. Watson, who is standing in open-mouthed wonder beside him, and, with a significant puff at his pipe, says casually:—

" ' Watson, I am now going out to arrest the Archbishop of Canterbury ! ' "

At the Lyons Prefecture there is a salon named after Sherlock Holmes. The Parisian chiefs are reported to have expressed the opinion that Conan Doyle would have made a first-class detective. An interesting commentary on this is to be found in the paragraph that appeared in the *Observer* at the time of Conan Doyle's death :—

> " Sir Arthur himself—and perhaps, as Lady Conan Doyle said to me yesterday, it is a point of which the general public are not aware—possessed in a most remarkable degree those very gifts of deduction he gave to Sherlock Holmes. ' I have known my husband,' she remarked, ' solve many mysteries which had been given up by the police.' One notable case, she recalled, was that of the disappearance of a young officer from a London hotel some years ago. It caused a great stir at the time. Many people thought there had been foul play. Sir Arthur, after examining all the facts, came to the conclusion that he would be found after three days in Scotland—and he was."

A biography of Dr. Watson has been penned, and an inconsistency in chronology has thus led to some scandal with regard to the worthy doctor's marital, or pre-marital, relations. An examination has been set on Sherlock Holmes. *Life and Letters*, following Calverley's immortal *Pickwick Paper Test*, produced some time ago a set of thirteen questions. Here, by your leave, is a selection from these questions at which you may like to try your hand :

" Give the context of the following passages, naming where possible the speaker and the person addressed :—
" ' You're too late. She's my wife.' No, she's your widow.'
" ' The next word is pig's bristles.'
" ' The aortic I may rely upon, but I should value your opinion on the mitral.'
" When did the following serve as clues : curried mutton, creosote, tarred string, a bell rope ?
" Solve the following problems :—
" Who was the British Government ?
" Whose task was it to copy the *Encyclopædia Britannica* ?
" Who or what were VV341, Kratides, the woman ? "

Sherlock Holmes was not, of course, a completely original characterisation. His prototype in real life was the famous Edinburgh surgeon, Dr. Joseph Bell [1] (born 1837 : died 1911), under whose ægis Conan Doyle came as a medical student.

" It is no wonder," the latter wrote, " that after a study of such a character, I used and amplified his methods when in later life I tried to build up a scientific detective who solved cases on his own merits and not through the folly of the criminal." The Press, scenting a good story, would seem to have regarded Dr. Bell and Sherlock Holmes as identical. To judge from his photographs, Dr. Bell had the nose, so to speak, in register, and the sharp, almost ascetic mouth that we associate with the detective. Conan Doyle described Dr. Bell thus : " He was thin, wiry, dark, with a high nosed, acute face, penetrating grey eyes, angular shoulders, and a jerky way of walking. His voice was high and discordant."

As far as character goes there appears to be one and

[1] From this account of Dr. Joseph Bell, I am drawing largely from *Dr. James Bell—An Appreciation by a Friend* (Oliphant Anderson & Ferrier).

only one important point of similarity. From the pages
of the *Appreciation*, Dr. Bell emerges as a modest,
jovial, good-natured man with a Galsworthian sense
of justice for the under-dog. I cannot quite imagine
Sherlock Holmes saying, as Dr. Bell is reported to have
said on one occasion, " I take no credit for it at all."
Dr. Bell at first detested the meretricious notoriety
which surrounded him as soon as the resemblance
became apparent. " Why bother yourself about the
cataract of drivel for which Conan Doyle is responsible ? " he once asked. On another occasion he said,
" I hope you folk see another and better side to me
than what Doyle saw." But Bell grew reconciled to his
caricature, for Conan Doyle tells us that he " took a
keen interest in these detective tales and even made
suggestions, which were not, I am bound to say, very
practical."

And now for the one point of similarity. Its importance may be judged from the fact that it is the
most familiar trait in Sherlock's character. For it is
the Holmes manner. First let me quote from Conan
Doyle's own account of Bell :—

> " He was a very skilful surgeon, but his strong point
> was diagnosis, not only of disease, but of occupation
> and character. . . . I had ample chance of studying
> his methods and in noticing that he often learned more
> of the patient by a few quick glances than I had done
> by my questions. . . . In one of his best cases he said
> to a civilian patient :—
> " ' Well, my man, you've served in the army.'
> " ' Aye, sir.'
> " ' Not long discharged ? '
> " ' No, sir.'
> ' ' A Highland regiment ? '
> " ' Aye sir.'
> " ' A non-com. officer ? '

" ' Aye, sir.'

" ' Stationed at Barbadoes ? '

" ' Aye, sir.'

" ' You see, gentlemen,' he would explain, ' the man was a respectful man, but he did not remove his hat. They do not in the army, but he would have learned civilian ways had he been long discharged. He has an air of authority and he is obviously Scottish. As to Barbadoes, his complaint is elephantiasis, which is West Indian and not British.' "

To supplement this extract, we take two quotations from the magazines. First from the *Strand Magazine* :

" Case No. 1 would step up. ' I see,' said Dr. Bell, ' you're suffering from drink. You even carry a flask in the inside pocket of your coat.' "

And secondly a statement of Dr. Bell's as reported in the *Pall Mall Gazette* :

" I recollect he (Conan Doyle) was amused once when a patient walked in and sat down. ' Good-morning, Pat,' I said for it was impossible not to see that he was an Irishman. ' Good-morning, your honour,' replied the patient. ' Did you like your walk over the links to-day as you came in from the south side of the town ? ' I asked. ' Yes,' said Pat. ' Did your honour see me ? '

" Well, Conan Doyle could not see how I knew that, absurdly simple as it was.

" On a showery day, such as that had been, the reddish clay at bare parts of the links adheres to the boot and a tiny part is bound to remain. There is no such clay anywhere else round the town for miles. That and one or two similar instances excited Doyle's keenest interest and set him experimenting in the same directions, which, of course, was just what I wanted with all my other students."

Conan Doyle revolutionised, possibly recreated, the detective story by making a character of the detective. We recall once more the history. Dupin was hardly human enough. Sergeant Cuff was not enough of the detective. M. Lecoq and Père Tabaret were efficient detectives, amusing and likeable, but hardly personal friends. We might easily fail to recognise them.

Conan Doyle, in his creation of Sherlock Holmes, compromised between this intellectualism and humanism. But, as the former element is so much more important than the latter, his remedy is in some ways ludicrously artificial. The thinking automaton necessarily takes precedence. Then comes an exploitation of mannerisms or a farcial caricature of logic and reason on holiday. Mr. Beverley Nichols quotes Conan Doyle as saying of Sherlock Holmes :

> " I've always felt that he's hardly human. He's got so few angles from which we can approach him. . . . I soon realised he was really nothing but a calculating machine. . . . As soon as you begin to make your detective too human the story flops. You have to be ruthlessly analytical about the whole thing.'

Eccentricity was the *deus ex machina*, as it did not involve any profound study of character in its expression, but was rather a cloak to conceal it. Again, a more subtle use might be made of eccentricity by innuendo. Once you admit the hypothesis that genius and eccentricity stalk hand in hand—and many readers of detective fiction are fortunately credulous enough to believe anything—you are inveigled into concluding that the very mention of the latter presupposes the existence of the former. It is a simple expedient but needs careful handling unless it is to tumble to the depths of the ridiculous. But its success is proved by the fact that it is a favourite target of Parody. The fashion at all events is now firmly established.

Observe, too, the more facile way of creating an impression by an exploitation of the peculiarities of personal appearance. Take the angular features of Sherlock Holmes, or the bland owlishness of Father Brown, or the conical head of Malcolm Sage, or the monocle of Carrington. The picturesque has got the better of the beautiful. Remembering the doctrine of Carlyle, cast your eyes also on the clothes favoured by the great detectives. Is their choice not in character ? Is it possible to imagine figures more *outré*, more outlandish ?

In the hey-day of pictorial illustration, I dare believe the detective had still a better chance of notoriety. Sherlock Holmes has always been indebted to the artists, and Martin Hewitt and Father Brown were equally fortunate in this respect. Nowadays our detectives are to be esteemed fortunate should their portrait adorn a dust-wrapper.

Although the second edition of a *Study in Scarlet* carried illustrations by Charles Doyle, the father of Sir Arthur, it was Sydney Paget who created the now familiar figure. Conan Doyle commented on the liberties taken by Paget, and described his own idea of Sherlock as follows :

" I saw him as very tall—' over six feet, but so excessively lean that he seemed considerably taller,' said *A Study in Scarlet*. He had, as I imagined him, a thin, razor-like face, with a great hawk's bill of a nose, and two small eyes set close together on either side of it. Such was my conception. It chanced, however, that poor Sydney Paget, who, before his premature death drew all the original pictures, had a younger brother whose name, I think, was Walter, who served

him as a model. The handsome Walter took the place
of the more powerful but uglier Sherlock."

At the same time, appearance and mannerisms are
hardly adequate to make a personality. Conan Doyle
started with a vengeance the romantic apotheosis of
the detective :

> " To carry the art (of ideal reasoning), however, to
> its highest pitch, it is necessary that the reasoner
> should be able to utilise all the facts which have come
> to his knowledge, and this in itself implies, as you will
> readily see, a possession of all knowledge, which, even
> in these days of free education and encyclopædias, is
> a somewhat rare accomplishment. It is not so im-
> possible, however, that a man should possess all
> knowledge which is likely to be useful to him in his
> work, and this I have endeavoured in my case to do.
> If I remember rightly, you on one occasion, in the
> early days of our friendship, defined my limits in a
> very precise fashion."

Then came Sir Arthur's timid apology in Dr. Watson's
rejoinder :

> " ' Yes,' I answered, laughing. ' It was a singular
> document. Philosophy, astronomy, and politics were
> marked at zero, I remember. Botany variable, geology
> profound as regards the mudstains from any region
> within fifty miles of town, chemistry eccentric, anatomy
> unsystematic, sensational literature and crime records
> unique, violin player, boxer, swordsman, lawyer and
> self-poisoner by cocaine and tobacco.' "

In time our writers dispensed with scruples of this
sort and the detective was raised almost to the plane
of philosophic perfection. He acquired, somehow, an
encyclopædic knowledge. He was a polyglot, a votary
of the arts, a scientist, a doctor—the incarnation of

omniscience. Occasionally, however, Holmes's utili-
tarian knowledge has been regarded as an adequate
equipment by our more conservative and thus less
exacting writers. Mr. H. C. Bailey's Mr. Fortune, for
example, knows a little of everything, " not thoroughly
according to himself, but quite thoroughly enough for
his own purposes."

Despite any conclusions to the contrary we may have
drawn from his personal appearance, it is but natural
that our detective should be an athlete. His creator is
not satisfied with bestowing on him a *mens sana* alone.
This further step is not a philanthropic or adulatory
gesture. It is a necessity ; for the detection of the
criminal is a hazardous enterprise and in a novel of
action it is too much a tempting of providence to rob
the hero of an attack and defence which is a second
nature to the villain. The more action there is, the more
athletic our detective becomes. We cannot get away
from the fact that our Muse still regards as delectable
superhuman feats of strength. Chinatown demands it.
Only it would be as pleasant for the detectives themselves as for us to have a brief respite from this vigorous
Philistinism. Their muscles would at least cease from
that interminable " rippling " on their backs !

In this context one thing has always perplexed me—
the mysterious immunity our detectives enjoy from
the exigencies of training. Be it admitted, by all means,
that Conan Doyle was alive to this anomaly.

> " Sherlock Holmes was a man who seldom took
> exercise for exercise's sake. Few men were capable
> of greater muscular effort, and he was undoubtedly
> one of the finest boxers of his weight that I have ever
> seen ; but he looked upon aimless bodily exertion
> as waste of energy, and he seldom bestirred himself
> save where there was some professional object to be

served. Then he was absolutely untiring and indefatigable. That he should have kept himself in training under such circumstances is remarkable, but his diet usually was of the sparest and his habits were simple to the verge of austerity."

Notice the misleading *petitio principii* in : " That he should have kept himself in training . . . is remarkable." Remarkable, certainly, if we recall Dr. Watson's stricture in the passage quoted before : " self-poisoner by cocaine and tobacco." Really, we expect Dr. Watson to be consistent. However that may be, training or no training, Holmes could run a record-breaking race after the Hound of the Baskervilles, and straighten out a bent poker with his " sensitive " hands !

" Where would Sherlock Holmes be in our memories without his drugs, his dressing-gown, and his violin ? " asked a reviewer in *The Times*. Where would our detectives be without their endearing quixotry, their disarming cynicism, and their thousand and one affectations ? Presumably part and parcel of disembodied reason. Either alternative is equally an impossibility : but, fortunately, there are degrees of attractiveness amongst impossibilities. Therein lies Holmes's *apologia*.

THE HOLMES METHOD

Holmes goes to the scene of the crime (hansom cab to Paddington), makes his investigations and takes his measurements. Then he returns to Baker Street and works out the conclusion from his data. From time to time he has recourse to an imaginative reconstruction of the crime, and he asks himself how so-and-so would

act in the circumstances. This may lead to a correspondence of his theory with the data, or to a new
interpretation of the data. . . . One never knows—
even Dr. Watson did not know—when or exactly how
Holmes arrived at a theory at all. Theory is born of
inference and Holmes's problem is to form the correct
inference. But this he cannot do until he has decided
which evidence is vital. In order to do this he must
have already formed *some* theory. But this is splitting
hairs.

Two justifiable accusations can be brought against
the Holmes method. The first is that he is occasionally
guilty of the *non sequitur*. He argues to suit the plot,
and the alternatives, the delight or bugbear of the true
logician, are disregarded. " A criminal," wrote E. M.
Wrong, " who had grasped his methods could have
defeated him. Holmes knew which way a bicycle had
gone because the back wheel's impression was deeper
than that of the front wheel ; the fact is true, but save
possibly on a hill, contributes nothing to the question
of direction. Holmes guessed that two persons, not
three, had drunk out of three glasses because all the
lees were in the third, but two clever men could have
drunk from all three, and avoided this, or three might
thus have masqueraded as two." The first great weakness of his method is that of inconclusiveness.

The second is the continual violation of the fairplay
method. Most of Holmes's discoveries are on the quiet.
He goes away in disguise to Limehouse, or suddenly
surprises Watson in the Baker Street flat. He never
tells him at the time what he is doing, where his " line "
is taking him. Everything is wrapped in mystery.
The realist despises Holmes for this : but the theatricality of Holmes is good exchange.

Dr. Watson

The detective's colleague also assumed a personality.
I leave it to you to decide whether this Boswell is
greater than the Johnson. It has frequently been said
that Dr. Watson is the typical Englishman of the
professional class. In the spirit in which it is said this
statement does not reflect much credit. But as a matter
of fact Dr. Watson could not help but be a good doctor.
The absurd charges of general dullness and stupidity
which are usually regarded as proven, are really un-
founded. The worthy doctor only showed that he could
not get the hang of detection ; could not readily apply
himself to processes of inference ; was a romanticist
rather than a logician. In similar circumstances the
majority of people would cut an even sorrier figure.
Mr. Edward Shanks writes very charmingly about
Dr. Watson :—

> "It is no less easy with a small use of the imagination,
> to see him going his rounds in that practice which he
> was always so ready to abandon for a few days to his
> accommodating neighbour. His manner was always
> more magisterial with his patients than with Holmes,
> from whom, besides, he gained some reflected glory,
> and a good many simple tricks of innocent bluff. He
> was too solid and valuable a figure for any one to re-
> sent those occasional absences from which he returned
> possibly with a good story, or, if not, with a most
> delightful air of importance and mystery. And he
> had qualities of heart ; there is something genuinely
> touching in his devotion for Holmes, and in the rare
> treasured glimpses of Holmes's devotion to him."

About the Baker Street ménage there is a deathless
attraction. The details impinge on the memory—

Holmes brooding over the mystery of London at night ; the blue packet on the breakfast table ; the reference files : the rug : the revolver in the drawer of the desk. The table talk is a most refreshing tonic. Its epigrammatic flavour : the intentionally provocative platitudes of the doctor : the crushing paradoxes of Sherlock : tentative suggestions and patronising superciliousness—these things will live as long as the language. The very style of their conversation became the standard for a host of imitators.

Several divergent views have been expressed on this pairing of the brilliant detective with a dull colleague. The idea has long since been worked to death and that is Dr. Watson's triumph. But would not the contemplation of a rather unexciting monochrome be more satisfactory than that eternal chequer ?

Even as Holmes had his Dr. Watson, so had Martin Hewitt his Brett, Thorndyke his Jervis, Poirot his Captain Hastings, Max Carrados his Carlyle, Philo Vance his Van Dine, and so on *ad infinitum*. It may be that the construction calls for his existence : that false theories mnst be propounded and false clues pursued in order that the problem may remain a problem for the requisite number of pages. It may be expedient to preserve the dignity of the detective, and to butcher his colleague in order to save his skin. It may be more fun to hunt in couples. Man may, as E. M. Wrong suggested, like to tell his secrets to an interested audience.

Again, it may be artistic that the detective should have a Boswell, and that the Boswell should in reality be as great a man as the Johnson. It may be a pleasant whimsicality for the one to be invariably right and the other invariably wrong, as in Mr. A. A. Milne's *Two Bears Who Lived in a Wood*. But I ask you in all

seriousness, is the relation not monotonous ? Why not
a turning of the tables ? Would it involve too weak a
pandering to melodrama to introduce some element
of luck and coincidence in order to vindicate honest
stupidity, since we grant intelligence to one and with-
hold it in its totality from another ?

I dream of the day when Dr. Watson will turn up a
trump, and what ample grounds he will have for being
rude in the extreme to his " distinguished friend " !
Holmes, indeed, behaves abominably to his foil. It is
a surprising fact that Dr. Watson stuck it so long. His
relations with Holmes were at times apt to be a little
strained, and once or twice they came very near to
quarrelling. (Incidentally, Mrs. Watson was the worst
sufferer.) The wonder is that Dr. Watson did not one
day, in a fit of exasperation, burn all his painstaking
notes. Fidelity knows no greater exponent.

Yet our Dr. Watsons have one feather in their caps.
They perform one of the functions of the Chorus in
Greek Tragedy : they reflect the average opinion of
" the ordinary man." They are the amateurs, while
the detectives are the specialists, the professionals.
They may commit obstruction or stand aside, wringing
their hands from an egregious incapacity. Still they
may plume themselves on the fact that they represent
what in their authors' minds will be the orthodox
theories entertained by the unwitting reader.

It was just this that got on our nerves. We became
sophisticated and could not brook to be so imposed
upon. In turn there arose a tendency to wipe the
specialist off the slate and the old feud between the
Gentlemen and Players was discontinued. Or, to put
it in a different way, Dr. Watson came into his own :
but in another way than the one already suggested.
The characters of the detective and Dr. Watson were

in a way fused. The one had lost what the other had gained. The solution of the mystery was entrusted to any Tom, Dick or Harry (perferably, you will notice, to a free-lance writer of detective fiction), who would make a presentable hero and fall in love with the girl so conveniently suspected by a benevolent Scotland Yard. So the young aspirant muddled through.

And now for a short account of the plot construction. Here, at least, we can rely on the author's own account. To Sir Arthur Conan Doyle the central idea came first —vague and unshapely it may be, but the essential and creative spark—and round this he constructed his story. Taken in itself the only claim on the attention that this idea has is its basis of novelty. If he was writing a murder story he needs must have imagined a new way of killing ; and a snake or a hound became the villain's instrument of death. Then began the construction proper, the *labor limæ*, the materialising of the idea, the development of it, refinement and limitation. We may well wonder at the frequency of these sparks, yet sympathise when we learn of the travail endured in creating them. Mr. H. Greenhough Smith, in an article in the *Strand Magazine* on *Some Letters of Conan Doyle*, quoted from a letter he received from Conan Doyle :—

> " I can write stories if I have good initial ideas but have rather exhausted my own stock. No wonder. I wonder if a competition for the best mystery idea would be possible—probably you would get no fish worth taking out of the net."

Concrete events, however, supplied him, on occasions, with ideas. Mr. Greenhough Smith relates how a German case supplied Conan Doyle with the idea and also the detection in *The Problem of Thor Bridge*, and how a child's scribble suggested the cryptogram in *The Dancing Man*." It is generally known, besides, that *The Man with the Twisted Lip* had his counterpart in real life.

In the report of an interview he had with Conan Doyle, Mr. Beverley Nichols has given us the latter's account of how he came to write *The Speckled Band* :

> " First of all I get my central idea—take *The Speckled Band* as an example. The first stage of that story was when, suddenly, and for no particular reason, the idea came to me of a man killing somebody with a snake. I thought the idea a good one, and thinking of it made it gradually grow. The man, I decided, should be an Anglo-Indian, and the person he should kill would be, naturally, somebody whose death would be to his advantage—preferably a woman. To heighten the gruesome effect of the story, I decided that it should be laid in remote surroundings, which would make the pathos of the victim the more acute.
>
> " Already, therefore, we had arrived after a very little thought at the conception of an unscrupulous man, who has lived in India, and has planned to murder his step-daughter by a snake in order that he may reap the benefit of a will that should rightly be hers. Well, there's the basis of the story. The rest consists of two tasks—the concoction of false scents to put the reader off the track and keep him guessing till the last minute, and the provision of clues as ingenious as one can make them for the detective to follow up."

Sherlock Holmes was the child of unemployment. Conan Doyle had taken consulting rooms in Montagu Street. Here from ten in the morning till four in the afternoon he endured enforced idleness, waiting almost against hope for the ring of his bell. In this inauspicious state of anticipation he created Sherlock Holmes.

In *A Study in Scarlet* Sherlock Holmes made his first appearance as Mr. Sherrington Hope : in fact, it was only after some chopping and changing about that Conan Doyle hit on the combination that satisfied him. The book is divided into two parts, and here he followed in the footsteps of Gaboriau. The first part consists of the statement and the problem, and the action paves the way for the second. This second part is an annalistic explanation of the conclusions already reached. The action is, as it were, reversed, and we have to spin backwards through time. Finally, we link up the past with the present. This retrogression detracts from the life of the action ; our suspense is allayed and we lose interest. Indeed Conan Doyle discarded this method at once. In the *Sign of Four* he borrowed some of the atmosphere of *The Moonstone* : got the story moving quickly at the start, and kept the speed up till the end. The action is now, so to speak, "present action," and the result is a capital thriller. The problem, however, is hardly up to the Holmes standard. In *The Hound of the Baskervilles* and *The Valley of Fear*, and chiefly the former, we have a perfect expression of tense atmosphere, the touch of the supernatural adding fuel to the spark of the original idea.

The idea of the fiery hound was taken from a Welsh guide-book, and the notion of introducing this traditional piece of folk-lore into a Sherlock Holmes story was one Fletcher-Robinson's. Mr. Greenhough Smith, in quoting from a letter of Conan Doyle's, adds that Fletcher-Robinson' name was fully acknowledged. The letter runs :

> " I have the idea of a real creeper for *The Strand*. It is full of surprises, breaking naturally into good lengths for serial purposes. There is one stipulation—

I must do it with my friend, Fletcher-Robinson, and his name must appear with mine. I can answer for the yarn being all my own in my own style, without dilution, since your readers like that. But he gave me the central idea and the local colour, and so I feel his name must appear."

It should be noted that in these four novels, he does not definitely, or at least for any length of time, dally with the red herrings. The art of the suspicious-game has not yet been cultivated. This is due to the fact that he has a habit of keeping his secondary characters rather in the background. He does not parade them before us in every chapter. Again he does not believe in a wide range of *dramatis personæ*, or in concentrating his attention either on the villain or on the principal suspect. It may be objected that artistically the attitude has its limitations. Possibly, but with Sherlock Holmes it makes the game more intriguing.

A competition in *The Observer*, on the popularity of the various Sherlock Holmes stories, resulted in the placing of the favourites in this order :

1. *The Speckled Band.*
2. *The Hound of the Baskervilles.*
3. *The Sign of Four.*
4. *A Study in Scarlet.*
5. *The Red-Headed League.*
6. *A Scandal in Bohemia.*
7. *The Naval Treaty.*
8. *The Man With the Twisted Lip.*

The *Strand Magazine* published Conan Doyle's own list, which is limited to the short stories.

1. *The Speckled Band.*
2. *The Red-Headed League.*
3. *The Dancing Men.*
4. *The Final Problem.*
5. *A Scandal in Bohemia.*
6. *The Empty House.*
7. *The Five Orange Pips.*
8. *The Second Stair.*
9. *The Devil's Foot.*
10. *The Priory School.*
11. *The Musgrave Ritual.*
12. *The Reigate Squires.*

Many people have attributed to the falling off the cliff a corresponding falling off in the detective's prowess, but an impartial review of the subsequent cases must surely induce us to qualify that statement.

Conan Doyle at that time himself commented, rather whimsically, on Holmes Redivivus :

"I was amazed at the concern expressed by the public. They say a man is never properly appreciated until he is dead, and the general protest against my summary execution of Holmes taught me how many and how numerous were his friends. ' You Brute ! ' was the beginning of the letter of remonstrance which one lady sent me, and I expect she spoke for others besides herself. I heard of many who wept. I fear I was utterly callous myself, and only glad to have a chance of opening out into new fields of imagination, for the temptation of high prices made it difficult to get one's thoughts away from Holmes."

As regards *The Case Book* it would only be fair to remember that the detective was in his senescence.

Conan Doyle blithely confesses in *Memories and Adventures* his liability to make mistakes :

"Sometimes I have got upon dangerous ground
where I have taken risks through my own want of
knowledge of the correct atmosphere. I have, for
example, never been a racing man, and yet I have
ventured to write *Silver Blaze* in which the mystery
depends upon the laws of training and racing. The
story is all right, and Holmes may have been at the
top of his form, but my ignorance cries aloud to heaven.
I read an excellent and very damaging criticism
of the story in some sporting paper, written clearly
by a man who *did* know, in which he explained the
exact penalties which would have come upon every
one concerned if they had acted as I described. Half
would have been in jail, and the other half warned off
the turf forever. However, I have never been nervous
about details, and one must be masterful sometimes."

Hardly a single contemporary critic would have
taken the trouble to unearth these howlers. With the
development of the detective story, readers have
become hypercritical, and take a fiendish delight in
picking holes.

The errors which found their way into the Sherlock
Holmes text have been the subject of a voluminous,
but not unentertaining, correspondence in periodicals,
such as *John O' London's Weekly*. It is interesting
to note that none of these errors seriously affect the
plots. They are, without exception, errors of detail.
For instance, Canon Whitechurch points out that in
The Final Problem the special train was allowed to
dash through a station only a few minutes after a
previous train had left, whereas it would have taken
at least eight minutes before the line could have been
signalled clear. Again, in *The Valley of Fear*, Watson
knew all about Moriarty, yet in *The Final Problem* he
has never heard of him—which comes of writing out
of chronological order. A correspondent notes a dis-
crepancy of dates in *The Adventure of the Red-Headed*

League. Another has some hard words for Sherlock's filing system. In *The Case of the Sussex Vampire,* it is discovered that Sherlock has indexed " Voyage of the *Gloria Scott*" and " Victor Lynch" under V instead of under G and L !

Sherlock Holmes has made numerous appearances on the stage and screen. *The Speckled Band* is the favourite stage story, and after it an adaptation of the *Return*. Dramatic critics will aver that Mr. Eille Norwood's performances have been the most satisfactory. Mr. John Barrymore's characterisation was less in accord with the popular notions as to how the part ought to be played. Similarly Mr. Clive Brook's performance in the recent talkie was a failure in this respect. Even in his make-up he was at no pains to resemble the traditional figure, and there was no need for Mr. Basil Dean to dress this Sherlock Holmes adventure in a contemporary setting. The Sherlock Holmes we know does not grow old, and touring cars are a poor substitute for growlers. Although Sherlock Holmes lived through the war, his period must remain Victorian.

CHAPTER VI

THE DOMESTIC DETECTIVE STORY

I

A tragedy is not a tragedy until it moves you. . . . Detective novelists are subject to the same great principles as other novelists. One of these principles is that a good novel cannot be made out of puppets.—Arnold Bennett *in the* Evening Standard.

For character-drawing in general the detective novelist usually pays only a passing regard. His characters have to re-act—to say the least of it—to an unusual situation, and so what they say and do is forced and exaggerated. They are, of necessity, unnatural and false to type. But then our author is not interested in types. He is more immediately concerned with emotions and passions, to follow the Aristotelian division, than with states of mind and the development of traits and propensities. His analysis is limited to motive, and motive reveals only a section of character. Character is thus taken unawares at a ridiculous poise, like the bather who finds his clothes stolen. It follows that many of the characters we meet in detective fiction are theatrical with a traditional stock-in-trade.

This absence of portraiture has been felt to be a serious drawback to the detective story. Mr. Chesterton writes : " If Sherlock Holmes is the only familiar figure in modern fiction, Sherlock is also the only familiar figure in the Sherlock Holmes tales. Not many people could say offhand what was the name of the owner of Silver Blaze, or whether Mrs. Watson was dark or fair. But if Dickens had written the Sherlock Holmes stories, every character in them would have been equally arresting and memorable. A Sherlock Holmes would have cooked the dinner for Sherlock Holmes. . . ."

For a long time the detective story writer fought shy of the company of live men and women. The novel of character was outside his domain. The moment came when he began to ask himself whether he could take a leaf out of fiction's book? If fiction ran the love element in preference to any other—well, he would have to see what he could do about it. However callously and dispassionately detective fiction dissected elemental and primitive passions, love, as the most elemental and primitive, would of necessity wander into the detective's ken. As a reader of human conduct he would have to know something about it, and from experience—on that we are all agreed. Well, one could be tactful, make no allusion to the detective's *affaires* and take them for granted with a polite cynicism. In that case he would probe for motives in crimes of passion, and unite the happy lovers like a genial Haroun al Raschid, first making trial of them by the ordeal of suspicion. Even so, love is still on the shelf. We are still dissecting shadows.

But, being sociable, our Muse asked herself the question : Will people like it ? She was just a little tired of analysis after Poe and of analysis plus eccentricity after Conan Doyle. " Let's have a little love," she suggested in a weak moment—and she got it hot and strong. Her detective started to fall in love. But he was not given a sporting chance. He had, in fact, only a paragraph or two of it between the successive abductions of his darling. In Chapter I. he met the

girl, and fell in love with her at first sight. It had to
be then or never, for he would certainly never see her
at her best again until the last pages. For the rest
of the book she was *dérangée, décolletée* and all these
other delicious Gallicisms which seem so ethereally
suggestive to the Anglo-Saxon. Don't imagine I am
exaggerating. Even worse was the plight of Pearl
White's and Mabel Normand's heroines in the serial
films. Putting all the fifteen episodes together, the
love-making cannot have lasted much longer than
five minutes.

Our Muse was not altogether pleased with the way
things were shaping. It was really undignified and
common. Her detective had sacrificed his superhuman
throne to go after a slip of a girl. Genius ought not to
fall in love with insipid beauty. (Poor girl, she had to
remain insipid !) Besides, what business had he to
fall in love ? It was defensible, although a mistake at
this stage, to make out that the detective must have
been young once and was at perfect liberty *desipere in
loco*. It was worse still—a deplorable error of judgement
—to make Sherlock Holmes (as portrayed by Mr.
John Barrymore) a slave to the conventional fade-out
in the film *Moriarty*. To imagine the face of Sherlock
Holmes—however platonic the profile—in close
proximity to a woman's is gross degradation. It is
to be admitted that at this time in his life Sherlock
Holmes was supposed to be an undergraduate at
Cambridge, but even this extenuation is not sufficient
cause for his peccadillo.

Far better the detectives should remain at a static
middle age. We do not expect them to fall in love.
It is *not* their business. Cynically we require them to
show more sense ; romantically they are not worth
the " self-abnegation " that Miss Mannin in the

evening papers so sweetly bestows on woman's love. Who, indeed, would be a detective's wife ? They are untidy, they are absent-minded. They are often dyspeptic. They are not clubbable, and the lioniser would not stand a chance with them. Their hours are impossible, their tobacco is rank. They riddle the walls at their revolver practice, or their enemies do it for them.

If you argue in this strain you are taking it for granted that the mould of the detective story is set ; that the conventions—the unnecessary conventions, not the canons—have got to stay. Once this attitude is questioned and action taken, new avenues and vistas of the best Lloyd Georgian kind are unrolled before our eyes.

2

Mr. E. C. Bentley's *Trent's Last Case*

There have been several attempts to civilise the detective story. Realism was the pressing inducement, for the phantasia of the super-sleuth had began to grow stale. The detective story was thus obliged to become domesticated. The introduction of character study was at first not an entirely satisfactory innovation. The *dramatis personæ* would behave for the major part of the book rather like W. J. Locke's characters—pleasantly evasive. Then the climax would turn Hyperion to a satyr. In a paragraph the smooth solicitor would be translated to a snarling maniac with an unprepossessing rictus. To this maladjustment, it must be confessed, the detective story is frequently subject. It is the greatest flaw in the theme of " the most unlikely person."

Mr. E. C. Bentley, however, in *Trent's Last Case* (1913) evaded this bogey of Inconsistency. To do this he had to spirit away his villain by making him the " murdered " man, and the posthumous influence of his malignity was just sufficient and no more to take the characters out of themselves. *Trent's Last Case* is a solo excursion by Mr. Bentley into detective fiction,* with the exception of a short Trent story, *The Clever Cockatoo*, published in the *Strand Magazine* (1914) and included by Miss Sayers in her anthology. Mr. Bentley is also famous for his *Biography for Beginners* in which he collaborated with Mr. G. K. Chesterton. *Who's Who*, curiously enough, omits to mention Mr. Bentley, and so little is known of him to the public that his existence has actually been scouted as a myth ! A recent reprint of *Trent's Last Case* (1929), however, bears with it a portrait of the author which reveals such clearly intellectual features as the high forehead and sharp, decisive mouth. Actually Mr. Bentley is on the staff of the *Daily Telegraph*.

Like so many detective tales, *Trent's Last Case* was, the story goes, the outcome of a wager. Mr. Bentley does not seemingly regard this as a " really noble motive." The only really noble motive he had in writing it, he tells us in the dedication to Mr. G. K. Chesterton, was that the latter might enjoy it. He further informs us that he " unfolded the plan of it— surrounded by Frenchmen "—a remark full of meaning, but unfortunately impossible to appreciate. Mr. Chesterton politely returned the compliment in kind, by writing enthusiastically about *Trent's Last Case*.

Miss Sayers declares it to be an acknowledged masterpiece of the genre, and considers the love story is " handled artistically and with persuasive emotion." The back cover of the reprint carries a formidable

---

* No longer true. *Trent Intervenes* (1938) is a collection of short stories.—E. F. B.

symposium of panegyrics from such writers as Dr. Austin Freeman, Mr. Wills Crofts, Mr. J. S. Fletcher and J. J. Connington.

In some respects the story is unique. The detective Philip Trent—who falls in love with one of the suspects —fails to solve the problem, and the solution is tendered gratis. For this violation of the rules the staggering dénouement is for once ample compensation. It is true that it also causes a second infringement. The " murder " turned out to be a less " sensational," but in the circumstances equally exciting, justifiable homicide. In fact, Mr. Bentley turned the tables very neatly. Instead of adhering rigidly to the rules and thus sacrificing his characters, he preferred the human drama and an elastic code. Otherwise the orthodox features are present. For many reasons it is the perfect detective story ; and not least for its construction. Indeed, so meticulously is it pieced together, that it fails to discourage the analyst ; it even invites the knife. That is at least a defence, however poor, for attempting rather callously to analyse the plot. Suppose we imagine, for the fun of it, the unfolding of the plan.

Could a detective story be worked out (we remember it was a wager) from the idea of a man committing suicide, in order to bring to the gallows an innocent man of whom he was blindly jealous ? Well, it had been done before. Planting was an old-fashioned dodge. One would have to consider at all events the motive to jealousy. Suppose the villain suspected the dupe of being in love with his wife. On the strength of these suspicions he determines either to commit suicide, or preferably for his own sake to build up a perfect case of circumstantial evidence of robbery, assault, etc., against the innocent party. A straight novel might easily be made out of that triangle. Observe how the

entry of the detective complicates matters. Two
alternatives at once suggest themselves :—

(1) The detective should arrive at the correct solution
of the problem, or,

(2) He should solve the problem as the villain meant
it to be solved—by reliance on circumstantial evidence.
The second alternative would, however, mean the
violation of a perfectly sound canon of detective fiction,
the happy ending. Therefore, we must be content with
(1).

Now, the circumstantial evidence will be based
willy-nilly on an examination of the wife and the
innocent " lover." These relations might be described
so as to make the reader believe that an illicit love
affair was responsible for the " murder " of the
husband. Or again, it might be hinted that the husband
was a brute and beat his wife, and thus the sympathy
of modern humanitarianism be enlisted. The latter
method would be the more natural one considering the
husband's real character. But what was the detective
to think ?

Then possibly was born Mr. Bentley's great idea—
that the detective should fall in love with the wife,
that it should be a grand passion. There would be
drama in this situation : the detective in love with the
wife (or widow), tormenting himself now with the
thought that his loved one was guilty of her husband's
death, now with the no less agonising suspicion that
the dupe had fired the shot from love of her. (One
recalls in this context a less dramatic and less artistic
situation in *Blackmail*.)

The opening of the story is surprising. As far as the
construction goes the first chapter is superfluous.
Sigsbee Manderson is dead. Plain, stark fact. No
ominous thuds. No shots ringing out in the tenebral

stillness. The story might have opened in the offices of the *Record*. Yet, for one reason only it is a brilliant piece of technique. Mr. Bentley, possibly underrating his power of creating the correct atmosphere, evidently determined at the outset to make in an indirect way the most of the dramatic and sensational possibilities.

We are immediately on the tiptoe of suspense. Sigsbee Manderson is dead ; the great financier is dead (Sigsbee *is* such a good name for the murdered man. It is also an additional motive to murder.) The world totters at his sudden demise. The " vortices of finance" (whatever they are) are in chaos. Thus is the importance of the issues magnified, and one of De Quincey's conditions of a perfect murder ignored. Listen to the Chestertonian thunder.

> " At the news of his death panic went through the markets like a hurricane. . . . All over the United States, wherever speculation had its devotees, went a waft of ruin, a plague of suicide. In Europe also not a few took with their own hands lives that had become pitiably linked to the destiny of a financier. In Paris a well-known banker walked quietly out of the Bourse and fell dead upon the broad steps among the raving crowd of Jews, a phial crushed in his hand. In Frankfurt one leapt from the Cathedral top leaving a redder stain where he struck the red tower. Men stabbed and shot and strangled themselves, drank death or breathed it as the air. . . ." [1]

Now we are in the offices of the *Record*. The press is on the job ; the salient facts are coming in. The editor decides to put Trent on the case. It is to be observed that Fleet Street is still regarded as superior

---

[1] Classical scholars will compare this with several passages in Thucydides !

in detection to Scotland Yard. This was of course before the latter had seen the commercial prospects in writing " shop " ! Curiously enough Mr. Bentley stoops to the old cliché of making Philip Trent unnecessarily reluctant to " take up the case."

The characters have now to be assembled. First comes Mr. Cupples, the genial, who conveniently supplies information about the Manderson ménage. This information amounts to the following :—

(1) The " murdered " man was not on good terms with his wife.

(2) Mr. Cupples had remonstrated with Sigsbee about it.

(3) Mr. Cupple's good words for Mrs. Manderson, suggesting that he is at pains to shield her, force the reader instantly to harbour a low suspicion against the latter.

(4) Mr. Cupple's frank admission that the death of Sigsbee was a pleasant little surprise serves to whitewash him.

Trent soon meets Inspector Murch in a spirit of friendly rivalry ; and just when we are expecting the death blow to the old antagonism and a victory for co-operation, the inspector softly and silently fades away. It is now Trent's business to show his mettle. Note-book in hand he creeps from room to room, taking finger-prints and measuring distances in splendid style. As far as the " psychological " aspect of the case goes, *Trent* starts by suspecting every one. Mrs. Manderson, Marlowe the secretary and intended dupe, Bunner the American, and the butler. As though aware of this, Bunner decides to simplify matters by producing so absurd a theory that he almost cries out to be suspected. All this time Mr. Bentley is working up a strong case against Marlowe and Mrs. Manderson.

The first movement closes with the suspects in this order (1) Marlowe ; (2) Mrs. Manderson ; (3) Bunner.

Mrs. Manderson had yet to make her entrance. The description of Trent's first sight of her is beautifully persuasive. We are immediately sentimental and, like Trent, drawn to her. Then we wonder for a moment if this persuasion was not really meant to consolidate our suspicions. The inquest soon follows, and Mrs. Manderson creates the expected sensation. Trent then ceases to be sentimental and becomes logical. False teeth and a pair of shoes occupy his attention ; and we return to the spade work. Trent, despite his logic, is fundamentally an intuitionalist. " Swiftly and *spontaneously* when chance or effort puts one in possession of the key fact in any system of baffling circumstances, one's ideas seem to rush to group themselves anew in relation to that fact, so that they are suddenly rearranged almost before one has consciously grasped the significance of the key fact itself."

The key fact once established, the process of inference proceeds apace. Trent's report is in many ways the most satisfying portion of the book. (Miss Sayers quotes from it at length to illustrate the shifting of the viewpoint from (1) " The Watson viewpoint " to (2) " The detective's " and to (3) " The middle viewpoint.") It is in a way all the more satisfying because, as we find later, the hypothesis was faulty ; and it is cleverer in a detective story to appear in these circumstances *plausible to the reader*, than to start from a true hypothesis and delude him by the way. Why this is so, I have never quite been able to understand. The final conclusion, prompted by the circumstantial evidence, is that Marlowe must have been the murderer.

The reader sits back, but finding that there are roughly 150 more pages to the book sits up again, and naturally wonders what the devil has happened. Is Trent wrong after all ? Was the deduction of pure reason all at sea ? The character of the book now changes. We forget we are reading a detective story. As Trent's love for Mrs. Manderson unfolds, the plot becomes one of character. Yet not for a moment does this development seem out of place. The farrago is exquisitely composed. The third movement ends in the united happiness of the detective and the woman once suspected.

And still suspected, for we suddenly remember that the problem has not been solved. Trent's theory of Marlowe's guilt suffers shipwreck when an intimation of the latter's engagement is brought to Trent's notice ; as Marlowe's motive was supposed to be his love for Mrs. Manderson. Trent has now a very good reason for getting to the bottom of the problem. He calls a council of war, and Marlowe is asked to attend. A diabolical suicide is exposed and the fourth wave is spent.

But what we supposed to be the real dénouement was merely a shadow ; and Mr. Cupples, dear old Cupples, in the last chapter of all provides the surprise of the book, upsets all calculations and beats every reader on the post. Without this grand finale the story would have had a satisfactory and effective conclusion ; but the last chapter raises it to the pinnacle of technique. By this stroke of genius the detective story is emancipated and claims a climax of its very own.

Even from this crude résumé it is not, I hope, impossible to recognise the sterling qualities which won that consensus of approbation. Never have the virtues of the genre been quite so elegantly displayed. The formal problem intertwined with the character problem ; the sincerity of the character study ; the

honeyed morsels of sensationalism ; the trail of the
red herrings, inside and outside the plot ; the natural-
ness of the "motivation ; " the tenseness and also
the humour of the situation ; and over and above all,
that supreme climax. It is rare that a solution hoaxes
both the detective and the reader. Mr. Bentley has
won that wager.

3

LYNN BROCK

Almost as much mystery enshrouds the identity of
Lynn Brock as of Mr. E. C. Bentley. Lynn Brock is
the pseudonym of Anthony Wharton, which in turn
is the pseudonym of Alister McAlister. But whether
Alister McAlister is a pseudonym or not I have not
been able to discover. It certainly sounds like it. At
all events Lynn Brock is an Irishman, born in Dublin
in 1877. During the war he served in the Machine Gun
Corps, and also, like so many other novelists, in the
Intelligence Service. He is rumoured to live near
Bristol, so if you have the hankering you might indulge
in a little bit of detective work. As Anthony Wharton
he is the author of a number of plays including *Irene
Wycherley, Nocturne, At the Barn, Benvenuto Cellini.*
He has, besides, written several straight novels—*Be
Good, Sweet Maid, The Two of Diamonds* and *The Man
on the Hill*—and contributed short stories to the
Saturday Evening Post and *Nash's Magazine.* His first
detective story, *The Deductions of Colonel Gore,* ap-
peared in 1924, and was followed by *Colonel Gore's
Second Case* (1926), *The Kink* (1927), *The Slip Carriage
Mystery* (1928), *The Dagwort Combe Murder* (1929),
The Mendip Mystery (1929), and *Q.E.D.* (1930).

Lynn Brock can introduce character study because he spurns indecent haste (his novels are roughly fifty pages longer than the average detective novel). Still the plot is only in a very small degree a character plot. Sensationalism is the mainspring, a sensationalism which Colonel Gore, the detective, admits ought, but fails to nauseate him : " There were moments when Gore accused himself—or rather thought that he ought to accuse himself—of an almost cold bloodedness in these speculations of his. The business was a horrible business. One ought to have been decently shocked by it." On the other hand the puzzle element as distinct from the action, is based on character. The reason for this is a simple one. Colonel Gore is not, and never could be, a detective. One can imagine his wrestling with Torquemada, or solving B.B.C. problems. But real murder—never. " Human sleuth " his publishers magniloquently but also mysteriously style him. What is the significance of the caption ? Does " human sleuth " mean merely that the sleuth is a man ? or that " humans " are his quarry ? Or does human mean humane, or most probably human in the sense *humanum est errare* ? Still, perhaps, they have ground for the epithet, for in the *Deductions* occurs the sentence, " It has been said that Wyck Gore was a very human person." Yet never by any stretch of the imagination could it be said that he was a sleuth. I dare say it sounds rather nice and Sexton Blakeish, but the indignity of it !

The Colonel, as a man of the world, finds the attraction of his first problem due to his interest in the actual *dramatis personæ*. And this, as with Philip Trent, makes him a psychologist after a manner. As a second point of similarity, he is at bottom an intuitionalist—chiefly for effect at the end of a chapter. " It's perfectly simple," he says once, " provided you reason logically, and stick to what you've reasoned, and don't get guessing about things blindly because at first they don't seem to square up all right. Perfectly simple—and quite infallible—provided you stick to it". But then the Colonel never does, thank heaven !

It wouldn't be as plain as a pikestaff either for the professional " sleuth " who could read character as a clairvoyant. To be candid, the Lynn Brock characters have little business in a *character* detective novel. They dress for dinner ; they play golf, and bridge, and dine together. They appear to be on the best of terms with each other. But we are asked to imagine secret intrigues and blackmail the moment the guests are gone, and descry bloodstains on the dreamiest and Toriest of golf courses. This is going too far ; make-believe is all very well up to a point. The wholesale massacre in the *Second Case* is almost comic. Possibly the *humanity* of the Colonel is responsible for this. Sociability and the holiday spirit are all very well, but scandal has to be so delicately wooed when it touches the professional classes and the Bath-Cheltenham brigade.

The Colonel might with justice bear a grudge against the attitude of his critics that he " makes plenty of blunders," that he has some " naïvetes " to smile at, some miscalculations to deplore. This criticism can only mean one thing—that the reader knows too much ; that the fair-play method has been pushed to the other extreme where the reader knows more than the detective. For example, in *The Deductions* the reader is aware, and the Colonel is not, that Cecil Arndale was a spectator in the highly dramatic scene between " Pickles " and Barrington. Miss Sayers finds fault with this state of affairs :—

" It is needless to add that the detective must be
given fair play too. Once they are embarked upon an
investigation, no episode must ever be described which
does not come within their cognisance. It is artistically
shocking that the reader should be taken into the
author's confidence behind the investigator's back.
Thus the reader's interest in *The Deductions of Colonel
Gore* is sensibly diminished. . . . Those tales in which
the action is frequently punctuated by eavesdropping
of this kind on the reader's part belong to the merely
sensational class of detective story."

This is not unequivocally true. The last sentence
might apply with some truth to a Gaboriau novel like
L'Affaire Lerouge, but it would not apply to a Thorndyke story. The real weakness seems to be rather that
we have a less intriguing substitute for the old problem
—a problem this time concerned with the means to
the solution. A much greater fault in *The Deductions*
was the hiding of Thomson through most of the action.

Our enjoyment in the Lynn Brock novels is due to
our liking for the Colonel. He is a " capital fellow."
Just a little too advanced in age to be a strong silent
hero, he is thus debarred from converting " Pickles "
into a second Mrs. Manderson. A platonic devotion—
they played together when children—drove the Colonel
to detection. A taste of it and he was like Mr.
Betteridge of the *Moonstone*, infected with the " fever."

. . . " The thing had now so caught hold of him,
that he had come to regard the actors in it as merely
pieces of a puzzle baffling and engrossing to the verge
of monomania. . . . ' I'm not going to be beaten by
the damn thing,' was his defence. ' I want to know.'
. . . He came to the conclusion—once more—that
all along he had made one fatal mistake. Instead of
following up any one of his theories he had allowed
himself to be distracted by every red herring."

That is an admirable commentary and apologia for Lynn Brock's method.

From the point of view of realism it is possible to be captious. No self-respecting colonel would draw graphs recording the process of the mind from " no record to certainty, through surmise to degrees of suspicion and belief," unless he were qualifying for a tutorship at Balliol. Nor would he write such copious self-analytical notes as he went along—unless it was to help the author to produce the red herrings.

There is every reason to suppose that Gore's platonic friendship with Pickles—like most platonic friendships —is about to be materially modified. In *Q.E.D* Lynn Brock had Pickles's husband murdered, so that the coast is now clear for the Colonel. Lynn Brock is now faced with an interesting dilemma. Pickles is prejudiced about private detectives, and hates to think of Gore engaged in the exposure of dirty linen. Unless she revises her opinions, the Colonel will have to make a fatal choice. Which is it to be, Matrimony or Detection ?

The Mendip Mystery and *Q.E.D.* suggest an attempt by Lynn Brock to reinstate the long detective story on the French model, to do for detective fiction what Mr. Priestley and Mr. Walpole have been doing for general fiction. For *The Mendip Mystery* and *Q.E.D.* are two parts of the same story, and Gretta Higgins is the arch-murderess in both. In *The Mendip Mystery* the Crown's case against her failed, but instead of thanking her lucky stars for her acquittal and curtailing her murderous activities she determined in *Q.E.D.* to go one better. It is unfortunate in a way that these two stories were published separately. In *Q.E.D.* Lynn Brock had to provide a review of *The Mendip Mystery* for the benefit of those who had been unfortunate

enough to miss it. Otherwise he might have been
accused of sharp practice. This tell-tale review spoilt
the problem. The plot became superficially complicated, and just too sensational. (The conclusion of
The Mendip Mystery was naturally unsatisfactory.)
We do, however, owe Lynn Brock a debt of gratitude
for having Dr. Melhuish murdered on the Clifton
suspension bridge. Bridges are eminently suitable for
murders, and the more famous the bridge, the more
dramatic the murder. What about the Forth Bridge
now ?

4

MR. PHILIP MACDONALD

Mr. Philip Macdonald is a grandson of George
Macdonald, the author of numerous Celtic phantasies
and romances. During the war Mr. Philip Macdonald
served in Mesopotamia, in which campaigns he got
copy for his *Patrol*—one of the best British war books.
Indeed, had *Patrol* been published during the 1930
boom, it would have been much more successful than
it actually was. Mr. Macdonald lives in Hertfordshire.
He is an authority on horses, and when he is not
engaged in writing detective stories he attends to the
breeding of hunters. I imagine him to have a good
deal in common with Michael Lawless in *The Link*.
His one ambition is to write " good " as distinguished
from detective novels. He finds no difficulty in writing
the latter. At the present moment he is said to be
carrying in his head no fewer than thirty-seven plots
for detective stories. His only fear is that some of
these ideas may be seized upon by others before he
has time to put them on paper.

To appreciate *The Rasp* (1924) to the full, one must first have read *Trent's Last Case*. This is the reason : Trent had started by suspecting Mrs. Manderson, and in the end had married her. Colonel Anthony Gethryn— the detective of *The Rasp*—started by suspecting Lucia; and he too fell in love at first sight. Thus, the reader who was familiar with Trent's love story had certainly grounds for harbouring the notion that Lucia might turn out to be a fraud. A second point of similarity is the formal report. Anthony is much more business-like than Philip, for he types his manuscript and indents the alternatives. The motive of the murder (this time it is a Cabinet Minister who is killed) is quite original. The victim is murdered by a colleague who is eaten up with jealousy, and who has had to play second fiddle to him from his school days. The murderer should not have had a double-barrelled name, for that is getting too common with criminals besides prejudicing the reader against them. One admired particularly the trick of the toupé which was put in position on the top of a chair's back to provide an alibi. Dummies have always had a run from the days of Sherlock Holmes, but custom simply cannot fade their infinite variety.

Colonel Anthony Gethryn has his nerves strung to fever pitch, and the *pizzicato* and the breathlessness of the narrative is inimitable. The interest is held almost by the style alone. Anthony is another of the intuitionalists ; he keeps his information to himself and waits for the momentous occasion when he can most theatrically divulge it.

In *The Noose* he defends his behaviour thus :—

" ' I'm constitutionally unable to spill the beans before they're properly cooked. P'raps I ought, but

I can't. That's all there is to it. I wouldn't, mind you,
Pike, keep you or any one else in the dark at a point
where your being in the dark might prejudice the
chance of success. But until that point, or until I'm
dead, cold, utterly sure—whichever is the earlier—
my beans remain unspilt. Sorry and all that. Expect
it comes from reading too many detective stories.
My sub-conscious ego—a monstrous brute—wants to
identify itself with Lecoq and Rouletabille and Gore.
They all hold their tongues to page three hundred
and four. They've got to, or no one would read them.' "

Anthony seems to be sacrificing accuracy to rhyme,
for Gore was certainly not that type of detective.

Thus Gethryn is always hot and bothered, storming
about the place and wrestling with problems which, as
far as the reader can make out, are non-existent. He
is a colonel with just a shade too much in common with
that type in choice of expletives. After all the only
lawful occasion for introducing the word " bloody "
into a detective tale is in the description of the corpse.
One can let it rip then ! Possibly it was the Colonel's
language which endeared him to Scotland Yard, for
he was on intimate enough terms with the Big Four
to call them by their Christian names.

In *The White Crow* (1928) (I hope the mention of it
in this chapter will not be regarded as a serious intrusion) Mr. Macdonald switched over to sensationalism
—to unsavoury night clubs, private cinematograph
shows of films not borrowed from the Kodascope
Library, to dagoes and niggers. A Napoleon of
finance is murdered this time, by his mistress, an
American blonde, assisted by " The Gem." We did not
guess the solution here because we never thought of a
blonde typist as " killer " in the more literal sense of
the word. *The White Crow* is not so good as *The Rasp*.
The unpleasant atmosphere dilutes the humour.

Anthony gets more worked up than ever and his language becomes more sanguinary. He is not too pleasant either as a lady's man. But it was a stroke of genius on his part to get Miss Fanthorpe to type out the final report which revealed her guilt.

Mr. Macdonald had some altercation with the critics over *The White Crow*. The bone of contention was whether or not *the* criminal had been kept away from the reader's interest, and been introduced at the end when he is about to be captured. The critics' accusation was a false one—a *suppressio veri* as Mr. Macdonald styled it—and the latter's refutation was convincingly pat. Two sentences in his defence are interesting as showing the cruel limitations by which our more scrupulous authors feel bound :—

> " . . . The accusation, which is not true, has been made against me that I have not followed the canons of detective story-writing. I have, to my mind, followed these canons—which I consider absolutely esential—with rather painful scrupulousness."

The Noose (1930) was the first choice of the Crime Club, and ran in serial form in *The Evening Standard*, thus securing some valuable publicity. In *The Noose* the action is accelerated by the setting of a time limit to the detective. An innocent man is condemned to death on circumstantial evidence, and is to be hanged in ten days. His wife manages to persuade Anthony Gethryn that he is innocent. The magnanimous Anthony and the languorous Lucia collect the band and proceed to investigate in double quick time. Anthony has at last a real excuse for his abruptness. The headings of the chapters even, which indicate the passing of the days, jerk us out of our complacence.

The idea is not absolutely original. In *The Old Age*

of M. Lecoq Du Boisgobey set Lecoq a time limit in which to save his son from the guillotine. Similar situations have been exploited by film producers from the early days of *Intolerance*. But Mr. Macdonald is the first to do real justice to the idea, and to mix us just the proper quantity of sentiment.

Mr. Macdonald is always original in his choice of motives. In *The Link* (1930) he surpasses himself. He causes to settle in Samsford several American ex-gangsters who have come to England for a quiet life and the (good) beer, or so they say. The actual link between the Canadian and the American soon became obvious ; and the collision, alleged in order to fake an alibi, made us doubly certain. *Rynox* (1930), " an exercise in crime," is a hoax, delightfully executed, but a hoax and therefore a disappointment. There is no detection, and a solitary police report. The actual faking of the murder was magnificently done, but how was the reader to know about the incurable disease ? Will Mr. Macdonald's next novel be " an exercise in detection " ?

5

With the exception of his play, *The Fourth Wall*, *The Red House Mystery* (1922) is Mr. A. A. Milne's only exercise in detection. *The Red House Mystery* is a fine example of the " Lord, what fun ! " type of detective story where detection is the amateur's recipe against rainy day ennui, and the murder is acclaimed as a happy stroke of Providence. Like Father Ronald Knox, Mr. A. A. Milne delights in house parties, and the whimsicality characteristic of *Mr. Pim Passes By* serves to mask the artificiality of the theme and of the characters alike. It is a summer afternoon problem and the very opening sentence with its drowsy cadences is redolent of July. This is equivalent to saying that Anthony Gillingham, the amateur Holmes, is guilty of some temporising. And, now one comes to think of it, what's in a beard? Anthony stumbles quite accidentally across a murder, and catches the murderer practically *flagrante delicto*. Curiosity gets the better of him and with the help of a conscript, Dr. Watson, he proceeds to grapple with a kind of problem of which he had no previous cognisance. His is a common enough type nowadays— the type the services are supposed to produce, humorous and endowed with a devilish intuition. As regards Anthony's methods " he had an uncanny habit of recording things unconsciously." For example, he might be engaged in conversation when a tray was brought in, and although he might continue this conversation without so much as a *conscious* glance at the tray, he could tell you all about that tray later. " His eyes seemed to do it without the brain consciously taking any part." It does not concern us whether this is strictly possible within human experience ; but it is a moot point whether it is justifiable in the detective story. For in its essence it is the very antithesis of the fair-play method. Mr. Milne is too wise to take, as he might easily have done, an unfair advantage of this " useful " perquisite of the amateur.

Two subtleties make *The Red House Mystery* a success. In the first place Mr. Milne selected a well-worn cliché and, as it were, turned it upside down. The cliché was the unexpected appearance from Australia of the black sheep of the family. In nine cases out of ten this character is introduced at the end to spring the surprise, and is as many times the culprit.

But Mr. Milne had a different use for him. The murdered man, Mark Ablett, for purposes of petty revenge wished to impersonate his brother, Robert, from Australia. So he grew him a beard. And this just suited to perfection his secretary, Caley, who hated him like poison. Caley and Mark were the only people, of course, who knew that Robert had died some years ago. That, by the way, takes some swallowing. So Caley shot Mark when he was impersonating Robert. Thus the murdered man was suspected of being the murderer of his deceased brother! His only too necessary disappearance forced this conclusion.

The impasse introduced the second subtlety. The real murderer, Caley, was suspected of being an accessory to the murder owing to his behaviour in the business of the key and croquet shed, and his midnight boating expedition on the pond. This leads Anthony to suspect Caley of shielding Mark. When we have had our suspicions levelled on one character for the greater part of the story, it seldom occurs to us that that character can be the murderer, and that our suspicions, though wrong in kind, were yet right *in personam*. A pleasant surprise!

Enter Sir John, by Miss Clemence Dane and Miss Helen Simpson, has been dubbed " the artistic thriller." It would have been an improvement to label it " the artistes' thriller," as the real interest of the book lies in the first-hand cameos of touring theatrical companies. The puzzle element is dwarfed, and Miss Dane and Miss Simpson would have given the show away if they had mentioned sooner—as they should have done—the " colour streak." Nor is the love idyll between the detective and the condemned girl very much above the standard of the novelette. (Mr. Hitchcock in his talkie adaption, *Murder*, intensified very successfully the emotional values.) Sir John Saumarez, the actor-manager, is an interesting detective. But he would have been the first to admit that the humdrum of detection cruelly assaulted his sensibility. Can you imagine Sir Gerald du Maurier making a successful detective ?

Two other examples of the domestic detective story we cannot afford to pass without mention are Mr. George Pleydell Bancroft's *The Ware Case*, which has been adapted for the stage and the talkies, and Mr. C. H. B. Kitchin's *Death of My Aunt*.

CHAPTER VII

THE REALISTIC DETECTIVE STORY

I

DR. AUSTIN FREEMAN

" An effort has been made to keep within the probabilities of ordinary life."

THERE was another opening for the writer of detective fiction, more glamorous to the nimble-witted and mathematically minded reader than " domestication " and the love element. This was the cult of realism which we may sub-divide into scientific realism and matter-of-fact realism. Note, however, that the murder issue remains statically real and its values from this point of view are the same whether Sexton Blake or Thorndyke is on the case. What is now aimed at is to set the seal of authenticity on the *process* of detection. The detective has to forgo his innuendos, and his theatricalities. He has to behave exactly as we would *expect* him to behave. A harrowing restriction this, for has not the *Evening News* told us what manner of men our detectives are ? Thus, the detective story—with a smattering of empiricism and logic—comes again into its purer form.

Dr. Austin Freeman started with a long handicap of specialised experience. *Who's Who* gives us some interesting facts :—

" Born in 1862 ; qualified as M.R.C.S. House physician at Middlesex Hospital ; Acting Deputy

Medical officer at Holloway Prison ; Assistant Colonial Surgeon Gold Coast ; Surveyor and Naturalist to the Expedition to Ashanti ; Member of Anglo-German Boundary Commission," etc.

" Recreations : modelling in clay and wax.

" Published Works (my own selection) : *The Red Thumb Mark*, 1907 ; *John Thorndyke's Cases*, 1909 ; *The Eye of Osiris*, 1911 ; *The Mystery of 31 New Inn*, 1912 ; *The Singing Bone*, 1912 ; *A Silent Witness*, 1914 ; *Helen Vardon's Confession*, 1922 ; *The Cat's Eye*, 1923 ; *Dr. Thorndyke's Case Book*, 1923 ; *The Puzzle Lock*, 1925 ; *The D'Arblay Mystery*, 1926 ; *A Certain Dr. Thorndyke*, 1928 ; *Mr. Pottermack's Oversight*, 1930.

Dr. Freeman certainly makes the most of his varied experiences. Thus, in any of his novels there is the ring of authenticity in his description of an autopsy or when he is dealing with such a subject as toxicology. In *The Mystery of 31 New Inn* he gives us a way to find our bearings in the dark, a trick which he had learnt in his capacity as a surveyor. In *The Red Thumb Mark* he regales us with an inside picture of Holloway prison. His recreations allowed him to speak with authority in *The D'Arblay Mystery* on wax modelling. But that, as we shall see, is by no means all.

We read in the Preface to *The Singing Bone* :—

" In the conventional detective story the interest is made to focus on the question, Who did it ? The identity of the criminal is a secret that is jealously guarded up to the very end of the book, and its disclosure forms the final climax.

" This I have always regarded as somewhat of a mistake. In real life the identity of the criminal is a question of supreme importance for practical reasons ; but in fiction where no such reasons exist, I conceive the interest of the reader to be engaged chiefly by the demonstration of unexpected consequences of simple

actions, of unsuspected casual connections, and by
the evolution of an ordered train of evidence from a
mass of facts apparently incoherent and unrelated.
The reader's curiosity is concerned not so much with
the question, Who did it ? as with the question, How
was the discovery achieved ? That is to say the
ingenious reader is interested more in the intermediate
action than in the ultimate result."

Dr. Freeman is here laying down the general law to
suit his own particular ideas. He knew very well that
his power lay in the tracing of the intermediate steps ;
that this uncanny gift of his would constitute his main
title to a seat among the worthies of the genre. So
without turning a hair he became dogmatic. . . .
" That is to say the ingenious reader is interested
more. . . ." Now, I wonder why " ingenious." And
what is an ingenious reader, anyway ? I cannot bring
myself to believe that Dr. Freeman implies that the
reader's ingenuity is a reflection of the author's—the
ingenuity being the capability to follow with interest
the various steps. It sounds precious like self-advertise
ment ; which, of course, it is not.

Yet is Dr. Freeman's theory a tenable one ? We
have regarded the problem of the detective story as
the answer to the question, Who did it ? and in
formulating this idea we did not clutch at the events
in real life as at a last straw. Now, we are informed
that that is not so interesting a problem as " How did
the detective solve the problem ? " In the first we have,
as it were, one known quantity—the data ; and in
the second two, the data and the conclusion. With the
latter it is as if we were set a problem and were told
that we might look at the end of the book for the
answer if we were so inclined. That very fact simplifies
the problem, even although we have to cook the

answer. Consider what we have to sacrifice if we are to be " ingenious." Suspense, excitement, the dramatic dénouement—all these go overboard. Instead we are asked to thrive on the vegetarian dish of science without tears !

In a first-rate detective story we expect both the interest of the intermediate action and the interest of the ultimate result. And as Dr. Freeman is one of the great artists of the genre, our expectations are not damped. The construction of the stories in *The Singing Bone* was a remarkably successful stunt (the last word is not used in a derogatory sense). The fact that Dr. Freeman has seldom essayed this type of story since seems to suggest that for him at least the novelty soon wore off. It remains, however, to repeat—and this was my reason for quoting at length—that whether the identity of the criminal is known or unknown, one's chief interest in an Austin Freeman novel is concerned with Thorndyke's methods.

Dr. Freeman subordinates all else to the scientific treatment ; and scientific, moreover, in the narrower sense, as all Thorndyke's triumphs are won in his laboratory or by means of his portable set, " the invaluable green case." This was a salutary reform. It was in fact the very best thing that could have happened to the detective story. The touches of academic pedantry, the chemical formulæ, the microscope, Farrant, the forceps, the dusting powder—all these constituted an admirable reaction to the wild guess-work of some of Thorndyke's contemporaries.

But a general public uninitiated into the mysteries of chemistry and physics likes its doses in small quantities. In the preface to *John Thorndyke's Cases* the author politely informed his readers that the experiments detailed in the book had been personally carried out

by himself—that Thorndyke's lustre was his own. A
critic had evidently jumped at this opportunity ; for
in the preface of *The Mystery of* 31 *New Inn* Dr.
Freeman sententiously takes up his cudgels in self-
defence :—

> " Commenting upon one of my earlier novels, in
> respect of which I had claimed to have been careful
> to adhere to common probabilities and to have made
> use only of really practicable methods of investigation,
> a critic remarked that this was of no consequence
> whatever, as long as the story was amusing.
> " Few people, I imagine, will agree with him. To
> most readers, and certainly to the kind of reader for
> whom an author is willing to take trouble, complete
> realism in respect of incidents and methods is an
> essential factor in maintaining the interest of a
> detective story. Here it may be worth while to
> mention that Thorndyke's method of producing the
> track chart, described in Chapters II. and III., has
> actually been used in practice. . . ."

The trouble with Dr. Freeman is just this : he takes
too much pains. Taking trouble to please one's
readers means taking trouble to please one's self.
So far as one may gauge the average detective story
fan's reaction to a Thorndyke novel, it is one of mild
annoyance coupled with a genuine admiration for one
who works at science and plays with it afterwards.
But as regards the practicability of the experiments,
the general public would just as soon have him confess
in a monthly magazine the impossibility of them. One
and all would acclaim him as the perpetrator of a
capital hoax. And this means that there was after all
something in the critic's submission and that Dr.
Freeman is apt to write above his public.

Dr. Freeman must have felt that so far he had been

quite original enough and that for the rest he had better abide by the conventions. The Thorndyke household is based on Sherlock Holmes's. Thorndyke lives more doucely in chambers, but prospective clients show the same eagerness to ring his bell. As a character Thorndyke cannot hold a candle to Sherlock. He occupies the chair of Medical Jurisprudence at St. Margaret's ; and he is a capital don, for he appears to have no eccentric weaknesses. He is an easy winner of the detectives' beauty prize. The symmetry and comeliness of his face, we are told, " make it akin rather to some classic mask wrought in the ivory-toned marble of Pentelicus." With this asset he could afford to make pretty speeches to characterless young women who owed him eternal gratitude. Here is Polton's description of his master's methods :—

> " The Doctor, sir, God bless him—is the most exasperating man in the world. He fairly drives me mad with curiosity at times. He will give me a piece of work to do—something to make perhaps—with full particulars. . . . But he never says what the thing is for. . . . He doesn't think like other men. . . . It isn't a question of Quantity at all. It's a different kind of intelligence. Ordinary men have to reason from visible facts. He doesn't. He reasons from facts which his imagination tells him exist, but which nobody else can see."

Jervis, the medico, lacks Dr. Watson's humanity. But Dr. Freeman has shown great discretion in refusing to exaggerate the Dr. Watson characteristics in order to get a laugh from the gallery. Even Jervis knows too much.

" Excluding, quite properly, I think—Raynaud's disease, we arrive at frost-bite and ergotism."

I ask you, is it fair ? Nor must we forget Polton, Thorndyke's laboratory assistant, photographer, butler, Jack-of-all-trades. Here Dr. Freeman has really missed the chance of his lifetime ; for Polton might have introduced a welcome burst of comic relief between the experiments. What a character Mr. Edgar Wallace might have made of him !

It can easily be seen why Dr. Freeman is more successful in his short stories. He is an exponent of the unexpected means, not this time so much the unexpected means of inflicting death, but the un-expected means of detecting it. The narrative consists of experiment upon experiment based on facts which Thorndyke has singled out from his data with an unerring sense of their significance.

It is impossible to deny that Thorndyke is one of Fortune's favourites. He always finds some clue, or his microscope does—whether it is an infinitesimal piece of glass or a speck of dust. One's ignorance prevents one from questioning the probability of these finds. For example, in *A Wastrel's Romance* the criminal is traced to a certain locality from three different types of dust that are found in a discarded overcoat. In *The Red Thumb Mark* and *The Old Lag*, Dr. Freeman describes a very clever method of forging finger-prints by a line-block process. Yet I have heard an authority on process-engraving express grave doubts as to the chances of such forgery proving really misleading. Now and again Dr. Freeman has the last laugh, as in *The Moabite Cipher*, where the reader expects that one of the more complicated forms of " mathematical cipher " is to be solved, whereas the real message is written in invisible ink.

There are times, too, when Dr. Freeman can be attractively simple, as in *The Singing Bone*, where the main items in Thorndyke's deduction are as follows : A pipe is found near the body. But as the mouth-piece of this pipe indicates that its owner has a good strong set of teeth whereas the corpse certainly had not ; and as the tobacco found inside the pouch was different from that found inside the pipe, the obvious conclusion—the one instance in a thousand where it is the right one—is that the pipe does not belong to the corpse. Then who else can be the owner but " the other ? " Simple, my dear Jervis. I bless Dr. Freeman for *The Singing Bone,* for it is the one and only Thorndyke story which I have prematurely solved *in detail.*

The full length novels—in particular *The Red Thumb Mark, The Eye of Osiris, The Mystery of* 31 *New Inn, The D'Arblay Mystery*—suffer by reason of three serious faults.

(1) Two series of concurrent events are described as if they had no connection. Now although the characters cannot for a long time trace any inter-relation, the reader can.

(2) The excitement is provided by the numerous, sometimes quite unnecessary, attempts on the life of the secondary hero—in most cases a young doctor—who has come by some important evidence and thereby frightened the villain out of his mind. Austin Freeman villains always wax nervy after doing the deed. Their excessive zeal to cover up their tracks has been the efficient cause of their downfall.

(3) The minor characters have the " annoying " habit of falling in love. " Annoying " is E. M. Wrong's mild epithet ; " exasperating " is perhaps a more fitting description. Perhaps on second thoughts Dr. Freeman concluded that he had misjudged the intensity of the scientific appeal. One cannot blame him for this decision. But love does not thrive in the laboratory,

and the scientist is rarely an artist in analysing the emotions. Dr. Freeman's lovers are excessively wooden, excessively sensitive, and excessively honourable. *Helen Vardon's Confession* is the Victorian novelette in miniature. And all through *The Red Thumb Mark* the refrain of the music-hall ditty rang in one's ears— " O kiss the girl if you want to, but let her go home to bed."

In passing one may mention the startling similarity in the circumstances surrounding the cremation in *The D'Arblay Mystery* and *A Silent Witness* and in the " substitution " of the bodies.*

2

MR. FREEMAN WILLS CROFTS

" He will present you with a magnificent alibi, an alibi that cannot be gainsaid." GABORIAU : *L'Affaire Lerouge.*

The greatest apostle of the matter of fact is Mr. Freeman Wills Crofts. Mr. Crofts is an Irishman, born in Dublin of an old County Cork family. He is a keen musician ; was organist at Coleraine Parish Church, and has trained many prize-winning choirs. By profession, however, he is a civil engineer, having worked for many years on the L.M.S. Railway as chief-assistant engineer to the Northern Counties Committee. This fact will at once account for the important part played by the railways in his novels and for his extraordinary knowledge of different localities.

Indeed, Mr. Crofts's' writing derives much of its effectiveness from the introduction of local colour. His novels have their setting in some precise district.

* The criticisms seem pointless.—E. F. B.

Thus, to those who already know that particular district, there is an added charm. Whether the scene is the Welsh coast, or the Yorkshire moors, or Southampton, or Castle Douglas, he retains throughout his uncanny accuracy. The dénouement of *The Starvel Tragedy* takes place in the Waverley Station at Edinburgh, and not in some imaginary Grand Central. If he describes a lane, a level-crossing, or a bridge in some district, you can take a train there and see these self-same objects for yourself. For Mr. Crofts goes over his ground before he pens a line. I have seen actual snapshots taken by Mr. Crofts of several key positions described in *Sir John Magill's Last Journey*. Not the least interesting point about them was the pencilling on their backs of the most intriguing stage directions—" Path taken by So-and-So."

Mr. Crofts prefers the unvarnished narrative, and it is only when he would adorn his tale with these geographical asides, or when he would plunge into the treacherous waters of sensationalism, that his style seems to lose its hundred per cent. efficiency. Even his crimes, cold and premeditated as they appear in the dispassionate telling of them, lack that gusto which would serve to make them more attractive and also more credible. There is no careless rapture about his criminals, no sense of humour, no emotion. His writing is for the most part succinct and business-like, and resembles a well-informed newspaper article.

This treatment has two prominent weaknesses. In the first place the more matter of fact Mr. Crofts becomes, the more liable is he to fly to clichés of expression. Thus Inspector French is persuaded to " have something to fortify his inner man ; " L'Affaire Magill is " terribly baffling," and so forth. The be-sprinkling of his text with these paste-jewelled phrases

is an unnecessary fault, and, therefore, hard to forgive.
Secondly, Mr. Crofts is so carried away by his love
for detail that he exalts the trivial to a false prominence.
Where any other writer would simply have said, " He
travelled by night to Stranraer," Mr. Crofts gives us
pages of description made up of paragraphs like the
following :—

> " He began, therefore, by engaging a sleeping berth
> at Euston. On inquiry he was directed to a station-
> master's office on No. 6 platform. There a clerk made
> the reservations, handing him a voucher. This voucher
> he presented at the booking office when taking his
> tickets. . . . The train left at seven-forty from No. 12
> platform. . . . His name was on the list on the
> window of the sleeping car."

Take again such a paragraph as the following :—

> " But later the excellent dinner served while the
> train ran through the pleasant country between
> Abbeville and Amiens brought him to a more quiescent
> mood, and over a good cigar and a cup of such coffee
> as he had seldom before tasted, he complacently
> watched day fade into night. About half-past six
> o'clock next morning he followed the example of the
> countless British predecessors, and climbed down on
> the long platform at Bâle to drink his morning coffee."

One is at liberty to argue that by such devices the
action is held up, that the rattle of coffee cups is out
of place in the detective story. Yet (Mr. Crofts might
reply) what better respite from concentration is there
for the detective who scorns Trade Union hours ?
What more pleasant rest-and-be-thankful for the
conscientious reader who takes a hand in the case ?
Along with Dr. Austin Freeman, Mr. Crofts
has acquired the unenviable reputation in certain

quarters of being a "highbrow." This is a comic anomaly, for they both cultivate unashamedly a prosaic reality. The charge of highbrowism—always snobbish or else it is a misnomer—denotes a strong dissatisfaction with certain alleged poses. Mr. Crofts cannot be a highbrow *qua* realist. Let us dismiss this absurd charge ; but let us also mention the imputed faults which have given birth to the libel.

The sensational element, it is true, is minimised in the typical Wills Crofts novel. There is plenty of action, but not apparently of that type of action in request by the fault finder. The reports of pistol shots are often in "indirect speech." The suspense is thus sometimes more the detective's than our own. But even so there are exceptions. Several of his novels, in particular the early ones, combine adventure with detection. Even when in more serious vein, Mr. Crofts does let himself go at the dénouement. A Mills bomb nearly wrecks the saloon bar in the penultimate chapter of *The Starvel Tragedy*. And Inspector French all but finds his quietus at the end of *The Sea Mystery*. In these close shaves, one must confess, Mr. Crofts seems rather off colour. He cannot keep his cake till it seemed a permanency, only to gobble it up for an effect so long despised.

Then again, the action being moulded to fit certain measurements, there is a similarity of situation, a clockwork movement. In reading the average Wills Crofts novel one is conscious each time of experiencing very much the same "thought-process." His plots run like his railway trains. This allows one's reason or intuition to take one a chapter ahead of Inspector French. The "leads," the "startling new lines" along which the detective plunges out of the blue at regular intervals beckon to one's intelligence and shout for premature recognition. To forecast the state of affairs twenty pages after is genuine solace to the reader ; it is flattering. But there, as a rule, his self-sufficiency ends. If the solution of each step in the investigation actually coincides with his pretty prognostications, the dénouement will shatter his complacency.

In construction he is the supreme technician. It is this quality that has earned for him an international reputation in Europe and America, and made him an Oracle of Detective Fiction, for whose praise publishers would go far to bartering their souls—this quality,too, that all but drew enthusiasm from the *Saturday Review*. No writer of detective fiction has ever produced a neater plot. Every brick fits exactly into the edifice. The plots of Gaboriau are not more exquisitely complicated. In Mr. Crofts's technique there are two great merits. The first is the cunning creation of the central idea, and the other the round-about rediscovery of it. A lesser artist than Mr. Crofts would have been severely handicapped by the conscientious deference to realism just mentioned.

To set off the sombre background he has his fireworks. He is an admirable conjurer, and a prolific "ideas-man." And because he is prolific, his tricks are seldom expanded into themes. Here is a haphazard selection—the changing of the numbers on the lorries and the smuggling of the pit-props in *The Pit-Prop Syndicate*. The drugging, and the solution of the diagrammatic cipher in *The Cheyne Mystery*. The solution of the dictionary cipher in *Inspector French's Greatest Case*. The planting of the twenty-pound notes in *The Starvel Tragedy*. The adventures with the rope ladder in *Sir John Magill's Last Journey*.

The realist having made his bed has got to lie in it. Of a necessity it must ever be sagging, for all the time he must be in the know. A knowledge of medicine and chemistry was indispensable to him even in the days of Sherlock Holmes. He must besides be as familiar with police methods as Mr. Edgar Wallace. Like Miss Sayers he must have common law and legal procedure at his finger tips. All this knowledge emanates without any gushing from Mr. Crofts. He is a criminologist and a cryptologist. I imagine he is a close student of the technical press, and files of *Police Journals* and *Reviews* adorn his shelves. He can tell one all about banking and brokerage ; customs and excise ; distilling ; motor engines ; seacraft, and a hundred and one different subjects. He approximates to the old-fashioned sleuth on whose omniscience emphasis was so plaintively but so necessarily laid.

In short, there are few writers in whom one could find such a wealth of interesting detail. If one were to count up to a hundred technical details in a story of his, one would be hard put to it to find a single flaw. I have heard that legal and medical experts have sat in judgement on his novels, prior to their publication and have picked out at the most three or four possible, but by no means certain, errors.

The *pièce de résistance* of his realism is his characterisation of the detective, that is of Inspector French, for the Burnleys, the Tanners and the Willises are only other editions of this favourite. The Inspector French that frowns on one from the insets on the dust wrappers seems quite an ordinary young man, clean-shaven, sharp of feature, well groomed and neatly dressed— just such a young man, in fact, as might adorn an advertisement of Austin Reed's or Three Nuns Tobacco. In the Elysian Fields he will assuredly be prejudged a

gate-crasher by Sherlock Holmes and the super-
detectives. His private life can boast no quixotry, no
æsthetic capers. Being an ordinary sort of chap, it
did not surprise us to learn that he was married.
His Emily—true to the associations that that name
has accrued—sits at home in their suburban villa
knitting his socks. Mr. Crofts, seldom obsequious to the
conventionalities, throws an unnecessary bouquet to
contemporary fashion.

> " When Inspector French felt really up against it
> in the conduct of a case, it was his invariable habit
> to recount the circumstances in the fullest detail
> to his wife. Sometimes she interjected a remark,
> sometimes she didn't . . . but she listened to what
> he said, and occasionally expressed an opinion, or, as
> he called it, ' took a notion.' And more than once it
> happened that these notions had thrown quite a
> different light on the point at issue, a light which in
> at least two cases had indicated the line of research
> which had eventually cleared up the mystery."

In the circumstances it was natural that Mr. Crofts
should have had no use for " the superior amateur."
His detective is the professional expert, the C.I.D. man,
caring more for the material guerdon of advancement
and an increase of salary than the fulsome flattery of
a neighbour. So far he remains in the force (although
merely from the point of view of realism Mr. Crofts
must have recently considered French's resignation).
He is energetic, ambitious, but not infallible; deferential
to his superiors, he recognises the guiding genius of
Chief-Inspector Mitchell and the Big Four.

The Inspector's methods are a true reflection of the
man. He worries things out and is always " up against
it." He never jumps to a conclusion, and that is the

great difference between him and the Father Browns and Hanauds. If one theory fails, he tries another. This point is of some importance ; for it is tantamount to the laying of all cards on the table. The fairplay method inaugurated by the fragmentary *Mystery of Marie Roget*, and both tentatively and temporarily adopted by various hands, has at last found its complete expression. The data are given. The detective's inferences are assembled in detail and from time to time a résumé is presented demonstrating the point reached in the investigation, and the points remaining to be solved ; the cruxes, as it were, underlined, and the " leads " tabulated. This is something to be going on with. This is business.

To the puzzle-worm the subjectivity of French's reasoning is reassuringly natural. Yet it would be strange if he did not from time to time realise that the other fellow was doing all the work ; that the mystery was being taken entirely out of his hands ; that all the clues with which his imagination might have dallied for brief intervals between the chapters, were exposed in detail one after the other.

French looks for his information in the likeliest quarters. He does not don fancy dress and slouch off to Soho or the docks. He does not readily impose upon people by facile impersonations of antiquarians desirous of seeing the reredos. One has usually not long to wait for the curt, formal introduction, so much more dignified after all than the Transatlantic seizure of the lapel. He spends many hours in hotels, chatting to their managers and studying the register. He is frequently to be seen in shops and banks. Somehow he reminds one of a commercial traveller, so ingratiating a way he has with tradesmen.

The alibi was Mr. Crofts's first love and he made

it the pivot of his plots. In life the mere presentation
of an alibi is three-quarters proof—thanks chiefly to
politeness and a disinclination on the part of normal
people to make a scene. The alibi has only to pass an
elementary test of probability, and circumstantial
evidence gains another victory. This was Mr. Crofts's
chance and this his angle of approach. If the novelist
never wearies of turning the handle of circumstantial
evidence to incriminate the too innocent hero, why
should the use of circumstantial evidence to shelter the
villain be not equally legitimate ? The comforting
maxim that the prisoner is innocent until proved
guilty—logically an impossible restriction to all juries
as being prejudice ridden—was another string to Mr.
Crofts's bow. Yet another fact exacted the alibi. To
the public, press-fed and expecting sensation, the
vital attraction is always the human interest of the
trial. Public interest soon wanes if the criminal is not
forthcoming. It is the pros and cons of the alibi,
and failing that, as a bad second, the veracity of the
statements of the accused, that lead from one pint
to another at the Rose and Crown. And circumstantial
evidence, by the way, although the object of the super-
detective's contumely, will yet turn a one-reel Movie
into an " attraction."

Circumstantial evidence's strongest foothold in
fiction thus rested with the possibility of concocting a
" cast iron " " honest to goodness," " unobjectionable "
alibi—all these epithets meaning, of course, the very
reverse, that the alibi was pre-arranged. In Gaboriau's
L'Affaire Lerouge, Père Tabaret discourses on the
theme :—

> " He (the suspect) will present you with a magnifi-
> cent alibi, an alibi that cannot be gainsaid. He will

show that he passed the evening and the night of Tuesday with personages of the highest rank. He had dined with the Count de Machin, gamed with the Marquis of So-and-So, and supped with the Duke of What's-his-name. . . . In short, his little machine will be so cleverly constructed, so nicely arranged, all its little wheels will play so well, that there will be nothing left for you but to open the door and usher him out with the most humble apologies."

But Père Tabaret's method of putting a cog in the wheels of the little machine presupposes a most alarming knowledge of the circumstances, and besides, if adopted to-day, would immediately bring into being a commission to report on third degree methods, ending in the dismissal of the detective.

" I have my man arrested. . . . I go right to the mark. I overwhelm him at once by the weight of my certainty, prove to him so clearly that I know everything that he must surrender. I should say to him, ' My good man, you bring me an alibi. It is very well, but we are acquainted with that system of defence. It will not do with me. Of course, I understand you have been elsewhere at the hour of the crime ; a hundred persons have never lost sight of you. It is admitted. In the meantime, here is what you have done. . . ."

But the parallel is of value with reference to Mr. Crofts's alibis. He constructs his little machine so cleverly that the reader does feel that there is nothing left for him but to dismiss the alibi-mongers from the circle of suspects. This is because the work of pre-arrangement is so deft, and because again we are misled by a false law of probabilities. Then the Inspector proceeds to break the little machine to pieces, and we " knew all the time "—but not quite honestly—that there was a snag somewhere.

With this new element as the central *motif*, the construction was bound to be modified. The suspects, for example, might be marshalled with promptitude as in *The Ponson Case* and their alibis be tested one after the other, and the artistic values of these alibis be enhanced by the juxtaposition. Or suspicion might be postponed until the tardy testing of the star alibi as in *The Cask*. In the earlier novels the alibi was a new toy to Mr. Crofts. Systematically he ran through a number of variations. In time he saw the tinsel, for if his plots were to be built up from the testing of un-objectionable alibis, the secret would soon be out ; so he gave his tale a twist with the introduction of bogus impersonations and dual rôles.

In the execution of the alibi theme Mr. Crofts exploited to the full his professional knowledge of the railways and found in Bradshaw an indispensable *vade mecum*. The original composer cannot even in his fondest flights of fancy have imagined to what diverse uses his *magnum opus* would be turned—to the com-position of Latin hexameters and the concoction of alibis for detective stories. The principal alibi in *The Ponson Case* was worked out from a careful examination of the L.N.E.R. main line to Scotland—the " Flying Scotsman's " track—and the local service from King's Cross to Grantham. Boirac's alibi in *The Cask* was also based on the railway time-table, and in *The Cheyne Mystery* a similar trick is played, although strictly speaking it is not an alibi. You see Mr. Crofts trades upon the reader's gullibility. The little machine is perfect. The reader never dreams of opening his Bradshaw. He is too lazy—or too polite. In passing, Mr. Crofts has not had the heart to keep his inspectors from the restaurant car whenever he has noticed in his time-table a capital " R " adjacent to the selected train. Realism achieved so easily has its points.

The Cask, Mr. Crofts's first book, is his most famous detective story. In fact *Trent's Last Case* and *The Cask* are judged by the critics to be the most scintillating stars in our crowded constellation. Mr. Crofts's own account of how *The Cask* came to be written is interesting :—

> " In 1916 I had a long illness, and it was after this that I tried writing a novel as a relief from the tedium of convalescence. I wrote most of *The Cask*, but on recovery, put it away and thought of other things. Some time later I re-read it, and thinking it did not seem so bad as I had imagined, I set to work to finish it.
>
> " I was delighted when Messrs. Collins accepted it, even though this acceptance was accompanied by an extremely kind note from no less a person than Mr. J. D. Beresford, suggesting that Part III. was unsatisfactory, and would I re-write it ? "

The Cask, like all Gaul, is " quartered into three halves." In the first part we read of the arrival of the cask ; the clerk's discovery of the gruesome contents and disappearance of the cask ; Inspector Burnley's discovery of it at Felix Leon's house ; the opening of the cask and Leon's " My God ! It's Annette," as the final curtain. An exquisite sandwich of action and detection.

In the second part Inspector Burnley and his colleague, Lefarge of the Sûreté, carry out exhaustive researches. The information acquired, in particular the fact that the victim, a Mme. Boirac, had *prima facie* tried to elope with Leon, leads to the building up of a perfect case against him. Perfect but in one important detail—the question of motive. In the circumstances thus imagined, it would be Boirac who would have cause to hate his wife. But Boirac was found to have an unassailable alibi. So Leon is arrested. The reader naturally asks himself whether the unfortunate Leon has not had too large a share of suspicion or whether it is a " double bluff." Boirac is the only alternative, as there is no other character important enough to fill the rôle of the villain. Is the alibi really cast iron ? Thus the problem consists in the choice of one of two characters. In this respect *The Cask* is unique.

In the third part we are introduced to Georges La Touche, a private detective engaged by Leon's legal adviser. La Touche's task is to prove Leon's innocence. To do this he had to assume that Boirac is the murderer, just as Burnley and Lefarge had come to assume that Leon was guilty. (Had there been more than two suspects it might have been necessary to call in a fresh supply of detectives, constituting a small crime circle like Roger Sheringham's in Mr. Anthony Berkeley's *The Poisoned Chocolates Case.* Mr. Crofts happily steers clear of an obvious pitfall. He makes all three detectives contribute to the solution.) The final section consists in the breaking down of Boirac's alibi. La Touche was lucky at the start, for there was no real reason why he should have noticed, *qua* detective, the dark typist. His interest in her led to his ascertaining that the typed message found inside the cask and a typed letter of Leon's had both been typed on one of Boirac's machines. La Touche's next step was to show that it was possible for Boirac to get to England, etc., and to check up the " times " of his alibi. Thereafter it was plain sailing.

The Cask is a splendid illustration of Mr. Crofts's unsurpassed exercises in detection. Maybe he relies now and again on catches (the faked telephone message, for example), but as a rule he relies more on the *minutiæ* furnished by the evidence which the careless reader will not notice. " Careless " is used relatively, otherwise it would be gross hyperbole. Mr. Crofts believes in making it hard for the reader. In one particular he goes too far—his time schedules. He may be as optimistic as the B.B.C., but the average reader will not feel disposed to take out his pencil. Life is too short for that. In justice to Mr. Crofts one is obliged to emphasise the significance that arises out of this attention to detail. And that is the *raison d'être* of the attraction that detection has for us. There is no fun in merely putting two and two together. I have in mind Burnley's inferences from the two footprints :—

" Well, I can only compare the heels (the sole of one of the footprints was missing) and there is not much difference between them. . . . ' By Jove, Inspector,' he went on, ' I've got you at last.' ' They're the same marks. They were both made by the same foot. . . . . The fourth nail on the left hand side is gone. That alone might be a coincidence, but if you compare the wear of the other nails and of the leather you will see they are the same beyond doubt. . . . How could Watty, if it was he, have produced them ? Surely only in one of two ways. Firstly, he could have hopped on one foot. But there are three reasons why it is unlikely he did that. One is that he could hardly have done it without your noticing it. Another, that he could never have left so clear an impression in that way. The third, why should he hop ? He simply wouldn't do it. . . . He walked up first with you to leave the cask. He walked up the second time with the empty dray to get it. . . ."

And this is only a detail ; only one link in the long chain. Unfortunately it is impossible without a tortuous explanation to enlarge upon this topic.

Mr. Crofts's other works consist of pure detective stories—such as *The Ponson Case, Inspector French's Greatest Case, Inspector French and the Starvel Tragedy, The Sea Mystery, Sir John Magill's Last Journey*, and the hybrids—*The Pit-Prop Syndicate, The Cheyne Mystery* and possibly the *Box Office Murders*. The latter being a mixture of detection and adventure have several recurring features. The adventure portion is the excuse for the detection. The amateur, the conventional hero, has danger thrust upon him ; for a time he struggles, quite effectively, with his antagonists. Suddenly he considers he is " up against it "—a conclusion prompted by the fact that he has fallen in love—and he rushes in a taxi to Scotland Yard. The professionals there magnificently smooth over the troubled waters ; and detection is vindicated. (Really rather a pleasant allegory denoting the superiority of the intellectual detective story !) Whether it was necessary for the professionals to do it is another question. The amateurs were going great guns and the inspectors hadn't really very much to do.

The Ponson Case, The Starvel Tragedy and *Sir John Magill's Last Journey* are for many reasons the most interesting of the others. The success of the first is due to the brilliant central idea of accidental death upsetting a cart-load of alibis. In the invention of the plot, it looks as if the alibi tricks preceded, and the original plot was suddenly modified by the afterthought. To be uncharitable, there is an outstanding weakness in the plot. The irritating love theme— reminiscent of Dr. Austin Freeman at his second best —is the only valid excuse for the continued silence of Austin and Cosgrove. As far as the latter is concerned, the thread is very slender. The love element does, however, become pivotal when Lois Drew, the

Wordsworthian heroine, steals a march on Inspector Tanner in the exposure of Cosgrove's alibi. Mr. Crofts makes great play with Cosgrove as a suspect. Observe the readiness with which one's suspicions immediately fasten on the business man whose finances are not too stable, and who has a liaison with an actress. The business man, as Van Dine discovered, is the perfect suspect.

Inspector French and the Starvel Tragedy is probably the most satisfactory of all double murder plots. In the historical method Mr. Crofts shows his superiority to Gaboriau. For although Dr. Philpot's first murder —the murder of his wife at Kirkintilloch—and the Ropers' discovery of it—are the hinges of the plot, the earlier event is never allowed to dwarf in interest the Starvel affair. The confusion and suspense in the reader's mind as to the real identity of the victims of the fire are splendid proof of Mr. W. Crofts's technique. The conduct of the coroner at the inquest is, however, extremely questionable ; and I believe that it is possible nowadays to tell the sex and age from a small piece of charred bone, let alone a complete skeleton. I should have liked to hear Sir Bernard Spilsbury on the Starvel Case.

Sir John Magill's Last Journey is in many respects the most typical of all Mr. Crofts's novels. It is a railway murder and never has he demonstrated his professional knowledge to greater advantage. The atmosphere has never been so vividly conveyed, and the descriptions of Stranraer, Castle-Douglas, Campbeltown, Larne and Whitehead help to intensify the realism. The problem is again paramountly a time-table one and involves the most intricate checking up of innumerable times. We have to contend with a quartet of alibis ; and poor French has to follow up the itineraries of each member of the gang both on land and sea. The actual murder went off like clockwork—a particularly brilliant murder this. It is hardly necessary to add that all the details were worked out beforehand with the most extraordinary accuracy. The " Sillin " by-plot is one of the best red herrings ever dangled before a wary reader. One has only two minor grievances. When a villain is made to impersonate somebody, what obligation is there to mention that he had once been an actor ? It gives the show away. Secondly, was it necessary for Mr. Crofts to borrow from *The Cask* the idea of the typewriter clue ?   But these are trifles, and the last journey of Sir John Magill is certainly French's greatest case to date.

CHAPTER VIII

THE ORTHODOX DETECTIVE STORY

MRS. AGATHA CHRISTIE

The Murder of Roger Ackroyd is dedicated "To Punkie, who likes an orthodox detective story, murder, inquest, and suspicion falling on every one in turn." Punkie must have derived no little entertainment from Mrs. Agatha Christie's novels, for she is in many respects a paragon of orthodoxy. She believes in a clean, slick murder and plenty of swift, exciting, low-brow action. Her detective, Poirot, belongs to the old school of super-detectives who keep things pretty much to themselves, and spar incessantly with the arrogant tribe of police inspectors. In Captain Hastings she has held the mirror up to Dr. Watson. The dedication shows that she is an advocate of the most unlikely person theme. As a final example of her orthodoxy, she is the perfect matrimonial agency in pairing off the right couples.

But granted that Mrs. Christie writes "down" rather than "up," that she keeps her crow a crow— in Mr. St. John Ervine's phraseology—and does not seek to make it a flamingo, that she does not cast about her for spurious effects, it is not difficult to discern a delicious vein of satire in her stories. Even before she essayed the burlesque of *Partners in Crime*, she had a hankering to poke fun at the various schools of detective fiction. She is certainly well read in the

Classics, as the adventures of Tommy and Tuppence show. It is almost as if she had set herself to learn all she could about the methods and technique of " How to Write a Detective Story for Profit "—and had then proceeded to pull legs.

Mrs. Christie is not a criminologist. She is not even a first-rate detective. Compared with Mr. Crofts she is in this respect a babe-in-arms. For the grouping of data, for the building up of a case from " purposeful " *minutiæ*, for the effects of belladonna on rabbits she has no time. And evidently she has felt unequal to the strain of assiduous bluffing. Her description of the data is, therefore, of the sketchiest. In lieu thereof she gives us a plethora of motives. Most of her *dramatis personæ* have quite a few motives concealed on them— motives white and black, motives satisfactory and unsatisfactory, so they be only motives. Mrs. Christie's skill lies in playing off motive against motive, and thus character against character ; for her characters are often merely pegs on which to hang these motives.

Neither does Mrs. Christie usually bother her head with character study. The recognised types are quite sufficient to be going on with ; big-game hunters of the Ethel M. Dell variety ; hard-boiled Americans after Mr. Edgar Wallace ; fencers and blackmailers of the Oppenheim School ; private secretaries and so forth.

Mrs. Christie was fully alive to the importance of the character of the detective. She had to be original here, for the dignity of the detective was at the time in the balance. It is true that she followed in Mr. Mason's wake by making her detective a Belgian and by calling him Hercule Poirot.* With true insight she banked on our blowing smoke rings round the unfamiliar. " Twopence coloured " wins every time. Then her sense of humour stood her in good stead. She

---

* The general characterization is inept, and Poirot's prototype is more likely to have been Robert Barr's Eugene Valmont.—E. F. B.

decided to make Poirot a comic figure. How she loves low comedy, does Mrs. Christie.

Mrs. Ackroyd's description of Poirot as a " comic Frenchman in a review " is perfect and to the point. His catch-words, his conversation, his conceit, his bravado, his sentimentalism, his gallantry—all these are deliberate playing to the gallery. But it is better theatricality than Gaboriau's or Mr. Edgar Wallace's, for it never ceases to be anything but a joke. And Poirot " gets it over." " My name is Hercule Poirot. I am probably the greatest detective in the world." The flourish is irresistible. To the ladies it is, " Trust Hercule Poirot, mademoiselle ; *he knows*," and like Zia in *The Mystery of the Blue Train* they all fall for it.

Poirot is one of the old brigade, because he was set the old kind of problem. Giraud, the fox, Poirot's police rival, says on one occasion :—

" I know you by name, M. Poirot. You cut a figure in the old days, didn't you ? But methods are very different now."

Poirot's answer is :—

" Crimes though are very much the same."

He is perfectly right, although his defence is not quite fair to Giraud. For all Poirot's harping on " the little grey cells," for all his insistence on method and symmetry, he is radically the intuitionalist. Only the Old Brigade could afford to be intuitionalists, for Fashion was now driving them out of court. Poirot sees a " girl with anxious eyes " or a chair out of position. The significance of these facts comes to him in a flash. Then, and only then, do " the little grey cells " get on with it. The intuitional detective starts with intuitions where the others start with a mass of data. Naturally, the former is rather jealous, for his evidence is intangible. But it is just because he can afford to take a leap in the dark without having to do the donkey work that he is so successful in his bluff. Poirot " had a certain disdain for tangible evidence such as foot-prints and cigarette ash, and would maintain that, taken by themselves, they would never enable a detective to solve a problem." The true work is done from *within. The little grey cells*—remember always the little grey cells, *mon ami* ! "

In one light Poirot's affected scorn for the new-fangled methods of detection is really a question of sour grapes. Here is his attitude to the Thorndyke method. Captain Hastings suggests to Poirot that " the study of finger-prints, and foot-prints, cigarette ash, different kinds of mud, and other clues, that comprise the minute observation of details " are of vital importance. Poirot replies : " I have never said otherwise. Yet you demand that I, Hercule Poirot, should make myself ridiculous by lying down (possibly on damp grass) to study hypothetical foot-prints and should scoop up cigarette ash when I do not know one kind from another."

Inspector French is treated with as much scorn— " ' I do not run to and fro, making journeys and agitating myself. My work is done within—*here.*' He tapped his forehead significantly."

Methinks Mrs. Christie doth protest too much !

From all this it will be concluded that Mrs. Christie does not believe in cluttering up the reader's mind with a mass of facts. She does not give us a time-table of alibis, an Ordnance Survey map and a chapter from *The Lancet*, as it were, in one spoonful. Her failure to do so has given rise to the idea that she does not play quite fair. Captain Hastings gets quite annoyed about it.

" ' No,' I replied with some ill humour, ' I neither see nor comprehend. You make all these confounded mysteries, and it's useless asking you to explain. You always like keeping something up your sleeve to the last minute ' "

The rules of fairplay vary according to their context. When the detective works from intangible evidence, naturally they must be stretched even to their limit. But the principle remains the same. Poirot has the last word :

" My friend, in working upon a case, one does not take into account only the things that are ' mentioned.' There is no reason to mention many things which may be important. Equally, there is often an excellent reason for *not* mentioning them. You can take your choice of these two motives."

Presumably for the benefit of the stupid Captain Hastings, Poirot talks in broken English—the broken English of the music-hall Frenchman. Undoubtedly there must be humour in this. To the average Englishman an incredibly small Frenchman with an incredibly pointed moustache and imperial beard, gesticulating superbly and always just failing to achieve *le mot juste*, is a spectacle worth paying a few shillings to see. Moreover, should this music-hall Frenchman intersperse his lines with a few phrases of his own tongue, the supporters of M. Hugo (the Correspondence King) experience a superiority complex : while the embarrassed monoglots captivated by the flavour of the genuine are compelled in self-defence to join in the laugh. But that is not quite all. For some strange reason, on the stage as well as in detective fiction, the

tradition holds that the comic Frenchman must inter-
polate into his prattle, *Monsieur's*, and *Madame's*,
and *que voulez-vous*, and *c'est bien's*, *irrespective of
whether he is addressing his compatriots or not.* Cut these
out, cut out also the " Zis's " and the " Ze's," and the
average Saxon intelligence, one is driven to conclude,
would fail to divine the nationality. Poirot talks
atrocious English : he cannot hold a candle to Hanaud.
But it *is* comic : it does help the caricature. And as
regards the italics, Mrs. Christie has been wise enough
not to expect more from her readers than a public-
school smattering of the French idiom.

The French idiom also adds a touch of the bizarre,
one might even say something of romance and mystery.
Take, for example, the most familiar " Sherlockism."
In *Silver Blaze*, Colonel Ross is talking to Holmes :

" ' Is there any other point to which you would
wish to draw my attention ? '
" ' To the curious incident of the dog in the night-
time.'
" ' The dog did nothing in the night-time.'
" ' That was the curious incident.' "

Translated it would become something like this :

" ' Is there any other point to which you would wish
to draw my attention ? '
" ' There is the dog,' he said. ' Always I think of
that dog in the night. Always it perplexes, that one.
It is of a mystery the most profound.'
" ' But the dog did nothing in the night-time.'
" ' *Précisément*,' he replied softly. (Poirot's replies
are usually ' soft.') ' That is the mystery, *mon ami*.' "

It is noticeable that when Hercule Poirot is " on the
case," he is often content to abandon these effects.
The longer paragraphs give him an eloquent mastery

of the English language, and even "*mon ami*" is toned down to "my friend."

In *The Mysterious Affair at Styles* Mrs. Christie evolved a scheme which she evidently felt would bear repetition. The murder was postponed for a few chapters to allow the reader to play the eavesdropper to conversations inevitably heated and inevitably interrupted. The murder out, she will probably toss a coin to decide on whom first to turn the searchlight of suspicion. It's really in a way immaterial, as they've all got to go through it. The plot gathers speed from the discovery of at least two significant incidents big with motives for the murder. This means that suspicion will rest in turn on all those implicated in these events. During this time Poirot flits about like a Tchehov character, casting the pearls of his innuendo before the pig-headedness of Hastings. The inquest will quicken Poirot's steps, for it means the veering of suspicion from the first star suspect to the second (the second being equally guiltless). All this time you will be feeling a shade uncomfortable. Two love affairs will be going in full swing ; not of the type, however, to arouse Evoe's nausea[1], for at least two of the lovers will be under a cloud. By a process of elimination, the field will be reduced to one or two "favourites." Then comes Poirot's hour. Not all the king's horses will prevent him from holding a salon. Certainly it is

---

[1] More about Murder Tales.—*Punch*, Nov. 6, 1929.
I cannot abide the Virtuous Young Pair. They are always present as soon as the butchery is done. They are always prigs. They have never done the deed of gore. There is not a chance of getting them killed, even at the end of the book. Apart from their morals, which are white as driven snow, they are chiefly remarkable for incredibly loving conversations and astounding callousness in the presence of a recently slain relative or friend. They sometimes work in collaboration with, sometimes in competition with, the great detective and the police. Their names are quite likely to be Richard and Joan.

impressive, with all the characters as his audience, to begin his exegesis with a *Messieurs, mesdames*. Impressive, too, is the grand climax when he points his finger to the villain, and the chair is overturned in the confusion.

The *Mysterious Affair at Styles* is a very good example of our old friend the " double bluff " ; but it is different from the ordinary species in that the very person responsible for directing suspicion at the start on the real criminal is actually an accomplice of the latter. Thus we have the amusing situation of the villain wishing to be arrested as soon as possible. He relied on securing an acquittal while the evidence was fragmentary and while he had, through the male impersonation of his accomplice, an unobjectionable alibi. Poirot was equally anxious in the circumstances to delay his arrest.

Poirot is over anxious in his first appearance to play fair. He actually details the evidence point by point to Hastings. (It is interesting to note that in *The Mysterious Affair at Styles* he relies more on concrete evidence than in any other investigation.) Only on one or two occasions (e.g., Poirot's " Sixth point," and the evidence of the chemist) does he keep any secrets to himself, and even then it is only for a few pages. Having described the evidence, he returns to his shell : " the human system " deducts in secret. It was clever to make the data afforded by the coffee cups *le point d'appui* of the deduction, but was it equally clever to make a mystery out of the number of coffee cups used ?

In *Murder on the Links* Mrs. Christie shapes to her own ends an interesting fact in criminal records :

> " Man is an unoriginal animal, unoriginal within the law in his daily respectable life, equally unoriginal

outside the law. If a man commits a crime, any other crime he commits will resemble it closely. The English murderer who disposed of his wives in succession by drowning them in their baths was a case in point. Had he varied his methods he might have escaped detection to this day."[1]

From Bluebeard to the Bavarian Butcher criminals have always been assuming that what has once succeeded will succeed again. On this fact the German police card system largely relies. A case in point was where a murderer was discovered simply because he would insist on having a meal after his dirty work, and on doing himself well with the marmalade.

Thus *Murder on the Links* is the second murder of a series. It would only be just to draw your attention to Mrs. Christie's cleverness in her choice of the murderess. Mme. Daubreuil, the blackmailer, was the obvious murderess—obvious, that is, after the facts had been divulged one by one. But Mrs. Christie goes one better. She gives an even stronger motive for murder to Marthe, the daughter, *via* Jack Renauld. (As a matter of fact it was the same motive that had caused Beroldy's death.) Mrs. Christie must have relied also on the fact that she had convinced the reader that Jack and Marthe were eventually to marry. To compensate the sentimentalist she had another lovely girl —for the greater part of the book under dark suspicion —ready to fill the vacancy. Mrs. Christie complicated matters still further by making Captain Hastings fall in love. Rare, indeed, is it that the Dr. Watson is allowed to fall in love in the middle of the detective story. There was plenty of method in this madness.

[1] See also Mrs. Tennyson Jesse's *Murder and Its Motives— Classification of Motives.*

The relationship immediately made Dulcie a star suspect. But it was not quite fair to introduce the twin Dulcibella sisters. No ! Emphatically we must not have twins in the detective story.

An appreciable part of the problem confronting the reader is the identification of the participants in the earlier, the *Beroldy Case*, and when this choice is made, in the further choice of the strongest motive. For we have at least three classes of motives fighting for recognition—the blackmail motives, the passion motives, and the " acquisitive " motives.

Poirot's solution is largely the " psychological " one. As a conversationalist he is in great form, especially in his skirmishes with Giraud. But as far as " concrete " detection goes he has little to do. The episode of the three daggers is trivial : and as for the watch with the broken glass we have had too many of these time problems. The incident of the overcoat shows admirably how Mrs. Christie is at pains to cover up her slight deficiency in actual detection. Conneau is found dead wearing only his underclothes and an overcoat thrown over, with a letter inside one of the pockets. Poirot strikes an attitude.

> " ' I thought for a moment,' said Hastings, ' that he was going to apostrophise it, to declare aloud his determination never to rest till he had discovered the murderer. But when he spoke it was tamely and awkwardly, and his comment was ludicrously inappropriate to the solemnity of the moment.'
> " ' He wore his overcoat very long,' he said constrainedly."

There is an interval of quite 150 pages, during which Poirot measures another overcoat, and then we have the following conversation :

" ' There was no mention of any name to show to whom the letter was addressed. We assumed it was to the dead man because it was in the pocket of his overcoat. Now, *mon ami*, something about that overcoat struck me as unusual. I measured it, and made the remark that he wore his overcoat very long. That remark should have given you to think.'

" ' I thought you were just saying it for the sake of saying something,' I confessed.

" ' Ah, *quelle idée*! Later you observed me measuring the overcoat of M. Jack Renauld. *Eh bien*, M. Jack Renauld wears his overcoat very short. Put these two facts together with a third, namely, that M. Jack Renauld flung out of the house in a hurry in his departure for Paris, and tell me what you make of it.'

" ' I see,' I said slowly, as the meaning of Poirot's remark bore in upon me. ' That letter was written to Jack Renauld—not to his father. He caught up the wrong overcoat in his haste and agitation.'

" Poirot nodded."

Both these incidents by themselves are effective ; but when one reflects that Poirot might have found all this out by a tactful question instead of " making himself ridiculous " by taking measurements, the brilliance of the detection seems to lose its lustre.

The Murder of Roger Ackroyd is Mrs. Christie's master-piece. Indeed it is one of the best half-dozen detective stories ever written. The stage version, *Alibi*, had a very successful run, and Mr. Charles Laughton, as Poirot, was responsible for a brilliant piece of character acting. *The Murder of Roger Ackroyd* is the perfect example of " the most unlikely person " *motif*. Logically, the most unlikely person to be the villain in the detective story is the detective. But this distortion causes a flaw in the construction. There has to be a second investigator to detect the detective. Mrs. Christie, however, hit on a character as " unlikely "

to be the murderer as the detective himself. She chose
the Dr. Watson : Dr. Sheppard this time, not our old
friend Captain Hastings.

The extraordinary cleverness of this idea grows on
one. It cannot have been a flash in the pan, but must
have been born only after much labour. And never did
an idea need such careful fostering. There are at least
three points which demonstrate Mrs. Christie's cunning.

(1) When the narrator is not the detective, he is
expected to flounder. We do not expect the candid,
nothing-to-hide Wills Crofts manner. This is largely
because Sir Arthur Conan Doyle has taught us not to
give Dr. Watson the credit of understanding Sherlock's
methods. Mrs. Christie took advantage of our education.
Here Dr. Sheppard's dullness was assumed because he
had something to conceal.

" I tried my best," said Dr. Sheppard, in the middle
of the story, " to read his (Poirot's) mind. As I know
now, I failed in this latter task. Though Poirot showed
me all his discoveries—as, for instance, the gold
wedding ring—he held back the vital and yet logical
impressions that he formed. As I came to know later,
this secrecy was characteristic of him. . . . I played
Watson to his Sherlock. . . . But after Monday our
ways diverged." The parting of the ways mentioned
in the last sentence refers, of course, to Poirot's process
of inference and is not a confession on Mrs. Christie's
part of illicit secrecy.

(2) Mrs. Christie deceived us in a second particular by
profiting from our association of ideas. Doctors, thanks
to the nobility of their calling, thanks also to the
sentimentalism of Sir Luke Fildes, have as a class an
enviable reputation—country doctors in particular.
The popular idea of a doctor is of a Dr. Watson—of a
large but infinitely gentle soul with a bushy moustache.

And when the narrator in the detective story is a doctor and has a wife called Caroline, one's previous impressions hold sway.

(3) Thirdly, it never enters our minds to suspect the narrator. We regard his existence possibly as an artistic necessity. It is, of course, a weakness in the plot that the villain should chronicle his villainy ; and Mrs. Christie, if hotly challenged, might find herself, *mirabile dictu*, at a loss for a satisfactory motive. It is amusing to find that she felt it necessary to mention that Dr. Sheppard kept his notes well "written up." To commit a murder first and then write a detective story about it is certainly one way of finding a plot.

Mr. W. H. Wright (Van Dine) in his introduction to *The Great Detective Stories*, regards the solution as illegitimate. "I fancy, however," Miss Sayers comments, "that this opinion merely represents a natural resentment at having been ingeniously baffled. All the necessary data are given. The reader ought to be able to guess the criminal, if he is sharp enough. . . ." Poirot's own claim : "Of facts I keep nothing to myself. But to every one his own interpretation of them " ; and Dr. Sheppard's statement quoted above : " Though Poirot showed me all his discoveries . . ." surely give the lie to Mr. Wright. Miss Sayers is certainly charitable. Although it is the fool's part to be wise after the event, it is perhaps a lesson in self-discipline to find some reasons why we should actually have suspected Dr. Sheppard all along. We might have paused, for example, to ask ourselves this little question: Why was Captain Hastings packed off to the Argentine ? If Dr. Sheppard was merely to be his *locum tenens*, nothing was to be gained by it. Another fact which should have put us on our guard was the failure of Dr. Sheppard to propound theories. Again, on no occasion does he betray the Watson denseness. Finally, we might have recognised for their worth these two very excellent red herrings—the telephone call, and the doctor's generous lending of his MSS. to Poirot.

No, there is no violation of the rules. Every character in the detective story, save the genuine detective and the necessarily *familiar* Dr. Watson, is a potential suspect. Both the detective and the reader enter the field in that frame of mind. In the doctor's description of the night of the murder, Mrs. Christie is at her artfulest. Dr. Sheppard has every reason for complimenting himself on his literary flair :—

> " What could be neater, for instance, than the following ?
> " ' The letters were brought in at twenty minutes to nine. It was just on ten minutes to nine when I left him, the letter still unread. I hesitated with my hand on the door handle, looking back and wondering if there was anything I had left undone.'
> " All true, you see. But suppose I had put a row of stars after the first sentence ! Would somebody then have wondered what exactly happened in the blank ten minutes ? "

The whole action is complicated (in much the same way as *The Murder on the Links*) owing to the fact that the murder of Roger Ackroyd was connected with the mystery enshrouding a previous death.

As regards the detection, it is interesting to note that the trick of the dictaphone being used to furnish an alibi, has been employed by Van Dine in *The Canary Murder Case*, and by J. J. Connington in *Death at Swathling Court*.

The Big Four was a surprise item. Here was low-browism with a vengeance. Mrs. Christie had already in *The Secret Adversary* and *The Man in the Brown Suit* won her spurs as a writer of the thriller pure and simple. In *The Big Four* she pitted Poirot against a syndicate of arch-criminals. This was a shock to Mrs. Christie's public, not to mention the shock to Poirot himself. For here he was living in a Sexton Blake atmosphere, in hourly peril of death, the recipient of " menacing missives " through the post or the skylight. The adverse criticism that has been levelled against *The Big Four* fails to take into account a not unimportant fact. It does not see the joke. This was Mrs. Christie's first sustained burlesque. Joyfully she pillories the novelette clichés. The miracle is that as far as excitement goes the book is one in a hundred. The gem of this tale is the parody on Mycroft Holmes. Mycroft, you remember, was Sherlock's brother, who would have made an even mightier detective than Sherlock himself had he (and Sir Arthur Conan Doyle) been bothered. On his superior knowledge the submissive Sherlock would sometimes depend, and was never for a moment reluctant to sit at the feet of this Gamaliel. Truly Sherlock had no business to have a brother, nor for that matter relatives of any kind. Poirot, caught in the inevitable trap, extricates himself by posing as his own brother (non-existent). The criminals too—it goes without saying—having read their classics fully expect another Mycroft.

Mrs. Christie is guilty of one grave error in this burlesque—an error of taste. She should never have brought Poirot into it. Far better had she created another Tommy, another Tuppence. Poirot, indeed, would have had to reconsider his answer to Giraud's " Crimes remain the same." Bombs in the coal scuttle, dynamite in the Dolomites are an insult to Poirot's dignity. In one sense *The Big Four* is Poirot's busman's holiday, but it is also his nightmare. At all events he shows a wise disinclination to recall this period of his career.

The construction of *The Mystery of the Blue Train* is similar to that of *The Mysterious Affair at Styles* and *The Murder on the Links*. Mrs. Christie again relies for her effects on the fusion of several plots. The two central motives are the same as before. Murder is committed on the Blue Train for the sake of an historic necklace. Again there is the usual background of intrigue. The chief point of interest in this tale is the perfect Wills Crofts train alibi—the murder being committed by two people, one of whom had an " unobjectionable alibi."

Mrs. Christie was also prompted to try her hand at the short detective story. Why not, indeed, except that the short story was not so suitable a medium for " the most unlikely person " theme, while it aided and abetted " the unexpected means." *Poirot Investigates* was, relatively speaking, not a success ; and Poirot soon showed his preference for a more leisurely march. In this series he has simply not time to get into his stride, and the villain to get out of his. One admires, however, Mrs. Christie's impartiality in her choice of the villain's sex. In a woman, this is indeed confusing.

The same general fault may be found with *Partners in Crime*. The texture of these stories is of the flimsiest. But really we have no business in this instance to be picking holes. Boredom and Mr. Blunt's delinquencies cause Tommy and Tuppence to take over the management of the said Mr. Blunt's Detective Agency. Blunt's Brilliant Detectives start in on the job, and the burlesque starts. Luck—as one might expect—has the lion's share in the solution of the problems. Tommy and Tuppence, like the well educated couple they are, have been spoon-fed on the classics. This enables them to imitate the methods of the *illuminati*—Sherlock Holmes, Father Brown, Hanaud, Bulldog Drummond, Roger Sheringham, Inspector French, Max Carrados, and, happy stroke, Poirot himself. Mrs. Christie reaps a rich harvest from this clever idea. Uusually she contents herself with a bold, at times rather an obvious burlesque. Thus :

> " Then he lay back for a minute, half-closed his eyes and remarked in a tired tone : ' You must find travelling on a bus very crowded at this time of day.'
> " ' I came in a taxi,' said the girl.
> " ' Oh ! ' said Tommy aggrieved. His eyes rested reproachfully on a blue bus ticket protruding from her glove. The girl's eyes followed his glance, and she smiled and drew it out.
> " ' You mean this ? I picked it up on the pavement. A little neighbour of ours collects them.'

But in the *Man in the Mist*, for example, which is a parody on Mr. Chesterton's postman, her touch is delicious :

> " He stopped suddenly, and stood still, and Tuppence gave a gasp.
> " For the curtain of mist in front of them suddenly parted in the most artificial manner, and there, not twenty feet away, a gigantic policeman suddenly appeared, as though materialised out of the fog. One minute he was not there, the next minute he was— so at least it seemed to the rather superheated imaginations of the two watchers. Then as the mist rolled back still more, a little scene appeared as though set on a stage.
> " The big blue policeman, a scarlet pillar box, and on the right of the road the outlines of a white house."

It was rather a pity that Mrs. Christie did not keep throughout to the style of *The Case of the Missing Lady*, instead of introducing the blood and thunder of red ink and tea trays. Bluff, for the sake of bluff, would have been preferable even in a story like *The Crackler*, and just as amusing. The nonsense detective novel from Bret Harte to Professor Stephen Leacock has always raised a laugh.

Poirot has been having a prolonged rest cure, for Mrs. Christie has started to experiment in her latest novels, *The Mysterious Mr. Quin* and *The Murder at the Vicarage*. In the former of these we have an interesting variation of the Dr. Watson theme, or rather a substitute for it. Mr. Harley Quin appears on the scene, mysteriously to be sure and somewhat spasmodically, merely to make the ordinary Mr. Satterthwaite realise the significance of the facts before him.

In *The Murder at the Vicarage* Mrs. Christie has given us an entirely new kind of detective, and a lady detective into the bargain. Miss Marple is an incorrigible Cranfordian, a spinster and a gossip.* The neighbours disliked her because " she knew everything," and because " she always thought the worst." The structure of this novel is not altogether satisfactory. Miss Marple's detection is virtually her solution, and an exceedingly small part of the book is devoted to the actual solving of the crime. It is almost as if Mrs. Christie had suddenly looked at the clock and realised that the vicar's story-telling was as leisurely as his sermons. One certainly gets the impression that she originally intended to make the vicar the detective, and only changed her mind in favour of Miss Marple at the eleventh hour. She was not, therefore, able to do full justice to Miss Marple as a character. In a

* Questionable, as is what follows.—E. F. B.

mild way we are prejudiced against Miss Marple on her first appearance, and one cannot help thinking that she is not of the stuff of the great detectives. Inquisitiveness will not always come off, and intuitions arising from a more refined interest in human nature are cheap in these days. Moreover, Miss Marple can only hope to solve murder problems on her native heath. If Mrs. Christie is planning a future for Miss Marple, as is very likely, she will be bound to find this an exasperating limitation.

CHAPTER IX

THE THRILLER

" I have supp'd full with horrors."

WE must, first of all, explain our title, though we shall not bind ourselves by definition. Our subject is still the detective story. To us the thriller (species) belonging to detective fiction (genus) must contain some detection in it. (And that's a passable substitute for a definition !) In our thriller there must be a riddle. So we proceed with great gusto to eliminate ; and our task is lightened with every dismissal. The literary critic will tell you that all great literature thrills. We direct his attention to our signpost. He becomes more precise. Says he, " *The Odyssey* is a thriller : so is *Macbeth*, and *Jane Eyre, Dead Man's Rock* and *Romance*." Again we answer in the same vein. We must pass over, besides, the adventure story of gang warfare, the epic of a Bulldog Drummond. Perhaps we might manage Mr. Gerald Fairlie's *Octopus* stories with a squeeze in recognition of the initial problem. We must refuse admittance to the Spy Story : to Mr. Buchan's *Richard Hanay** and Mr. Valentine Williams's *Clubfoot*.** It may be thrown in our teeth that the spy story contains a problem, and bulges with ciphers and the furniture of the detective story. We reply that the problem is different. It is no longer a case of finding X, the unknown villain. The " murder " in the spy story is seldom murder at all. The " murderer " is just as seldom a criminal. The various characters fly their true colours from start to finish, and the suspicion game is not *de rigueur*.

* *The Four Adventures of Richard Hannay*, containing *The Thirty-nine Steps, Greenmantle, Mr. Standfast, The Three Hostages*.—E. F. B.
** *Clubfoot the Avenger*.—E. F. B.

The main attraction of the thriller is, however, derived from the excitement of the action, from a primitive and pugilistic romance. The first, second and third virtues of the thriller are, like the orator's, Action. Human life is cheaper in the thriller. The connoisseur has to bear with the " copious effusion of blood." But the mere multiplication of the number of victims in a detective story does not necessarily make it a thriller. The usual holocaust in J. J. Connington's novels does not necessarily turn the problem detective story into the thriller.

The recipe for the thriller contains three principal ingredients.

It follows from what has been said that careful attention must be paid to create the nerve-racking atmosphere. Otherwise there will be no catharsis, and at the best we will be mildly amused. This terrorism, being second-hand imitation, prospers with elaboration. The great masters like Edgar Allan Poe and Wilkie Collins used every artifice they could lay their hands on.

The second ingredient is a brisk simple narrative (unvarnished save with horror). It should, moreover, be continuous : that is, the action should be so pieced together that we are not conscious of the necessary gaps between the episodes. These gaps are, in fact, necessary because the plot of the thriller is patchwork : the stringing together of appealing situations which must at all costs be brought in, since so much effort has been expended to think of them.

The last ingredient—which has something in common with the first—is the exploitation of the dramatic effect. This may be effected, as we saw in the first chapter, by raising the issues at stake and by introducing state documents, synthetic-chemical formulæ, and Guy Fawkes conspiracies. Forlorn hopes, narrow shaves, last-minute rescues, " tense " situations, all the frills and furbelows of sensation come under this heading.

There are at least four plots which the thriller shows a reluctance to abandon :

(1) After the murder the identity of the criminal is soon revealed, and there ensues a terrific chase which lasts until the last chapter, when the criminal is overtaken. (Mr. Valentine Williams's *Mr. Ramosi* ; Mr. Gerald Fairlie's *Scissors Cut Paper*, etc.)

(2) After the murder the criminal hears of the surprising progress of the detective. Considering that this is not in the interests of his health he proceeds to make repeated attacks on the detective's life. These assaults may last for two or three sequels. The identity of the criminal may be known, as in M. Sax Rohmer's *The Book of Dr. Fu Manchu* ; or unknown, as in Mr. John Rhode's *The Ellerby Case.*

(3) The daughter of the murdered man determines to avenge her father's murder. Very often she is physically attractive to the villain, and there follows abduction upon abduction until the lust of the villain is frustrated by the efforts of the hero. (Mr. Arthur B. Reeve's *The Exploits of Elaine.*)

(4) The rescue of a beautiful girl who has got into the clutches of a criminal gang. (Mr. Louis Tracy's *The Black Cat.*)

There are countless variations, as one might suppose. For example, in Mr. John Arnold's *Murder* we step into the shoes of the hunted man, for the hero is wrongly taken to be the murderer and the circumstantial evidence is damning. Again, in Mr. J. Jefferson Farjeon's *The Master Criminal*, the detective's own brother is the leader of a murderous gang. After a dramatic duel, the bad boy commits suicide, while the detective changes into his brother's clothes and masquerades as the Master until he has rounded up the gang. The idea is ingenious enough ; but this adaptation of *The Prisoner of Zenda* is hopelessly impossible. Few authors who delight in these coincidences of identity seem to bother much about the telltale voice and the vast gaps in the masquerader's knowledge. In Mr. Walter S. Masterman's *2LO* most of the excitement is caused because an innocent man has been condemned to death and the chances seem to be ten to one that the detective will be too late to save him. One must mention in passing the highly dramatic exit of the villain (a playwright) who confesses before the microphone in the B.B.C. Studio—presumably to the British Isles. A variation of (3) is *The Master of the Microbe* by the Canadian poet, Mr. Robert W. Service. Here a mortiferous microbe in a silver cylinder falls into the hands of a maniac who soon inaugurates his campaign of annihilation. An American student, somewhat addicted to the bottle, gets wind of it, and the usual warfare ensues midst apache dens and the Parisian sewers. The book, however, is remarkable for the excellence of its technique. Mr. Service has inherited Poe's power of making our flesh creep and of accumulating horror upon horror. It is a full-length edition of *The Pit and the Pendulum*.

The thriller teems with impossibilities and improbabilities. It is seldom that the writing—the style —is a good enough excuse. If the thriller is to come up to form, there should be a credibility about the events described. There *has* to be a " pathetic fallacy." It is all very well to talk like Mr. Francis D. Grierson's Professor Wells :

> " It certainly sounds a tall story. But most of the
> stories you deal with *are* tall stories—or you would
> not be dealing with them."

but if one's apprehension is to be roused, one has to
believe for a joyous two hours in the Swiss navy.
Mind you, we can be malleable in the extreme. We
accept the possibility of hedgehogs roaming the country-
side, their quills touched up with a spot of poison ;
of teeth being filled with a stopping infected with
canine rabies ; of clocks so mechanically contrived
as to shoot to kill. We allow the police to be even
more callously victimised than elsewhere. Houses are
attacked with bomb and machine-gun fire within a
couple of miles of a police station, and the constabulary
stirs not a step until the last chapter. Then and only
then, the Black Marias arrive opportunely midst the
smoking ruins. We gladly suffer the electrification of
garden walls and the construction of secret passages
to the Bank of England. Really, we can congratulate
ourselves that we are capable of this dream fugue.
But it requires no little skill to put us in this frame
of mind. The spell is broken so soon as we catch ourselves thinking, " How far-fetched " or " How stupid."
It is to be confessed that this discovery is not in-
frequent.

Inconsistency has also a good innings. It was once
said of *The Egoist* that so involved is the dialogue that
it is advisable for the reader to have a pencil in his
hand if he wishes to be quite sure who is speaking.
The dialogue in the thriller does not rise to these
heights ; but the pencil is just as necessary, for one
character always seems to be saying what the other
was intended to say. Again no man waits for time in
the thriller. In *The Ellerby Case* we start our adventures on the 31st of July, and a few weeks later no one

seems upset because August has not arrived. One
of Mr. Edgar Wallace's ladies changes her name from
" Lila " to " Millie " (or *vice versa*). I suppose she had
some justification. It is unnecessary and puerile to
labour the point. There is one bright spot in the
Cimmerian gloom. The contemporary scholiast is
given such glorious chances. If you are a member of a
circulating library you will have noticed the frequent
marginal glosses (no longer, alas, in rubric) finished off
with a gigantic exclamation mark.

Clichés are two a penny in the thriller. Every one
can recognise the villain of the thriller. He has the
usual tapering fingers, the maniacal laugh, and an
expressionless cruelty in his eyes. He is a killer, but
usually by proxy, and keeps a dwarf, a scientist, or a
chimpanzee to act on his behalf. But there are two
people in the world he will not kill, for all his blustering,
the hero and the heroine. Time and again he has them
at his mercy trussed up on the rack ; always he refuses
to drop the handkerchief. And yet one is asked over
and over again to believe that it is his lust for a sweeter
revenge, or for torture long drawn out that makes him
procrastinate. He lives in luxury and keeps a sinuous
vamp on his premises either to act as a decoy or merely
to ornament his salon. For he is a perfect devil for
effect. He is a connoisseur in wines. He has a high-
power grey touring car.

Considerable difficulty is naturally experienced in
starting the chase. Recourse is often made to the
personal columns of the Press. This cliché has, in
turn, led otherwise sensible people to read through
these columns religiously every day in the hope of
detecting a real adventure. It is certainly amusing to
weave romances round a dozen words inserted in all
probability for a rather prosaic reason. If we could

see what was happening at the other end our giants would soon become windmills again. If a " young man wants adventure : will do, risk anything," he might be found a week or two later attempting to sell vacuum cleaners to harassed housewives. In the thriller the same advertisement will bring him a sheaf of replies. From these he will select one, knit his brows and pass it to his friend, with a " Looks interesting." The reply will be to this effect :

> " Meet me beside the picture post cards in the British Museum at three. Wear a white carnation in your buttonhole. Don't speak to any one until I have spoken to you."

He will accordingly repair to the rendezvous and there meet his future wife, the victim of an immediate murder, or the arch-criminal himself.

A large percentage of the criminals in the thriller are Chinamen. " Chinamen have long arms," says Cherry in *The Kang-He Vase*.* " I've heard of them stretching all the way from Pekin to Piccadilly." Father Knox has a natural enough antipathy to this invasion, and regards it as essential that there should be no Chinaman in the detective story. But this proposed ostracism is too extreme a nostrum. The Chinaman of the *Mr. Wu* and *The Chinese Bungalow*** variety makes a splendid villain. Oriental mysticism is a good excuse when one is at a loss for a motive or an explanation. But still there are too many Chinamen : there are, besides, too many Hindus who come next in popularity. Would the choice of a criminal from a country nearer home be a violation of the Kellog Pact ?

Dr. Fu Manchu is the greatest Chinaman of them all. Sax Rohmer's *The Mystery of Dr. Fu Manchu, The Devil Doctor, The Si-Fan Mysteries* have run into

---

* *The Kang-He Vase* by J. S. Fletcher.— E. F. B.
** *Mr. Wu* by L. J. Miln. *The Chinese Bungalow* by Marion Osmond.—E. F. B.

countless editions, and now the doctor has a large
omnibus volume devoted to himself. In this series
we at last have an instance of a contest where the villain
is more than the equal of the detective. Indeed
Commissioner Nayland Smith, the detective, and Dr.
Petrie, his Dr. Watson, are in luck's way all the time.
Chapter by chapter they escape death by the skin of
their teeth. Although it required considerable ingenuity
in addition to their good fortune to remain alive, it
really required considerably more ingenuity on the
part of the doctor to set so hot a pace. Oftimes, too,
Nayland Smith and Petrie were saved by the slave girl,
Karamaneh, whose exotic sensuality may weary us
but never the susceptible Petrie.

Dr. Fu Manchu is a born genius. When you discover
that he possesses such attributes as *vril*, *force*, that he
has a radiating aura and glamour which " hangs like
a miasma over the neighbourhood," you know what
the Commissioner is up against. He has, too, the
features of a born ruler.

> " And even in that moment I could find time to
> search my memory, and to discover that the face,
> saving the indescribable evil of its expression, was
> that of Seti I., the mighty Pharaoh who lives in the
> Cairo Museum."

The doctor is at his best when he is devising new
methods of murder. He has a partiality for keeping
strange creatures and reptiles in reserve as most of his
myrmidons fall before Nayland Smith's fire. The
doctor's servants, by the way, are usually brown,
not yellow, are naked to the waist, hairy, and have a
silent tread. But his Fred Karno's Circus is much
more amusing. He has a pack (or is it a herd ?) of
Cantonese rats, a rare specimen of the *Cynocephalite*

(it has to go in italics when it makes its appearance), and damnable insects which carry about them the subtlest of alkaloids. Nor must we forget the doctor's pet marmoset which leaps and gambols about the place " uttering its shrill whistling cry." Other methods of extinction favoured by Fu Manchu are wire cages and mediæval torture chambers. One has only to read such chapter headings as " Questing Hands " (not an essay on the Cinema) and the " Coughing Horror "—and one knows all.

It is superfluous at this stage to devote any time to the historical development of the thriller, since we have done as much in our incidental sketches. It is virtually impossible all the same to guard against serious hiatus. We offer a skeleton résumé as a peace offering.

As we saw, the thriller prospered in the salad days of our Muse. _The Moonstone_ is the first genuine thriller, though some of the novels of Gaboriau (and later of Du Boisgobey) may be included in this category. Dickens's _Edwin Drood_ might have been our prize catch. But, owing to its fragmentary state, we are not quite at liberty to claim it. " There are some," said E. M. Wrong, " who even deny there is a corpse to be discovered, and speculation ranges still over the identity of Datchery." As we are not certain that there is a corpse and not certain either that there is a detective (although Datchery inspires one with that confidence), we must not be too greedy. Miss Sayers pays tribute in her Introduction to the novels of Mrs. Henry Wood. " Through _East Lynn_, crude and sentimental as it is, she exercises an enormous influence on the rank and file of sensational novelists, and, at her best, she is a most admirable spinner of plots." It is unfortunate that _The Ebony Box_—Miss Sayers's choice in her collection—does not bear this out. But, in general,

Mrs. Henry Wood had certainly the knack of spinning an intriguing plot. When shorn of their padding her novels reveal a first-class technique. An interesting figure, with even greater claims to our appreciation, was the Irish Sheridan LeFanu, at one time a hack journalist.* LeFanu's *Uncle Silas*, which is included in the *World's Classics*, is one of the best examples we have of the Victorian thriller—hair-raising, steeped in the supernatural, and just a trifle long-winded. Sir Arthur Conan Doyle and his contemporaries of the nineties were partial to the thriller, but, with the turn of the century and the introduction of the scientific detective story, there grew up a tendency in the best circles to eschew it. Notwithstanding, it would be untrue to suggest that the thriller ever went out of fashion. The prolific William LeQueux and Mr. E. Phillips Oppenheim, issuing their volumes with an almost benign regularity, continued to hold their public. Similar in many respects to the French *roman policier*, their novels contain more mystery and intrigue than genuine detection. Much as we may admire the cleverness of the plot or the excitement of the action in such tales as William LeQueux's *The Three Glass Eyes, Hidden Hands* and *Sant of the Secret Service*, or Mr. Oppenheim's *The Conspirators, A Prince of Sinners* and *The Great Prince Shan*, we cannot rightly regard them as detective stories. Since the war the thriller has prospered increasingly.

The subject-matter of this chapter provides us with a convenient opportunity for grouping, in spite of their striking dissimilarity, three outstanding masters of the thriller, Mr. Edgar Wallace, Mr. A. E. W. Mason, and Mr. J. S. Fletcher.

* LeFanu was never a hack journalist, but a fairly well-to-do owner of newspapers and periodicals.—E. F. B.

2

THE WALLACE COLLECTION

To many people detective fiction is nowadays synonymous with the novels of Mr. Edgar Wallace. Born in 1875, Mr. Wallace has had a varied career. He has served as a private soldier, been a miner, war correspondent, journalist on the staff of at least two London daily papers, and has experimented in numerous other occupations. Then three or four years ago his detective stories suddenly became popular ; now he is one of the world's celebrities. If my memory does not play me false, it was only a few years ago that he was enlivening the columns of the less dignified Sunday papers with the adventures of an *Aberdeen Annie* : but he has put on his three-league boots since then. His international popularity is probably greatest in America and then Germany. He edits a German magazine of detective stories, and the enterprising bookseller of even the small German provincial town dresses his windows with an attractive display of *Romanen von Edgar Wallace*. Germans will smile at you when you inform them that of their contemporary writers you read only Ludwig, Feuchtwanger and Remarque. But you cannot afford to smile in return when they tell you they read Shaw, Galsworthy, and Edgar Wallace.

Mr. Wallace's output is the wonder of our age. Over two years ago, the *Daily Mail* published the following statistics of " returns " :

140 novels (though he might have forgotten ten or a dozen).

Half a dozen plays (at least).
Two hundred (or it might be four hundred) short stories.
About 9,000,000 words.

Recent figures are not to hand, but although there has been a slight falling off in output, the figures quoted have been very considerably increased. This mass production means an uncanny precipitancy in execution, and no doubt Mr. Wallace's experience on the staff of the *Daily News* (1900) and the *Daily Mail* (1901-02) stood him in good stead.   Mr. Wallace gives the following as his record speed :

> " A firm of publishers asked me on a Thursday for a novel of 70,000 words by noon on Monday. Working seventeen hours a day, dictating it all to a typist, with my wife doing the corrections, I delivered *The Strange Countess* on Monday morning."

One remembers, too, " The Midday Wallace " joke in *Punch*, and Mr. Wallace's favourite excerpt from the *Wabash Monitor* :

> " Edgar Wallace, world's most prolific writer, was called on the long-distance at the Marquery Hotel, Park Avenue, ' Sorry,' said his secretary.   ' Mr. Wallace has just started a new novel.' ' Great ! ' said the voice from Cincinnati, O. ' I'll hold the wire till he's through.' "

Let us take a peep into the Wallace *phrontisterion*. We must be careful not to enter in the D. B. Wyndham Lewis spirit, or we may rouse Mr. Wallace to biting sarcasm. The Wallace Collection is run on strictly business lines. Which is a pity, for the very introduction of the business element is tantamount to a sacrifice of quality. But Mr. Wallace prefers quantity to quality,

and the critic *will* have him follow in the steps of
Dumas. " The Wallace library is extensive, especially
on crime subjects." Yes, decidedly that is a selling-
point. Apparently, if Mr. Wallace cannot lay his fingers
on certain details, reference works in public libraries
needs must be consulted. Better still ! A dictaphone
stands in the corner. Of course it may not actually
occupy that position : but there *is* a dictaphone, and
in detective stories the corner is always the position
allocated. It is rumoured that there are innumerable
files with cross references and subsections which play
a not inconspicuous part in the great fight against
time. Mr. Wallace has a stenographer : now and then
he calls him a typist, but he will probably hear about
that. This stenographer is one of the champions of
Great Britain—and he would need to be. In and out
and round about the sanctum creep strange men.
" It is no new experience for me," Mrs. Wallace has
admitted, " to come face to face with a criminal on the
staircase. Down-and-outs, hoboes, people-with-stories-
to-tell, and others keep calling on Edgar, and the
result of their visits is sometimes manifest in articles,
sometimes books, and occasionally in plays." Does it
not seem *infra dig.* that criminals who can always
turn a dishonest penny should have preferred this
labour exchange ?

Mrs. Wallace is the lady with the blue pencil. She
sins on the side of the angels. Work for the day usually
begins at seven in the morning : during the rush
season at four or even at midnight. It is alleged that
all Mr. Wallace's plots are thought out before the
dictaphone is used : and that he does not write on
the spur of the moment.

Mr. Wallace's work is curiously varied, both in theme
and in style. He is a most unequal writer. " When

he is good, he is very very good, but when he is bad he is horrid." On the credit side he has these virtues :

(1) His narrative is straightforward, and there is no padding, and no nonsense.

(2) He is genuinely exciting, and relies on no artifices for his creation of atmosphere. He follows the old saw, *Ars est celare artem.*

(3) His humour is never strained. " The Sparrow " and " J. G. Reeder " are inimitable characters, naturally humorous.

(4) He has an inside knowledge of Scotland Yard and police methods.

(5) He is familiar with the lingo of crooks.

On the other hand :

(1) He is too fond of " the most-unlikely-person " theme.

(2) Impossibilities and improbabilities occur too frequently.

(3) He is by no means word-perfect. He calls a napkin a serviette, and is guilty of a phrase like " she shrugged milky shoulders." His grammar, also, is not unimpeachable.

(4) His sensationalism is often extremely crude, and not in perfect taste.

Mr. Arnold Bennett finds one very grave defect in Edgar Wallace :

> " He is content with society as it is. He parades no subversive opinions. He is ' correct.' Now, it is very well known that all novelists who have depicted contemporary society, and who have lived, abound in subversive opinions. Look at Defoe, Swift and Fielding. Feel their lash. Remember the whips and scorpions of Dickens, and the effort of even the Agag-footed Thackeray to destroy utterly the popular convention of the romantical hero. And Hardy's terrible rough-hewing of the divinity that shapes our ends.

. . . It may be counted a maxim that good modern
literature is never made out of correct sentiments.
If there are exceptions to this rule they must be
extremely few. . . . Perhaps I am unfair to Edgar
Wallace. Perhaps in earlier years he has chastised
society with intent to be immortal."

This criticism seems to be very wide of the mark.
It is absurd to require the detective novelist to be a
social reformer. Besides, Mr. Bennett starts from the
assumption that society in Mr. Wallace's novels is
his idea of actual Society! If Mr. Bennett does not
make this assumption, one asks whether he can force
us to attach any substantial meaning whatsoever to
his objection. For if he does not, it would seem he
finds fault with Mr. Wallace for not being in his writing
a social reformer as well as a writer of detective stories
—a conclusion which cannot cast any reflection,
whether for good or ill, on his detective stories as such.
As it is, the joyous absence of any subversive opinions
might well be considered a merit instead of a defect.

For convenience' sake we might classify the Wallace
novels in five main groups. Perhaps I should admit
that, as I cannot claim to be a member of any Edgar
Wallace Club, I have read only a fraction of the grand
total. This classification is therefore " E. and O.E."

(1) *The Four Just Men Series.* (*The Four Just Men,
The Four Just Men of Cordova, The Law of the Four
Just Men, The Three Just Men.*) In these stories
murder is regularly committed from the highest
motives. The Four Just Men form a Crusade to rid
the world of its most noxious members. They are the
champions of moral as opposed to legal justice. Thus
the police, as the upholders of an inadequate system,
become the villains. The Four Just Men began badly,
for they put to sleep a " fairly harmless Secretary of

State." Of course, it cannot be said they did not warn him, but the unfortunate politician had to think of the Press. The quartet improved fortunately with experience, and ran a highly successful Co-operative Murder Campaign. One notes the close affinity of this series to the Arsène Lupin stories.

(2) The Police novels, such as *The Crimson Circle*, *The Ringer*, *The Squeaker*, *The Terror*, etc. It is here that Mr. Wallace overdoes " the most unlikely person " theme, the detective finally emerging as the villain or *vice versa*. Gaston Leroux's *Le Mystère de la Chambre Jaune* is parent to this engaging family.

(3) Just thrillers, which need no further comment. *The Green Archer*, *The Avenger*, *The Black Abbot*, *The India Rubber Men*, *The Sinister Man*, *The Yellow Snake*, *Room 13*, *The Clue of the New Pin*, etc.

(4) The J. G. Reeder stories—*The Mind of J. G. Reeder*, *The Orator*.

(5) *The Sanders of the River stories—Sanders of the River*, *Bosambo of the River*, *Bones*, *Lieutenant Bones*, *Bones in London*, etc.—which do not come within our purview.

Mr. Wallace's detective dramas such as *The Ringer*, *The Terror*, and *The Flying Squad*, caught the public favour ; and the West-End, thereupon, suffered from a spate of police plays. (*On the Spot* was more an amusing satire on Chicago than an honest detective play.) Then followed a tendency to substitute for sheer excitement social propaganda, as in Mr. Vosper's *People Like Us*, or humour, as in *Sorry You've Been Troubled* ! It would not be out of place to pause for a moment to consider the æsthetic of the detective drama, and to see whether it gains or loses in its new surroundings.

In the first place it is a question how far it has

retained its integral character in such adaptation.
Drama has always exulted in murder and violence :
but bloodshed was, as a rule, spilt at the final curtain—
the tragic climax and loosening of the knot. In the
detective drama it is the preliminary tying of it. On
the stage the atmosphere of the detective story is
skilfully produced by an accumulation of dramatic
effects. The producer likes to bathe his " sets " in
shadows, to throw the tiny light of an electric torch
on a giant staircase, to rouse our pity and fear by
strangled cries and " dull thuds," and to increase them
still further by switching on the lights for brief intervals.
This is simply *Grand Guignol*. We might have guessed
as much. How in the world can the drama present
analytic reasoning, the mainspring of detective fiction ?
The answer is that it cannot : all it can achieve is to
present us with the setting and leave us to take it
for granted—in the face of grave disadvantages—that
we are witnessing a great deal more. Indeed such
illusion is in cold blood ludicrous. We watch the detective prowling and prying about the stage. Poor
fellow, he cannot sit still to think ! Logic does not
partake of the dramatic, and even if it did there would
still be serious technical difficulties such as the presentation of the evidence, and the portrayal of
character. The screen suffers from the same disability
to " project " logical analysis.

There are three main reasons why detective plays
and films prove such an attraction. Their popularity
is in the first place a borrowed one, and an adaptation
is always a source of interest. Secondly there will
always be, and quite naturally, a public for *Grand
Guignol*. Thirdly, in witnessing a detective play or
film we are subject to a strange illusion. The detective
has not got the time to think (nor, we might add, the

inclination either) so that *the audience has to reason for him*. All he has to do is to appear mysteriously profound and to strike the right dramatic attitude at the proper moment. And this can be so supremely taking that we are inclined to give him the benefit of the doubt and allow that we had no hand in helping him to his discovery.

The detective play may be either a thriller pure and simple like *The Flying Fool, The House of Danger*, etc., or it may make some pretence of containing a problem, in which latter case only one *motif* is virtually possible, that of the most unlikely person. Mr. Wallace again shows his preference for the latter, as in *The Ringer*. It was a piece of folly on the part of the producers of *At the Villa Rose* to make this a straightforward thriller instead of keeping it in the second category. The physical limitations of the theatre are less suited to the requirements of the thriller than the screen is. The screen, on the other hand, cannot make so much of the problem play, as it does not express character so clearly, and also because certain stars insist on being either heroes or villains. The talkie version of the detective story retains the weaknesses of both the stage and screen versions. How the Van Dine murder cases have suffered !

3

Mr. A. E. W. Mason

Compared with Mr. Edgar Wallace, Mr. A. E. W. Mason is an infinitely more painstaking artist. He will spare no effort to achieve the picturesque and will employ all manner of elaboration and artifice to heighten the dramatic effect. Where Mr. Wallace is complaisant,

Mr. Mason is not content till he has hitched his wagon to a star. He must have realised that, after all, a pot-boiler is only a pot-boiler, and that it remains for the conscientious craftsman to use a little camouflage to make it as attractive as possible. Combined with these stylistic charms Mr. Mason has the gift of story-telling. On this score the author of *Clementina*, *The Four Feathers* and *The Broken Road* can rest on his laurels.

It is only the Hanaud trilogy—*At the Villa Rose*, *The House of the Arrow* and *The Prisoner in the Opal*—that falls, strictly speaking, within our purview. In these three stories are to be found all the essential ingredients of the thriller recipe. He threw the veil of romanticism over his action by transporting us to Aix-les-Bains, to Switzerland and the Riviera. He keeps the problem unanswered till the end, and he regales us with excitement caused by abduction and assault. He cultivates the-most-unlikely-person theme, but rather overdoes the diverting of suspicion to some other character. But he has the grace to explain Hanaud's reason for this. If Hanaud had no reason for it, then his infallible intuition would have been at fault—and so we may continue to argue pointlessly in the vicious circle. In *At the Villa Rose* the presentable lover of the chloroformed girl becomes the villain : in *The House of the Arrow* we have an exchange of sex, and Betty Harlowe, who has captured young Frobisher's heart, is suddenly discovered to have committed the murder. This time, however, there was a happier ending, as far as Frobisher was concerned, for it turned out to be a case of " How happy could I be with either," and Hanaud sent him into the arms of the other girl. This was only a fair return, because it was Hanaud who had made Ann Upcott the chief suspect. In *The*

Prisoner in the Opal Mr. Mason revived the orgies of the Black Mass somewhat in the style of Mr. John Buchan's tales. The plot structure is not much changed. We have first the murder, then the abduction, and lastly the frustration of a second murder (when one of the characters begins to know too much). After all, it was merely fear of discovery that gave Robin Webster, the renegade priest, his two associates ; whereas the original murder was his own doing. It is possible that Mr. Grierson's short story *The Sign of the Serpent* may have suggested the Black Mass theme to Mr. Mason. The basis of the plot is the same in both.

Mr. Mason's Hanaud is one of the most effective portraits in our gallery of detectives. In many ways he is similar to Mrs. Christie's Poirot (or perhaps we should put it the other way round as Hanaud appeared years before Poirot). Hanaud, as we have already mentioned, is an intuitionalist. He does not claim any supernatural power. He has been " trained," as he modestly explains on one occasion. He thinks quickly, and he thinks to the point. Hanaud does not, however, always play fair. That is Mr. Mason's chronic weakness —he has a tendency to get off-side. For example, he notices frequent changes of facial expression when murder, for example, " blazes out " of an unsuspected face ; but he waits till the dénouement before he parts with this knowledge. We recall, too, the episodes of the clock and the mirror, of the pen with the poisoned shaft, and of Hanaud's talk with the Edinburgh professor—all occurring in *The House of the Arrow*. If put on his defence, Mr. Mason would find some difficulty in rebutting this charge.

Hanaud is theatrical but with more dignity than Poirot. We have spoken of Mr. Mason's love of effect.

The conclusion of *The Prisoner in the Opal* is a perfect example of the picturesque style :

> " Hanaud drew Ricardo's attention to their (the lovers') slow progression with a good many chuckles, and digs with his elbow, and playful archnesses ; all of which were quite detestable to one of Mr. Ricardo's nicety. But Hanaud's manner changed altogether when the four of them stood together in the street under the lamp of the hotel. He took off his hat as Joyce thanked him in warm and trembling tones, and with a great simplicity he said to her :—
> " ' Mademoiselle, I have served.' "

Hanaud has less difficulty with the English language than Poirot. (There is the same conventional interspersion of French words). Only when he learns the word " Gorblimey " from Ricardo's chauffeur, and plays with it as a new toy, is there any indulgence in low comedy. Although Hanaud has something of the *gamin* in him, he is never drawn with the crude bold strokes of caricature. He lacks the quips and cranks of Poirot. To his peacock vanity are not allied the oft-repeated mannerisms. Hanaud is a police official. He is not given the same latitude to follow his own whims. Incidentally, he must have been unpopular at the cinema, for he found it the best rendezvous for a discussion of the case.

Mr. E. B. Osborn, in a review in the *Morning Post* of M. René Cassellari's *Dramas of French Crime*, referred us to an interesting account of Mr. Mason's originals :

> " As you may learn from A. E. W. Mason's mystery stories, the best models for the detective of fiction are to be found among the experts of the Sûreté Générale of Paris. *Dramas of French Crime* introduce us to M. René Cassellari, who was for twenty years a Commissary of that radio-active body and is now established

in a flourishing private detective agency of his own, which carries on business all over the world. ' These French detectives,' observes his biographer in a too brief introduction, ' have a way all their own. They sense the drama that underlies their work, and they frequently stage the *finale* in a manner that would bring them vast credit if they were to devote their talents to the theatre. . . . The successful detective officers of the Sûreté are invariably men of first-class education and, more often than not, excellent linguists. But then they are not recruited as are the officers of the Criminal Investigation Department of Scotland Yard. In France a detective is not compelled to patrol the streets before he is eligible for the investigation of crime. He enters the Sûreté as a clerk, engaging himself principally in keeping records and gaining a technical knowledge of criminals and their ways before he is entrusted with cases of his own.' "

Hanaud has in Mr. Ricardo a new type of Dr. Watson. Ricardo, the connoisseur, is not the kind of man who would really be attracted by the detection of crime—he has more the cosmopolitan's interest in character. Thus we do not expect him to be of much service to Hanaud, although the spirit of the chase does so possess him that he makes orderly notes now and again for the benefit of the reader. The two have so little in common that it does occur to one that Mr. Mason has his tongue in his cheek. I mean that Mr. Mason may have intended a parody independently of the humour of the association. Hanaud is indeed a master of " crural tension " : and Ricardo's finicking propriety is too good material to be wasted. To sum up, the contrast is one of character. It is no longer a contrast between a deductive ability and disability.

4

Mr. J. S. Fletcher

One of the most interesting figures in our list of authors is Mr. J. S. Fletcher. Mr. Fletcher, who was born at Halifax in 1863, is an historian and antiquarian first ; his detective stories we must regard as the fruit of his leisure hours. He has written *A Picturesque History of Yorkshire*, a work on *The Cistercians in Yorkshire*, and several historical novels in which he displays a remarkable knowledge of eighteenth century history. He is also an authority on rural life and has contributed articles on this subject to the *Leeds Mercury*, the *Star*, and the *Daily Mail* under the nom-de-plume, " A Son of the Soil." He has besides written several " straight " novels dealing with north country life. He is a great Yorkshireman, and the moors are a favourite setting for his novels. Mr. Fletcher is an enthusiastic book collector, but he does not find contemporary literature to his taste. Even the wares of his competitors fail to rouse his interest.

Mr. Fletcher knows his own mind, and follows his own whims. For this reason there is always an uncertainty about the solution to his mysteries, and that is unsatisfactory. In *The Mysterious Chinaman* he simply did not bother about explanations at all ; in *The Great Brighton Mystery* the villains turned out to be the most likely persons.

Mr. Fletcher is not a very good detective ; he has little use for minute tangible evidence, and has not the patience to build an intricate structure of hypothesis. He relies on hearsay evidence for the most part, on information received in public houses or in lawyers' offices. Any character in the Fletcher novel is capable of solving the problem—granted a little luck.

As our first choice we might select *The Charing Cross Mystery*, *The Mazaroff Murder*, and *The Kang-He Vase*. In the first of these we have a murder capitally staged, exciting abductions, and a new process for the making of ink as a key to the plot. In the second we have an up-to-date border feud in which the unexpected novelty of the motive compensated for its inadequacy. *The Kang-He Vase* is the refashioning of the *Treasure Island* type of story, the bill of entry into our genre being provided by murder and theft.

In the second rank we would place *The Middle Temple Murder*, *False Scent*, *Sea Fog* and *Green Rope*. Less attractive are *The Safety Pin*, where an unfamiliar character springs an eleventh hour surprise, and *The Great Brighton Mystery*, which is apt to drag.

5

JUVENILIA

It would be illiberal to ignore in this chapter the juvenile " bloods "—*The Adventures of Sexton Blake*, *The Nelson Lee*, *Dixon Hawke*, and *Nick Carter Libraries*. The penny dreadful is the *locus classicus* of the public librarian's epidemic dissertations. On the whole the brazen article is dealt with leniently by the reverend seniors. Not so in Germany, where a translated *Nick Carter* awaits academic recognition. " We fight," Dr. Behl has said, " the penny dreadful and the shilling shocker-sensation, written in often ludicrously bad German." Miss Sayers has already undertaken the defence of " the blood " in no eleemosynary or satirical spirit. " The really interesting point about them," she says, " is that they present the nearest modern approach to a national folk lore, conceived as the centre for a cycle of loosely connected romances in the Arthurian manner." These are detective stories told to the children. You will find in them much moralising of the kind that advanced educationalists would now call " priggish," but as you might expect blood and thunder come first. In these cheap romances it is anathema to be unconventional. The Sexton Blake household (including Sexton Blake, Tinker, Mrs. Bardwell—not to forget the Dog Pedro) is modelled, as Miss Sayers mentions, on that of Sherlock Holmes. The detective's methods from being simplified may strike one as somewhat crude and fortuitous. If there is an overdose of Philistinism or an over-escape of gas—why, bless one's soul—the same thing happens in a Wallace novel. Much of the work of these anonymous authors and syndicates is mature and competent, and you might easily fail to recognise an adventure of Sexton Blake if disguised in a seven and sixpenny dressing. At the same time Sexton Blake has a large adult following, much larger than you would possibly credit. The funniest thing about the stage presentation of *Sexton Blake* was the schoolboy self-consciousness of the elder members of the audiences.

The *Nelson Lee Library* is the most amusing to the adult. It is a combination of the detective story and the public school story. In the public school that never was, Nelson Lee, " the master criminologist," hopes to settle down as an idolised house master to a lotus-land retirement after the fitful fever of previous investigations. In vain ! for criminal gangs arrive weekly to ruffle the scholastic calm. Nipper, Nelson Lee's assistant, a boy of indeterminate age, takes a sort of post-graduate course. Naturally the whole school is infected with detectivitis. Of the boys, Tommy Watson plays Dr. Watson to Nipper's Sherlock, and Handforth is a police inspector in embryo. Had the head master been an ordinary head, he would have sent Nelson Lee packing as soon as the Yellow Peril appeared. But no, the presence of the great Nelson Lee on his staff was an honour to the school, besides adding spice to pedagogic routine. The wonder of it all was the docile acquiescence of the parents. Perchance Nelson Lee's timely rescue of Tommy Watson's uncle (he was kidnapped on a visit to the school) was meant to shatter any parental misgivings as to the wisdom of allowing the younger generation to be educated elsewhere.

CHAPTER X

TRIED FAVOURITES

I

THE purpose of this chapter is to fill up some of the painfully obvious gaps. Our defence before was that it was impossible owing to the vast volume of production to give anything like a complete account of the thousand and one detective stories clamouring righteously for recognition. We still cling to this defence like prisoner to the railings. But there is a way out. Let us take a charabanc tour, and make the most of the short time at our disposal. The guide, kind patron, is allowed to " hae his doots." He knows that unless he makes some sort of apology to disarm criticism at the start, his passengers will give him the very devil of a time. Many of them know the route as well as, if not better than, he does himself, only they haven't done the sights in this particular manner. The passengers are requested to refrain from talking to the driver, and to curb their ire should our conveyance pound past the monument and the village pump. And so, with as much shaking of the head as of this pen, we take the road.

Every honest excursion should include a church in its itinerary. We start with the church this time. We will choose Father Ronald Knox and Canon Victor Whitechurch as the principal representatives of the cloth. The former has a partiality for a detective story without a moral, which is to all intents and purposes a detective story without a murder. The " suicide "

in *The Three Taps* (1927)—the laxity of " reformatory " thinkers condones this form of " murder ")—
turned out to be an accident. The murder in
Footsteps at the Lock (1928) was a fake. In *The
Viaduct Murder* (1928) there was an honest murder ;
but then the murderer confessed just to teach the
amateur detectives a lesson, for these charming
investigators had begun to suspect each other. *The
Viaduct Murder* is probably Father Knox's best
detective tale. The beauty of it is the moral—just as
you can be too stupid to solve a murder mystery, so
you can be too clever. Sophistry won't get you anywhere. It will amuse you, but it will reveal only that
insignificant suggestion of character that is patent
when people argue and theorise for argument's sake.
And what has this to do with the detective story ?
Here is a quotation for an indirect answer :—

> " You have to start out by saying, ' This document
> consists of three parts One part is genuine, one part
> is spurious, the third part is faked evidence put in to
> make the spurious stuff look as if it was genuine . . .
> you reject altogether the parts of the document which
> you don't like. Then you take the remaining part,
> and find that it still contains a certain sort of
> dross—evidence which still conflicts with your theory.
> That dross you purge away by calling it a deliberate
> fake. The watch says four fifty-four—that is proof
> positive that, in the first place, the murder took place
> at three-forty-five, and, in the second place, the
> murderer tried to pretend it didn't. . . . Now, the
> more of that business you do, the more ingenious
> your theory becomes, and the more ingenious your
> theory becomes, the more easily will people accept it
> as true."

This paragraph contains an obvious allegory.
Father Knox was bound to be unconventional in

detail as well. His detective, Miles Bredon, is a private agent in the sense that he is not connected with the police. Detection is none the less his job, for he is an agent of The Indescribable Insurance Co., and he has to protect the interests of his company against fraudulent stratagems. To Miles and his amusing wife, Angela, detection is not an uncongenial occupation ; they adopt the A. A. Milne attitude towards it.

Father Knox's detective stories all go a-begging. *The Viaduct Murder* lacks a detective ; *The Three Taps* lacks a murder (and thus a villain) ; *Footsteps at the Lock* lacks a death. All three of them lack action and excitement. Theoretical detection is all very well, and we applaud the gymnastics of the sophist. But his antics can be as tedious as a " Greats " essay when continued for a long time.

Canon Whitechurch, on the other hand, is a sound conventionalist. His " secular " work—*A Bishop Out of Residence, The Canon in Residence, Downland Echoes*, etc.—is admired for its quiescent charm. In 1927 he forsook these pastures and got down to business, producing first *The Crime at Diana's Pool* and shortly afterwards *Shot on the Downs*. His former style fortunately did not desert him. Both these novels are as good examples of an unassuming, able technique as one might hope to find in a long day's march. Canon Whitechurch makes no secret of his methods. In his preface to *The Crime at Diana's Pool* he wrote :—

> " In most detective stories the author knows exactly what the end is going to be, and writes up to that end from the beginning. But, in reality, the solver of a problem in criminology has to begin at the beginning, without knowing the end, working it out from clues concerning which he does not recognise the full bearing at first.

"I have tried to follow this method in the construction of the following story. To begin with, I had no plot. When I had written the first chapter I did not know why the crime had been committed, who had done it, or how it was done. Then, with an open mind, I picked up the clues which seemed to show themselves and found, as I went on, their bearing on the problem."

What a splendid idea for a detective story competition —to present the entrants with the opening chapter. In a way the mention of the clues suggests that if the Canon did not know how the problem was going to be solved at least he was prepared to bind himself to one or two conditions. It follows that since the problem is formed and grows as the plot is unfolded, Canon Whitechurch proceeds at an ambling gait. That is to say, as he admits in his preface to *Shot on the Downs*, he has implicit faith in ordinary police methods, and has no need to introduce dazzling feats of deduction or to pile up crime on crime. His real secret is that he does not make the problem so hard to solve as all that, and is not in a hurry to set out his data in a tidy heap. The descriptive passages in *Shot on the Downs* are so charmingly written, and so rare an event is this in the detective story, that we would be churlish to pass it by without a word.

The Presbyterians have been strangely silent, and we have yet to welcome the advent of a Calvinistic detective. Dr. James Moffatt, however, the renowned translator of the Scriptures, published some little time ago his maiden detective story. *The Tangled Web* is rather disappointing. As one reviewer pointed out, the spider did not inveigle and made no pretence of being anything else but a spider. The web, is it necessary to add ? was drawn round a rectory family.

To complete this group there is the Rev. John Ferguson, the author of the deservedly famous one-act play, *Campbell of Kilmhor*. Mr. Ferguson in secular mood prefers to be sensational, as the mere titles will indicate—*The Man in the Dark*, *The Secret Road*, *Murder on the Marsh*. *The Stealthy Terror* remains my own favourite. Mr. Ferguson is one of the most delightful stylists in the genre, and this makes ample amends for the temporary banishment of enlightened detection.

2

The universities are strongly represented by J. J. Connington, and by Mr. G. D. H. and Mrs. Margaret Cole.

J. J. Connington is the pseudonym of Professor A. W. Stewart. Professor Stewart, the son of the Dean of Faculties in Glasgow University, is a professor of Chemistry in Queen's University, Belfast. He is the author of numerous studies in this subject with such formidable titles as *Stereochemistry* and *Recent Advances in Inorganic and Physical Chemistry*. But in his detective stories he is J. J. Connington, and refrains from talking shop although he must have been sorely tempted. Nevertheless, being a good professor mathematics entered his soul—and also his novels.

It is the numerical factor that complicates and makes his plots. In fact, by multiplying murder, the problem he presents is in the annals of detective fiction quite a singular one. For example, in *Murder in the Maze* (1927) two people are murdered, one immediately after the other. Observe the ramifications of this " double," and the extra conundrums :—

Were the two murders the work of the same man ?
Was the motive the same or different in each case ?
Were both murders premeditated ?
Was the first murder a mistake, and the second a correction of that error ?
Was the second victim the murderer of the first ?
and so on and so forth. In *The Case with Nine Solutions* we have a problem of permutations and combinations. Sir Clinton, the detective, takes the deaths of Hassendean and Mrs. Silverdale in every possible " combination." He finds that nine is the greatest possible number of combinations. To make this clear to any of my readers who are not familiar with the book, I will start to copy the table, viz. :—

Hassendean.	*Mrs. Silverdale.*
(1) Accident.	Accident.
(2) Suicide.	Suicide.
(3) Murder.	Murder.
(4) Accident.	Suicide.

(One was thankful that J. J. Connington did not make matters worse by adding the death of the maid to the list). Elimination is the next step, and in the actual work of elimination there is a return to conventional detection. The numerical factor is also present, though not to the same " degree," in *The Two Tickets Puzzle*.

This partiality for bloodshed has been misinterpreted and somewhat unjustly attacked. We pointed out in the last chapter that in spite of the number of persons killed, the Connington novel remained a problem novel. *The Mystery at Lynden Sands* (1928) is his only detective story that comes near to being a thriller. Mr. Arnold Bennett, however, finds fault with the inhuman, unemotional quality of *The Case with Nine Solutions*. He wrote :—

" But my main adverse criticisms of the story are that the human repercussions of its events are simply not handled ; and that only one character has any life, the chief constable of the borough. He lives. The rest do not. The book is inhuman. If a jig-saw puzzle has emotional quality, then *The Case with Nine Solutions* has emotional quality. It not, not. . . . It has some attraction, but no attraction of emotion. It has employed the invention of the author, not his imagination. A tragedy is not a tragedy until it moves you. This book has four tragedies, and you do not care twopence."

Mr. Bennett is within an ace of attacking the whole *raison d'être* of the detective story. We have already laboured this point. As regards *The Case with Nine Solutions* we reply that there are not four tragedies— no, not even one. But there are four deaths.

In *Death at Swaything Court* (1926) there is only one murder. This novel has an outstanding weakness, the lack of a proper villain. The murder is perpetrated by two likeable conspirators, and the black deed is white-washed in a sentimental way. The concoction of the alibis, the dictaphone records, and the telephone call are worthy of Mr. Wills Crofts. Much more, one feels, might have been made of the parrot. In the preface J. J. Connington upheld the fairplay method :—

" Unfortunately in many cases his (the reader's) labour is made futile because the author allows his detective to pick up some undescribed clue of supreme importance ; and this generally happens in the middle of the book after the reader has expended much energy in working his way through the tangle of incidents."

In *Murder in the Maze* J. J. Connington was not quite so self-conscious a stickler for this optional rule. As we have remarked, *The Mystery at Lynden Sands* is almost a thriller, an abduction and subsequent chase providing the requisite excitement. The problem here is perhaps not so much a numerical problem as one of time. There is an amusing reference to an old cliché of detective fiction. When a watch belonging to the murdered person is found, glass broken and the hands at rest, it is immediately taken for granted that the helpful hands of the said watch are good enough to indicate the precise time at which the murder was committed. It is amusing to reflect that often on the flimsy basis of such details an elaborate plot structure can be erected.

Mr. G. D. H. Cole is Reader in Economics at Oxford University, and a Fellow of University College. Mr. Cole is a member of the Economic Council, is a publicist of much distinction, and has the reputation of being one of the ablest economists in the socialist ranks. He can talk for hours on political philosophy and on his pet subject of Trade Unionism. Mr. Cole started writing detective stories by himself. But even as his detective, Superintendent Wilson, grew to rely on the assistance of his wife when things were not going too well, so Mr. Cole enlisted the services of his wife (though not necessarily for precisely the same reason), and the two have now been in successful literary partnership for a number of years. Mrs. Cole is a daughter of the late Professor J. B. Postgate.

The Coles's detective stories are really of the domesticated kind, and if we had aimed at perfect pigeon-hole classification we might have transferred them to Chapter VI. They combine, however, the qualities of so many different schools that perhaps after all it is better to have them here. The amusing social satire contained in their novels shows up the popular fallacy that a socialist cannot have a sense of humour. In

The Death of a Millionaire (1925) the creatures of high
finance are pilloried ; in *The Blatchington Tangle* (1926)
the more innocent intrigues of " society " are lightly,
ever so lightly, dealt with ; in *Poison in a Garden
Suburb* (1929) a terribly sensitive, but at the same
time conventional suburbia is satirised. In *Burglars in
Bucks* and *Corpse in Canonicals* it is the turn of the
" county." The extraordinary thing is that this
satire is so successful. One would imagine that satire
would be completely out of place in a detective story,
and would be inimical to the interests of the detection
element. But this is not so with the novels of the
Coles. Their characters are very much alive, and
belong to just these strata of society with which the
Cole must come in daily, or " vacational," contact.

As regards detection Superintendent Wilson is of
the Inspector French calibre. He is never brilliant. He
worries things out, and often makes mistakes. He is not
so painstaking as Inspector French, chiefly because
the Coles must yield to Mr. Wills Crofts as far as the
art of elaborate detection goes. I always think of French
and Wilson living in the same street, and of their
respective wives paying calls on each other, comparing
their husbands' cases (in the second spirit of feline
rivalry), the while they knit socks for their lords and
masters. It was a telling idea on the part of the Coles
to make Wilson hand in his resignation to the Yard
owing to Lord Ealing's appointment as Home Secretary.
In *The Death of a Millionaire* Wilson learnt just a little
too much about that gentleman's business methods.
So two birds were killed with one stone. Wilson became
the private agent ; yet he still had his official connections. Politicians should appreciate the sweet
irony of it.

Little need be said of the actual novels themselves.

There is with one exception no striking originality in the presentation of the problems or in the working out of their solutions. In *The Brooklyn Murders* (1923) a double murder is committed in such a way as to look, at the first glance, as if the two men had killed each other ; and at the second as if one of the other characters (the chief suspect) had done the deed. There is a faked murder (as one guessed) in *The Death of a Millionaire*. *The Blatchington Tangle* is the perfect house-party detective story, even although the " murder " turns out to have been almost an accident. The humour is capital, and the fun furious—" Murders *do* break up a house-party," as one of the characters says. Most of these characters were themselves concerned in the shady business, and Wilson had some difficulty in letting one of the blackmailers escape (for the peace of the peerage) from Inspector Peascod's clutches— a modern sequel to the old feud between the amateur and the professional.

In *Poison in the Garden Suburb* Wilson's task is complicated by the ineffective garrulousness, and the petty feelings which were naturally magnified in the circumstances, of grossly intellectual suburbanites. *Superintendent Wilson's Holiday* (1928)—a volume of short stories—is in the same light vein, mildly amusing, but not up to the standard of *The Blatchington Tangle*.

Burglars in Bucks is another typical example of the Coles's country house crimes. Here, however, they have introduced a novel manner of presentation. They have discarded the ordinary narrative method, and have instead provided the reader with the evidence as it came to hand, in the shape of newspaper cuttings, telegrams, etc. By itself this evidence would have failed to make a novel. Therefore, some series of letters are included to explain the evidence and adorn the tale.

This innovation does not entail a radically new technique. To claim that the reader is given a fairer chance by being presented with authentic documents is beside the point, for the author can be just as deceitful and selective as before, and can couch his telegrams in language as ambiguous as the answers of the Delphic Oracle. This new manner of presentation has been followed to some extent in *The Documents in the Case* by Miss Sayers and Mr. Robert Eustace, and in *The Bowery Murder*, by Mr. Willard K. Smith.

3

It is rather late in the day to return to the Old Brigade. Politeness decrees that since we originally took our hats off to them, at least we can spare a few minutes with them. The three masters whom we have chosen to buttonhole are Father Brown, Max Carrados and Mr. Fortune.

Mr. G. K. Chesterton's Father Brown stories— *The Innocence of Father Brown, The Wisdom of Father Brown, The Incredulity of Father Brown*, and *The Secret of Father Brown*—amount to an elaborate, at times a tortuous brief for simplicity in a world of chaotic complications. The simple insignificant little souls, of whom Father Brown is the picturesque representative, are at any moment liable to assume gigantic proportions. The grotesque setting, the atmosphere of men in sable outlined against a lurid sky suggest the pantasmagoria of a dream. It is all deliciously exciting. Postmen carry corpses in their letter-bags ; philanthropists who preach " the religion of cheerfulness " are suicidal maniacs. In such a world there is no place for the empirical criminologist

That would sacrifice the paradox. Father Brown is an intuitionalist. His simplicity—his " innocence " or " credulity " if you will—enables him somehow to regard complication as a subjective failing. He reads a man's character in a flash, and the recognition of the truth, of good and evil, is almost an æsthetic sense to him. As intuition is a fallible guide, Father Brown's intuition has got to be infallible.

It is often asked whether the Father Brown stories are detective stories at all. The answer depends on one's idea of what detection means or what it can be stretched into meaning.

The problem of a Father Brown story can seldom be stated in precise terms. One starts with a murder, but one learns precious little about it. In fact, the theorising starts before there are any data to theorise from. Thus the problem becomes a choice of theories ; and Mr. Chesterton has the last laugh because he has kept another theory up his sleeve. There is much more than this to it. There is a subtle use of superfluous evidence—and of common or garden padding when the subtlety fails.

The construction of these stories is similar throughout, though not monotonously similar. The component parts are in order—a weird murder, or a strange occurrence ; obvious theories with obvious evidence for them ; and, lastly, the correct theory, correct most often because it is *different* from the obvious theories. It may be different in either of two ways ; different because it is the least likely solution that would occur to one, or because it is still more obvious really than the obvious theories. No wonder the Chesterton plots are styled " impossible " and " fantastic " since they are shaped in this mould.

The critic who takes it upon himself to discuss the

works of Mr. Chesterton does not go very far before he finds himself discoursing on the paradox. The Father Brown tales are riddled with paradoxes. Let us catalogue the more important of these.

(1) Father Brown himself is a paradox. A Catholic priest is the last person in the world to be a detective in a detective novel.

(2) Father Brown's " detection " is most brilliant when he makes wild guesses—" His head was almost most valuable when he lost it."

(3) The police are incompetent because they are too clever (v. *The Three Tools of Death*).

(4) The plots often contain a paradox. *The Invisible Man* and *The Hammer of God,* are examples of the unlikely person theme explicitly stated.

Much of the theorising is mere trick-writing. Take for example this passage from *The Queer Feet* :—

> " He had seen men run in order to jump. He had seen men run in order to slide. But why on earth should a man run in order to walk ? Or again why should he walk in order to run ? . . . The man was either walking very fast down one-half of the corridor in order to walk very slow down the other half ; or he was walking very slow at one end to have the rapture of walking fast at the other. Neither of the suggestions seemed to make much sense."

Then think of the simple explanation of this strange behaviour. One must confess that many of the complications in Mr. Chesterton's plots are verbal, or at least " abstract." Mr. Chesterton would seem to start with a simple enough idea and then really to put himself out to make it *look* complicated. *The Three Tools of Death* is perhaps the best example of this bluff. In this story the police found evidence from which they could logically deduce that the dead man was killed three times over. In *The Man in the Passage* a looking-glass, of the treacherous kind so dear to the comic film, causes all the discrepancies in the evidence.

The characters in the Father Brown stories are even more fantastic than the plots. What a madhouse it is, tenanted by all sorts and conditions, from the man placidly eating his bath bun in the A.B.C. tea shop to the police-criminal of *The Secret Garden*, and the blackmailing numismatist of *The Head of Cæsar*. It is hardly necessary to add that the humour is irresistible. But the detective story fan is out for redress since he is debarred from working out these problems himself. He will be more disappointed still with *The Poet and the Lunatics* (1929), for it is even more grotesque. It is not really a detective story at all, whatever the critics have said. Gabriel Gale has not the slightest veneer of the detective. Only *The Shadow of the Shark* might have been included, with a stretch of the imagination, in the Father Brown cycle.

Mr. Ernest Bramah's Max Carrados mysteries— *Max Carrados*, *The Eyes of Max Carrados*, etc.—are really elaborate specimens of stunt writing. Carrados is the blind detective " who combines in one person " as E. M. Wrong said, " all the remarkable abilities of all the blind men of history." Carrados made his debut before the age of realism, and at a time when miraculous powers were appreciated merely because they were miraculous. The Carrados cases bear a distinct resemblance to those investigated by Sherlock Holmes and Martin Hewitt. The less violent kinds of crime were more in Max's line owing to his blindness. However, he found himself in pretty desperate company now and again (v. *The Game Played in the Dark*). The episode related in *The Comedy at Fountain Cottage* takes us back to the grand old days :—

" He said that you (Max Carrados) were once in a sort of lonely underground cellar near the river with two desperate men whom you could send to penal servitude. The police, who were to have been there at a certain time, had not arrived, and you were alone. The men had heard that you were blind, but they could hardly believe it. They were discussing in whispers which could not be overheard what would be the best thing to do, and they had just agreed that if you really were blind, they would risk the attempt to murder you. Then, Louis said, at that very moment you took a pair of scissors from your pocket and coolly asking them why they did not have a lamp down there, you actually snuffed the candle that stood on the table before you."

There is good enough reason for Max having a Carlyle as a Dr. Watson ; but it is not quite so clear why Carlyle was made so incompetent. Max had another assistant in his butler, Parkinson, who not only provides occasional genteel humour, but also acts as the eyes of his master.

The most interesting point about Mr. Bramah's stories naturally concerns the blind detective's methods. Mr. Bramah asks the reader to take a lot for granted. Max deduces " from certain observations." He is able to make these observations by keeping his ears " skinned " and by being American-wise, " aura-conscious." Here is how he deduced a man was wearing a false moustache :—

" The man carried a five-yard aura of spirit gum emphasised by a warm, perspiring skin. That inevitably suggested one thing. I looked for further evidence of making-up and found it—these preparations all smell. The hair you described was characteristically that of a wig—worn long to hide the joining and made wavy to minimise the length. All these things are trifles."

Having made these observations he is wont to rely more on intuition than on deduction.

The Knight's Cross Signal Problem, The Brookbend Cottage Tragedy and *The Ghost at Massingham Mansions* are his most spectacular prize winners.

Mr. H. C. Bailey is more widely known as an historical than a detective novelist. It was as late as 1920 that his Mr. Fortune appeared on the scene in *Call Mr. Fortune.* Mr. Fortune's encores were numerous, and he has reappeared in *Mr. Fortune's Practice, Mr. Fortune's Trials, Mr. Fortune Please* and *Mr. Fortune Explains.* Mr. Fortune, however, belongs to the old school. He is another of the infallible intuitionalists.

" These men," according to E. M. Wrong, " leap to conclusions while others limp behind. Those who like them like them very much indeed, even though they admit that many of the crimes discovered by Father Brown were impossible, and think Mr. Fortune perhaps too ready to assume the responsibility of granting life or death."

Those who do not like them so very much are often at a loss to account for the popularity of the intuitional detective. Mr. Fortune is lionised by the critics, yet there is not after all so very much in him. He is a good judge of character ; that we must grant him, but this perspicacity can be presented to any detective. It is too accidental a quality. His intuitional powers are sketchily described as a " sixth-sense," and as we mentioned in Chapter V. he has a practical sort of omniscience. Lomas—the head of the Criminal Investigation Department—is Fortune's Dr. Watson. The rivalry is rather too ambitious, is it not ? E. M. Wrong regards Lomas merely as a companion, but in this he seems to err. Lomas not being an intuitionalist becomes thereby a foil.

The Fortune stories differ from most other detective
stories of the intuitional kind in one respect. They are
slight in texture, and lack the loaded atmosphere of
Mr. Mason's or even Mr. Chesterton's novels. This is
due to Mr. Fortune's buoyance and racy conversation.
But he does raise such a pother to mesmerise us with
his mystery.

4

Miss Dorothy Sayers, who writes so charmingly
about the detective story, herself gained an enviable
reputation in the genre with her *Unnatural Death,
Whose Body?* and *Clouds of Witness.* Miss Sayers is
always original and always entertaining, and moreover
from her study of the subject she knows what's what
and does not lay herself open to attacks for inconsistency. In her Introduction Miss Sayers described the
detective story as, above all, a problem, and she has
stuck to the letter of this dictum. On one occasion she
perhaps went too far. One of her short stories—*Uncle
Meleager's Will*—was merely a dramatised cross-word
puzzle.

Her detective, Lord Peter Wimsey, is an amusing
mixture. He is not an original character as a character,
but he certainly is as a detective. He is the aristocratic
dilettante, cultured, an art collector, and an admirer
of the classics. All these are his superficial assets.
Twenty years ago the detective was at pains to reveal
his detective ability, Lord Peter is usually anxious
to conceal it. Let us believe that this is a sign not
of decadence but of polish. As a detective, Lord Peter
is related both to Anthony Gethryn and Philo Vance.
In *Strong Poison* Miss Sayers succumbed at last to
sentimentality in making Lord Peter fall in love, and

have to rescue his eventually happy Harriet from the gallows.

Unnatural Death is Miss Sayers's most interesting novel. It is a composite detective novel. It is divided into sections, and these sections represent in epitome the different aspects from which the detective story is most often written. Thus one section deals with the problem from a medical point of view and another from the legal point of view. It was unfortunate that the final section—the detective novelist's pigeon—was the least successful. Let us hope that the idea of providing the reader with a genealogical table is not copied. It was excusable in *The Forsyte Saga*, but in a detective story. . . .

In *Lord Peter Views the Body*, a collection of short stories which was not generally approved by the critics, Miss Sayers was responsible for some attractive fooling. Lord Peter's reputation may have suffered owing to these extravagances, for corpses had to be opened up and an escape to be made from an underworld gang. But I challenge anybody to deny that there is bouquet in *The Bibulous Business of a Matter of Taste, The Entertaining Episode of the Article in Question*, and *The Learned Affair of the Dragon's Head*.

The Documents in the Case was written in collaboration with Mr. Robert Eustace, who, you will remember, was joint author with Mrs. L. T. Meade of our earliest scientific detective stories. Thus it is natural to suppose that Mr. Eustace was responsible for the manufacture of the " synthetic muscarine," and the laboratory tests with beams of polarised light. If our supposition is correct, Mr. Eustace is certainly to be congratulated on the discovery of a plausible poison. Miss Sayers (and Mr. Eustace) postponed the murder until we had some idea of the wherefore and what it was all about ; and no attempt was made to hide the criminal. In this respect *The Documents in the Case* resembles a Thorndyke novel, though in justice to its authors one must add that the characterisation is more effective than Dr. Austin Freeman's.

As our charabanc trip is almost over it remains to draw the passenger's attention to the attractions which we are mercilessly passing by.

If you prefer the police novel then you are recommended to make, or renew, the acquaintance of *The Hampstead Mystery* and *The Mystery of the Downs*, by Mr. J. R. Watson and Mr. A. J. Rees, and *The Shrieking Pit* and *The Hand in the Dark* by the latter.

Or if you hanker after the conventional detective story you will admire Inspector Pointer's solutions of *The Clifford Affair, Footsteps that Stopped, The Cluny Problem, The Eames-Erskine Case* and *The Wedding Chest Mystery*, by Mrs. A. Fielding.

Mr. Anthony Berkeley's Roger Sheringham is a less serious edition of Philip Trent, and another journalist-detective. In *Roger Sheringham and the Vane Mystery, The Wychford Poisoning Case, The Silk Stocking Murders, The Piccadilly Murders* (which was chosen by the American Detective Club) and *The Second Shot* there is in each case an original idea, a twist to the plot, that crowns the detection. Mr. Berkeley's *Mr. Priestley's Problem* is probably the most amusing hoax in the genre.

Finally, before alighting, we really must not miss Lord Gorrell's *In the Night* and Lord Charnwood's *Footsteps in the Snow*.

CHAPTER XI

THE AMERICAN DETECTIVE STORY

I

WHILE Jack Diamond was in hospital he started to read detective stories. He did not take long to make up his mind about them. One day to a waiting world the news was broadcast, " Jack Diamond says detective stories are the bunk." I am not sure what this means, but it sounds uncomplimentary. Now, it is probable that he was at the time in no frame of mind to appreciate a joke against himself and his. Outside in the corridor the real detectives were on sentry-go, and now and then, maybe, a " wise crack " of theirs was overheard by the racketeer. It is equally probable that he did not approach the detective story as it should be approached. On the other hand it is just possible that the detective stories served up to him, being American, were " the bunk " (whatever it *does* mean). We have had some experience.

Poe gave the American detective story too spectacular a send-off. A relapse was inevitable, and for the next eighty years American writers succeeded in living down this reputation pretty effectively. Indeed it was only with the advent of Van Dine that the American ,detective story " made its grade." Prior to the happy event this country had been flooded with imports of cheap sensational stuff, and E. M. Wrong's complaint was not unjustified. In the preface to his collection he wrote :—

> " The (possibly pointed) omission from this volume
> of all American stories save those of Poe is due partly
> to ignorance on the part of the compiler, partly to his
> feeling that a detective story should have some
> literary quality. There are thousands of modern
> American detective tales, but in those that he knew
> the divorce between plot, often good, and style,
> generally execrable, seemed to him too complete to
> justify inclusion."

Moreover, our impressions of the American detective
and his methods were not exactly improved by studying
his behaviour on the screen. Bred on Sherlock Holmes
and the classics we were immediately up in arms
against this assiduous masticator of the cigar, who
extorted his information from languishing victims by
his brutal third-degree methods, and showed a strange
disinclination to take his hat off under any circumstances.

Miss Anna K. Green, as already mentioned, was Poe's
first successor.* Little need be said here of the novels
that have come from her facile pen. Criticism has on
the whole treated her kindly. She never quite succeeded
in combining convincingly the Victorian melodrama
with the detective interest—largely because she was
not a very good detective. The reprint of *The Leavenworth Case* attracted some attention. A post-prandial
pronouncement of Mr. Baldwin was presumably the
origin of this venture, for on the jacket we read in bold
black type from some continental laundry :—

" Mr. Baldwin—speaking at a dinner of the
American Society in London on the 29th November,
1928, said :—

> " An American woman, the successor of Poe, Anna
> K. Green gave us *The Leavenworth Case*, which I still
> think one of the best detective stories ever written."

* Not correct.—E. F. B.

Something must have been wrong with the dinner. *The Leavenworth Case* is not by any means a first-class detective story. The detection is singularly elementary. The plot is hopelessly drawn out, and the melodrama is a sample of unnatural and stilted writing. It may be unfair to cut out a sentence or two from its context, but the climax cries aloud for glorious isolation :—

> "A silence ensued which, like the darkness of Egypt, could be felt. Then a great and terrible cry rang through the room, and a man's form, rushing from I knew not where, shot by me and fell at Mr. Gryce's feet shrieking out : ' It is a lie ! a lie ! Mary Leavenworth is innocent as a babe unborn ! I am the murderer of Mr. Leavenworth. I ! I ! I !' "

A much better story than *The Leavenworth Case* is the same writer's *The House of the Whispering Pines.** This is in many ways a capital thriller. It has one grave defect. The criminal, Zadok, is hidden away from the reader's gaze for most of the action. Objection might also be taken to the fact that the action is set to the wrong tempo. It opens too quickly and has to slacken speed appreciably, whereas the ideal thriller gathers speed with every chapter like a runaway train. Of her other works one might select for mention *The Mill Mystery, Behind Closed Doors* and *The Step on the Stair*.

Then the plague of sensational, ill-written thrillers filled the land. Mr. Arthur B. Reeve, who now controls the prosperous fortunes of a group of detective story magazines, is the most notorious representative of this legion. His pseudo-scientific detective, Craig Kennedy, has always swayed Teutonic affections. Craig Kennedy's greatest successes were won in *The Exploits of Elaine* and its sequels, *The Romance of Elaine* and *The Triumph*

---

* The modern consensus is that Miss Green was an excellent plotter but a poor writer, and that *The House of the Whispering Pines* is among her poorest books.—E. F. B.

of Elaine. He is of the Nayland Smith type, rather strong and silent, athletic and egregiously resourceful. This last quality was essential owing to Mr. Arthur B. Reeve's ingenuity in devising original methods of destruction the scientific possibility of which is often problematical. Craig Kennedy committed one unforgivable sin. He had no business to fall in love with Elaine. He had just polished off the Clutching Hand (the family lawyer and a suitor—in rather a curious way—of Elaine) when he suddenly found that her eyes were limpid pools. Thereafter, he had to protect her against persistent Chinamen. If you like this sort of thing you will find ample amusement in Mr. Reeve's *Craig Kennedy, Detective* and *Craig Kennedy Listens In.* Mr. Reeve has also attempted with some success to impart a romantic flavour to the detective story, by giving us the cosmetic settings of Cuba and the South American republics.

Competence stamps the works of Isabel Ostrander, who also wrote under the pseudonym of Robert Orr Chipperfield. Her chief fault is her tendency to conceal some piece of vital information as in *Annihilation* ; and if she does not fall into this error she is tardy in surrendering her data. *The Neglected Clue* should not have been neglected for so long. *Ashes to Ashes* is probably her best work. " This shows," says Miss Sayers, " the clues being left by the murderer, who is then compelled to look on while they are picked up, one after the other, by the detective, despite all his desperate efforts to cover them. It is a very excellent piece of work, which, in the hands of a writer of a little more distinction, might have been a powerful masterpiece." In matters of detection Isabel Ostrander is rather a plodder. She has no room for brilliant analysts and psychologists like Terhune, but either pins her faith to the McCarty type or lets matters take their own course when a Geoff Peters or a Peterby investigates. Her most widely read novels besides those already mentioned are *Dust to Dust*, *McCarty Incog.* (Isabel Ostrander) ; *The Second Bullet*, *Unseen Hands*, *Above Suspicion* (Robert Orr Chipperfield).

In altogether lighter vein are the amusing novels of Mr. Hulbert Footner, from which we may single out for special mention *The Substitute Millionaire*, *The Owl Taxi* and *Officer !* Mr. Footner, however, deserves special mention for his gallant attempt to make a detective of a beautiful woman. His portrait of Rosika Storey in such novels as *The Doctor Who Held Hands* and *The Viper* is attractive, but unconvincing. This, as we have seen, was also a fault with Mrs. Christie's Miss Marple. The great lady detective has not yet been born. It is only a question of time, and it will be an interesting event this, without a doubt. Her creator will have some difficulty in deciding what her methods are to be, for intuitions are too common ; and extreme delicacy will have to be exercised in the handling of the most violent situations. Scotland Yard does not boast a sybil, but the beautiful women of the Secret Service are not mere figments, and the novelist might learn something from them—in a literary way.

Sam Spade, the ex-Pinkerton man of Mr. Dashiell Hammett's *The Maltese Falcon*, *The Dain Curse* and *Red Harvest*,* is an honest-to-goodness, 100 per cent. American detective. There does not appear to be much more than this to commend him. Mr. Hammett is himself an ex-Pinkerton man.

* This is Thomson's worst gaffe, both critically and factually. Sam Spade does not appear in *The Dain Curse* or *Red Harvest*.—E. F. B.

2

"Let us look at the psychological aspect of the case.—
PHILO VANCE.

In 1926 Van Dine opened the Philo Vance series
with *The Benson Murder Case*, to be followed by *The
Canary Murder Case* (1927), *The Greene Murder Case*
(1928), *The Bishop Murder Case* (1929) and *The
Scarab Murder Case* (1930). Van Dine (or Mr. Willard
Huntington Wright) is so important a figure in the
history of the detective story that the reader may
like to know something about him. The following is
an excerpt from an interview reported by Mark Larkin
in *Photoplay Magazine* :—

   "Six years ago he was flat broke and flat on his
back, his strength exhausted by the overtax of work.
And for two years and eight months this man was
confined to his bed, the victim of a shattering physical
and nervous collapse. For practically three years he
was not allowed to write a line. For almost one year
he was not allowed to read. Finally, however, he
prevailed upon the doctors to permit him to read
detective stories. And that started him on the road
to fame.
   " ' It is not in the least original to say this,' he told
me, ' but invariably some apparently inconsequential
thing shapes a fellow's destiny. I set out to write a
monograph, a small book outlining the history of
mystery fiction. I hadn't the slightest intention of
writing a murder mystery yarn myself. I merely
intended to do an analytical scholastic work bearing
on this type of story. The history of this kind of
fiction, you know, is comparatively brief, beginning with the works of Poe, who originated the
form.
   " ' After completely solving the mystery of the

mystery story, however, I determined to do one myself, so I turned from my mass of data and notes to this, for me, precarious undertaking.

" ' The result was *The Benson Murder Case.*'

" In addition to being a distinguished author, Mr. Wright is also a worthy mathematician Therein, perhaps, lies the secret of his great success as a deviser of mystery stories, for after all a mystery story is nothing more, he says, than an elaborate literary puzzle.

" Mr. Wright, like all who labour, has one consuming ambition. In a way, this ambition is quite unique. He hopes never to have to write another murder mystery story. Imagine that ! Each book that he does means a small fortune, yet he hopes never to have to do another.

" He wants to write about biology and anthropology. And his crowning ambition is to complete the philology upon which he was working at the time he collapsed and became rich and famous."

A murder from the Van Dine point of view is akin to a work of art. *In primis* it is a thing created of thought. Also it has a technique in the execution, and bears the impress of its author's character. De Quincey might have agreed with Van Dine on the last point, but he certainly did not have occasion to argue about it. Let us wrestle with this idea for a minute. We start with the statement that any given murder will have the stamp of the murderer upon it—the brand of Cain, so to speak, in reverse. From this you may conclude that the psychologist will be able to pick out the murderer from a study of those characters connected with the crime. As far as the detective story goes the psychologist will have to be infallible ; one cannot allow his psychology to be in any sense experimental. Very well then, let us have Philo Vance's own succint explanation :—

" Having determined the exact psychological nature
of the deed, it only remained to find some interested
person whose mind and temperament were such that,
if he undertook a task of this kind in the given circumstances, he would inevitably do it in precisely the
manner in which it was done."

This method is after all not so very far removed
from Père Tabaret's.

The technique of the crime is therefore the investigator's lodestar. It is possible that the psychologist
might have as much difficulty in settling the authorship
of a murder as the literary critic in deciding who wrote
The Poems of Ossian. The psychologist would more
than likely go astray in such cases as the following :—

(1) Where a person killed some one in mistake for
some one else.

(2) Where a person murdered another in a momentary
fit of aberration or of seeing red.

Does the æsthetic-psychological argument hold water
where much has been committed in a *Kubla Khan*
trance ? It is hard to believe that such a murder would
betray a tell-tale technique. We would not accept the
psychologist's retort that it would be possible to name
the person prone to this form of mania. You will
notice too, that Van Dine's murders are all premeditated ; the stamp has time to make the impression.

The solutions in the Van Dine novels are based on
a study of this technique. In *The Benson Murder Case*
Vance argues that the nature of the crime proves that
it was committed by a bold, fearless gambler, by an
aggressive, brutal man with no subtlety or imagination
about him. He casts his eye round the circle of suspects
and finds the head to fit his cap. A novel game of poker
resolves his doubts in *The Canary Murder Case*. He
knows the kind of man who committed the crime, but

he does not know the suspects well enough to pin, as it were, " the psychological indications " of the crime to the culprit's nature. So a game of poker is arranged, because Vance believes with " Doctor George A. Dorsey " that : " Poker is a cross-section of life. The way a man behaves in a poker game is the way he behaves in life." Clergymen have said the same thing about golf ; and we wait for the detective story wherein the detective stymies his suspects one after the other in order to observe how their physical organisms respond to " the stimuli supplied by the game." The poker game is pre-arranged so that Vance may discover the real gambler in the party of suspects.

In *The Greene Murder Case* it is rather different. There is a whole series of murders, and Vance has to regard these murders as a composite whole. Here there is an extremely interesting digression on the difference between a photograph and a painting. Vance is determined to regard the murders as a painting, but at first he has to be content with the unrelated facts of the photograph. How he manages to do this is surprisingly ingenious. He catalogues the facts, selects certain of them, numbers them and by shifting these numbers about he is able to arrive at a grouping which satisfies his æsthetic, or rational, or psychological, sense. Once he is satisfied with this arrangement he can put his old formula to the test. He returns in *The Bishop Murder Case* to the simpler process. As in *The Greene Murder Case* there is again a series of murders. But this time the solution is much less intricate, for Vance reasons from "the psychological aspects of the case " that the murders were committed by a man who would scoff at human values, but would play with infinity, e.g., the mathematician ; and his eye lights on Professor Dillard.

It must not be supposed that Vance's thoughts are all in the clouds of psychology. The application of psychology is the final master stroke, but the data and the classification of the various unrelated facts have to come first. It usually happens that the police experts, the doctors, the camera-men, the fingerprints and fire-arms specialists produce the several items of evidence. Markham and Heath, Vance's foils, fail to group these facts in the right order or to inter-relate them correctly. They attempt " to reduce human nature to a formula," a formula which makes room for circumstantial evidence. Quite often, however, Vance himself is not above trick exhibitions. One recalls the " bit of clever criminal mechanism "—the twine and the tweezers—employed to open the door from the " other " side in *The Canary Murder Case* ; and in *The Benson Murder Case* the substitution of the cartridges, detected owing to the peculiar brightness of one cartridge amongst its six tarnished fellows.

A word about the structure of the Van Dine plots. In *The Benson Murder Case* and *The Canary Murder Case* we note the following points :—

(1) The victim is a double-dyed villain, and a blackmailer to boot.

(2) There are, therefore, several people who would have a motive for the murder.

(3) The suspects are all mustered near the scene of the crime at the critical moment. These features are introduced so that Vance can play about with his ideas of the technique of the crime.

In *The Greene Murder Case* and *The Bishop Murder Case* the composition of the plot is widely different. Psychology is not at so highly valued a premium. In both stories there is a series of murders. In *The Greene Murder Case* a family is wiped out, and one

after the other the erstwhile suspects become victims.
It is worth mentioning that in many points *The Greene
Murder Case* bears a close similarity to the unsolved
Croydon Poisoning Case. The solution in *The Greene
Murder Case* is really reached by a process of elimination. Similarly in *The Bishop Murder Case*. Both
these novels are incidentally interesting studies in
criminology. The murders in the former are imitations
of historical murders described in the tomes of Tobias
Greene's lurid library. In *The Bishop Murder Case*, as
already mentioned, we have a study of a mathematician
whose sense of values has become distorted. Thus in
these two novels we have the abnormal murder, which
means a certain deficiency in motive. To make our
problem still harder, Van Dine peoples these stories
with neurotic chess champions, neurotic mathematicians
and neurotic young women (not to mention the rather
cranky old women capable of doing anything).

In *The Scarab Murder Case* (1930) Van Dine re-
introduced the subject of Egyptology into the detective
story. The killing is done in the darkness of the Bliss
Museum, and the murderer turns out to be, as we
rather expected, the antiquarian Bliss. There is
nothing startling in the plot ; it is a simple example
of " double bluff." Bliss, our first real suspect, tried
to give people the impression that he was the victim
of a plot, and built up a nice little case against himself.
As this was an American case, he was confident of
acquittal from lack of *real* evidence against him.
Van Dine is careful in his first attempt at a " double
bluff " plot to preserve his reputation for fairplay
with the reader. Thus he makes Vance claim :—

> " I did not say one word to give you the definite
> impression that I exonerated Bliss. Not once did I
> say he was innocent."

The cleverest thing in the book is the pre-arranged
death-trap. The idea of it is clever ; but cleverer still
is the way in which Van Dine uses it to play on the
foibles of the reader. This extract humbles a man,
especially the footnote.

> " ' When the experiment was made I realised how
> unlikely it was that he had actually been killed by the
> statue falling.' Vance's eyes twinkled. ' I did not
> raise the point at the time, for I wanted you to believe
> in the death trap. The truth is, Sergeant, I did every-
> thing I could to make you overlook this inconsistency
> of it. And Mr. Markham didn't see it either.'[1]
> " [1] Nor did I. But while this record of mine was
> running serially in the *American Magazine* several
> readers wrote to me pointing out the inconsistency."

Philo Vance is delightful company. He belongs to
no school, but has a certain affinity to Lord Peter
Wimsey. He is the aristocratic dilettante, a master of
refined badinage.

> " ' Vance was not yet thirty-five,' says Van Dine,
> ' and, in a cold, sculptural fashion was impressively
> good-looking. His face was slender and mobile ; but
> there was a stern, sardonic expression to his features,
> which acted as a barrier between him and his fellows.
> He was not emotionless, but his emotions were, in
> the main, intellectual. . . . He was an art collector
> in a small way, a fine amateur pianist, and a profound
> student of æsthetics and psychology. Although an
> American, he had largely been educated in Europe,
> and still retained a slight English accent and intona-
> tion. . . . His manner was cynical and aloof.' "

Philo's inconsequential remarks, his academic dissertations on æsthetics and psychology to the bored
Markham and the scornful Heath are delightfully
humorous. But the footnotes are the wittiest thing in

the Van Dine novels. Only in *The Greene Murder Case*
and *The Scarab Murder Case* might they be cut to
advantage. One is forced to admit that the diagrams
are superfluous.

The Mystery of the Roman Hat, by Ellery Queen (1929)
was " recommended " by our *Arbiter Elegantiarum,*
The Book Society. This work follows very closely the
Van Dine method. In fact, with a few alterations, it
might be taken as a Van Dine novel. There is a
foreword signed by J. J. McC. (for which initials
familiarity is apt to breed contempt) corresponding to
the first chapter in a Van Dine murder case. There is
a provoking but soon forgotten sketch plan. There are
one or two academic footnotes. A catalogue of
characters is also added to help the reader in this
" Problem in Deduction." Says E. Q. (not J. J. McC.
this time) :—

> " It is intended to simplify rather than mystify.
> In the course of perusing mysterio-detective literature
> the reader is, like as not, apt to lose sight of a number
> of seemingly unimportant characters who eventually
> prove of primary significance in the solution of the
> crime. The writer, therefore, urges a frequent study
> of this chart during the reader's pilgrimage through
> the tale, if toward no other end than to ward off the
> inevitable cry of ' unfair '—the consolation of those
> who read and do not reason."

Withal *The Mystery of the Roman Hat* is a first-class
detective story. Monte Field is murdered in the
Roman Theatre during the performance of a crook
play. The doors are closed and an exhaustive search
is made amongst the audience. As the title indicates,
the really significant question turns out to be the
disappearance of Monte's opera hat ; and with the
progress of the action the missing head-piece grows in

significance. It transpires also that quite a few people wanted the decease of Monte, for he was a blackmailer of a most disagreeable kind. This multiplication of the suspects and their motives again reminds one of the Van Dine problem. But here the similarity ends. Old Richard Queen and Ellery Queen—a new partnership in the annals of detection this of father and son—rely more on the accepted methods of the old detection. In spite of their proneness to long-winded dissertation their deduction is sound, business-like and delightfully realistic. As the paragraph already quoted indicates, the author is desperately anxious to play fair with the reader. In the main he nobly lives up to his intentions. Perhaps he protests just a little too much. Towards the end of the book an " Interlude " is enterpolated in the form of a direct challenge to the reader to answer the question, " Who killed Monte Field ? "

> " Mr. Queen agrees with me that the alert student of mystery tales, now being in possession of all the pertinent facts, should at this stage of the story have reached definite conclusions on the questions propounded. The solution—or enough of it to point unerringly to the guilty character—may be reached by a series of logical deductions and psychological observations."

The average reader does not like so pointed a challenge, and it puts him on his mettle. Otherwise he might have passed over one slight infringement of the fairplay rules. On page 207 Ellery is gleaning information from Mrs. Phillips, one of the stage hands :

> " The white-haired lady smiled and Ellery, taking her arm, led her off in the direction of the stage."

But it is only *after* the interpolation of the Interlude

that the reader knows what happened backstage. On page 298 he reads :—

> " When Ellery had reached this point in his reasoning he took Mrs. Phillips backstage and checked up on every hat in the actors' rooms and the wardrobe room. Every top-hat there—and all were accounted for, none being missing—was a property top-hat bearing on its lining the Le Brun insignia. Field's hat, which we had proved to be a Browne Bros. topper, was not among the property top-hats or anywhere backstage."

We mention this detail because it does after all seem " pertinent," and because being human we were a trifle suspicious about that challenge.

The French Powder Mystery (1930) by the same author is a competent murder story with a drug-traffic interest. The scene of the murder is effectively laid in a New York department store, and the villain turns out just once more to be the most unlikely person— the "house" detective of the store. Although the secret is exceedingly well kept till the end, *The French Powder Mystery* is not so good as *The Mystery of the Roman Hat.* In the latter Ellery Queen gets his second wind by discovering how the blackmailing documents were hidden away in a number of hats. In *The French Powder Mystery* the investigation is given a fillip by the discovery of a similar dodge. This time the dope merchants have been using the books in a library as a means of communicating to their clients where and when the stuff was to be had. It is worth bearing in mind that, however spectacular the discovery may seem, it is a comparatively easy task to work up a trick of this description and score full points for one's detective. The reader is again challenged to work out the solution for himself, and this time he has a fairer chance of success. For the rest the pseudo-classical

American vocabulary is almost as irritating to the
English reader as the more familiar slang. And the
idea of heading the chapters with excerpts from
nursery rhymes had already been used with considerable
effect by Van Dine in *The Bishop Murder Case*. However, Ellery Queen is always able to hold our attention,
the construction and the realism being admirable.

4

It is not unlikely that *The Famous Trial Series*
suggested to Miss Frances Noyes Hart the idea of
presenting the detective story in the form of a report
of a murder trial. There had been scores of trial scenes
within the detective story, but the whole action of the
detective story had not, previous to *The Bellamy Trial*,
consisted in the drama carried on within the four
walls of the court. It is really rather extraordinary
that no one had thought of this idea before, considering
that in real life the report of the trial is usually the
sole part of the story with which the public is familiar.
Thus a new kind of realism was acquired, and its
attractions were proved by the success on stage and
screen of *The Trial of Mary Dugan*, and *On Trial*, not
to mention *The Bellamy Trial* itself in talkie form.
In so confined a setting the detective story must
unavoidably malinger. The problem is made easier
since the accused is, or are, eliminated from the list
of suspects. It would be criminal to convict any one
who had stood in the dock for over 200 pages. The
excitement of the actual detection has vanished, and
in its place the reader is asked to attend to the lawyers'
logomachy and to sift the evidence as best he can.
If emotional and dramatic values are taken into

account the trial story might be highly rated. No doubt the English lawyer will smile and tell you that only the American Judicial System (and possibly the French, since the Branson murder trial) could have been responsible for this development.

The Bellamy Trial is excellently done. The secret is kept till the end, even if Miss Noyes Hart provides us with the solution to the problem after the trial had ended, and thus violates the precious unity of place. A detail this, but it did seem an unnecessary violation of the unity of place to whisk us off at the very end to Judge Carter's library. There is little detection in *The Bellamy Trial*, and the finger-print expert had short shrift. Again the erring schoolmaster was rather obvious a *deus ex machina*. But the court speeches and the manner in which the story is unfolded in the evidence are both admirable. Thanks are also due to Miss Noyes Hart for the genteel sentimentality contained in the modern version of a Christopher Sly induction.

Hide in the Dark (1929) by the same writer contains a clever idea marred by imperfect execution. There could not be a better setting to a murder than here. A reunion party ; the lights out ; and the position of all the characters known only to themselves. Unfortunately there was a deal of uncalled-for confession, the reconstruction of the crime being too much for some of them.

We could well do with a high tariff wall to impede the importation of two kinds of American detective stories—those based (1) on the nauseating vicissitudes of gang warfare, and (2) on the corruption of the police and legal systems. Of these subjects the British public is growing a-weary. But the realistic school is worth our attention. It is making a fair bid for survival.

CHAPTER XII

CONCLUSION

In one sense there is no future for the detective story. I mean that it is in no process of natural growth ; its development has already been perfected. Its success may be attributed to the attraction adventure always possesses, plus an adherence within certain limits to a set of rules. A violation of these rules may cause either of two results. " Commercialism " is doing its best to bring the detective novel down to the level of the blood-and-thunder adventure novel, and this alloy, as it were, will be the result solely of such disregard. Or the element of adventure and excitement may be thrown overboard and we may have an allegorical detective story after the manner of *The Man Who was Thursday*, and the merging of the detective story into a more intellectual genre. In either case the detective story perishes. Conventionality is an essential canon of our Muse. I use this in no depreciatory way. All art is placed under such restraint. Attempts to throw off the halter may rouse a passing interest, but they prove futile in the end. Exploitation works in a vicious circle, and harks back to convention like the biblical sow. No, the rules must remain.

Father Ronald Knox is pessimistic enough to believe that the days of the detective story are numbered— " before long, it is feared, all the possible combinations will have been used up. Stories become cleverer and cleverer, but readers are becoming cleverer and cleverer too ; it is almost impossible to think out any system of bluff which the seasoned reader will not see through."

The survival of the detective story, so far as the immediate future is concerned, will depend on the ability of our entertainers to produce really original ideas ; to stage their murders, as it were, on virgin soil ; to discover novel " tools of death." It will depend also on their ability to discover new methods of detection, new kinds of detectives, and new angles from which to tell their stories.

Publishers could a tale unfold about the present competition amongst writers of detective stories to be first in the field with new ideas. The most extraordinary fact is the tendency for these new ideas to happen in cycles, for a number of writers to hit on the same bright thought simultaneously. In the first half of 1930 at least three authors perpetrated their murders on a bus. In the latter half of the year at the very least three authors have chosen an ecclesiastical setting. In the present year I am informed there is to be a season of witchcraft and the Black Mass. Even in the choice of titles—an important selling point in the detective story —the same coincidences persist. There is no guarding against it. Coincidence affects equally the recognised master and the latest recruit. But keen competition in the literary, as well as the commercial, world is a healthy stimulant to the harassed producer.

Sir Arthur Conan Doyle had another reason for prophesying the death of the detective story. " We shall," he said, " have a clairvoyant in attendance at every police station, and every offence will be hunted down, so that crime will become very difficult, if not impossible." In reply to this a leader in the *Manchester Guardian* was amusingly reassuring :—

" If clairvoyants are to be attached to police stations
they can hardly help but become officials ; probably
they will have to be enrolled in the ordinary way,
and be sure to put a belt and tunic on before they fall
into a trance. In that case one can see very little
real future for their investigations—at least so far as
novels and magazines are concerned. If they are
official they are bound to be ineffective ; that is
almost the first principle of fiction of this character.
So there is, after all, hope for our older friends. Their
shrewder researches will continue to triumph—but
over accredited crystal-gazers and uniformed clairvoyants instead of the former sergeants and super-
intendents."

The psychologist may argue that the pulsometer
and the psychometric machine will prove the most
effective deterrent from crime (supposing, that is, that
the party to be experimented upon has been found).
Thus in this millennium crime itself will be an impossibility. From which we conclude that the detective
story will be shelved, and be treated by future generations as an interesting historical romance. Even if we
have this optimistic view on the future of the human
race, we must confess it will take some time. Possibly
by that time Literature herself may have perished.
It is, besides, questionable in the extreme, whether
psychological experiments can ever be conclusive even
in theory. Father Brown's scepticism has a satisfying
flavour :—

" ' What sentimentalists men of science are,'
exclaimed Father Brown, ' and how much more
sentimental must American men of science be. Who
but a Yankee would think of proving anything from
heart throbs ? . . . There's a test from the circulation
of the blood, discovered by the immortal Harvey ;
and a jolly rotten test too.

" ' You always forget that the reliable machine
always has to be worked by an unreliable machine-
man.' "

The realistic detective story marches with scientific
development, and the details in the various methods
of detection will change in accordance with scientific
invention. It is hardly necessary to remind you that
in his younger days Sherlock Holmes did not envisage
the development of aeronautics and dismissed as an
impossibility a death inflicted by a flying body. Again
there is no reason why the domestic detective story
or the story of intuitional detection should ever turn
the corner. Satire and the comedy of manners still
retain their juvenility. Thus in a sense, too, the
orthodox detective story may suffer a sea change,
and be transformed into something strange to our
present notions; but to future generations it will
be orthodox.

Thus there is no room for tears. Competition,
the striving for novelty, and these other factors will
accelerate the development of the detective story.
Already our writers have been put on their mettle.
It is most unlikely that human ingenuity will not
respond to the challenge.

INDEX OF DETECTIVE STORIES

(Including Detective Dramas, Films, etc.)

INDEX OF AUTHORS

INDEX OF DETECTIVES

287

A CATALOGUE OF SELECTED DOVER BOOKS
IN ALL FIELDS OF INTEREST

A CATALOGUE OF SELECTED DOVER BOOKS
IN ALL FIELDS OF INTEREST

THE DEVIL'S DICTIONARY, Ambrose Bierce. Barbed, bitter, brilliant witticisms in the form of a dictionary. Best, most ferocious satire America has produced. 145pp. 20487-1 Pa. $1.75

ABSOLUTELY MAD INVENTIONS, A.E. Brown, H.A. Jeffcott. Hilarious, useless, or merely absurd inventions all granted patents by the U.S. Patent Office. Edible tie pin, mechanical hat tipper, etc. 57 illustrations. 125pp. 22596-8 Pa. $1.50

AMERICAN WILD FLOWERS COLORING BOOK, Paul Kennedy. Planned coverage of 48 most important wildflowers, from Rickett's collection; instructive as well as entertaining. Color versions on covers. 48pp. 8¼ x 11. 20095-7 Pa. $1.50

BIRDS OF AMERICA COLORING BOOK, John James Audubon. Rendered for coloring by Paul Kennedy. 46 of Audubon's noted illustrations: red-winged blackbird, cardinal, purple finch, towhee, etc. Original plates reproduced in full color on the covers. 48pp. 8¼ x 11. 23049-X Pa. $1.50

NORTH AMERICAN INDIAN DESIGN COLORING BOOK, Paul Kennedy. The finest examples from Indian masks, beadwork, pottery, etc. — selected and redrawn for coloring (with identifications) by well-known illustrator Paul Kennedy. 48pp. 8¼ x 11. 21125-8 Pa. $1.50

UNIFORMS OF THE AMERICAN REVOLUTION COLORING BOOK, Peter Copeland. 31 lively drawings reproduce whole panorama of military attire; each uniform has complete instructions for accurate coloring. (Not in the Pictorial Archives Series). 64pp. 8¼ x 11. 21850-3 Pa. $1.50

THE WONDERFUL WIZARD OF OZ COLORING BOOK, L. Frank Baum. Color the Yellow Brick Road and much more in 61 drawings adapted from W.W. Denslow's originals, accompanied by abridged version of text. Dorothy, Toto, Oz and the Emerald City. 61 illustrations. 64pp. 8¼ x 11. 20452-9 Pa. $1.50

CUT AND COLOR PAPER MASKS, Michael Grater. Clowns, animals, funny faces ... simply color them in, cut them out, and put them together, and you have 9 paper masks to play with and enjoy. Complete instructions. Assembled masks shown in full color on the covers. 32pp. 8¼ x 11. 23171-2 Pa. $1.50

STAINED GLASS CHRISTMAS ORNAMENT COLORING BOOK, Carol Belanger Grafton. Brighten your Christmas season with over 100 Christmas ornaments done in a stained glass effect on translucent paper. Color them in and then hang at windows, from lights, anywhere. 32pp. 8¼ x 11. 20707-2 Pa. $1.75

CREATIVE LITHOGRAPHY AND HOW TO DO IT, Grant Arnold. Lithography as art form: working directly on stone, transfer of drawings, lithotint, mezzotint, color printing; also metal plates. Detailed, thorough. 27 illustrations. 214pp.
21208-4 Pa. $3.00

DESIGN MOTIFS OF ANCIENT MEXICO, Jorge Enciso. Vigorous, powerful ceramic stamp impressions — Maya, Aztec, Toltec, Olmec. Serpents, gods, priests, dancers, etc. 153pp. 6⅛ x 9¼.
20084-1 Pa. $2.50

AMERICAN INDIAN DESIGN AND DECORATION, Leroy Appleton. Full text, plus more than 700 precise drawings of Inca, Maya, Aztec, Pueblo, Plains, NW Coast basketry, sculpture, painting, pottery, sand paintings, metal, etc. 4 plates in color. 279pp. 8⅜ x 11¼.
22704-9 Pa. $4.50

CHINESE LATTICE DESIGNS, Daniel S. Dye. Incredibly beautiful geometric designs: circles, voluted, simple dissections, etc. Inexhaustible source of ideas, motifs. 1239 illustrations. 469pp. 6⅛ x 9¼.
23096-1 Pa. $5.00

JAPANESE DESIGN MOTIFS, Matsuya Co. Mon, or heraldic designs. Over 4000 typical, beautiful designs: birds, animals, flowers, swords, fans, geometric; all beautifully stylized. 213pp. 11⅜ x 8¼.
22874-6 Pa. $5.00

PERSPECTIVE, Jan Vredeman de Vries. 73 perspective plates from 1604 edition; buildings, townscapes, stairways, fantastic scenes. Remarkable for beauty, surrealistic atmosphere; real eye-catchers. Introduction by Adolf Placzek. 74pp. 11⅜ x 8¼.
20186-4 Pa. $2.75

EARLY AMERICAN DESIGN MOTIFS, Suzanne E. Chapman. 497 motifs, designs, from painting on wood, ceramics, appliqué, glassware, samplers, metal work, etc. Florals, landscapes, birds and animals, geometrics, letters, etc. Inexhaustible. Enlarged edition. 138pp. 8⅜ x 11¼.
22985-8 Pa. $3.50
23084-8 Clothbd. $7.95

VICTORIAN STENCILS FOR DESIGN AND DECORATION, edited by E.V. Gillon, Jr. 113 wonderful ornate Victorian pieces from German sources; florals, geometrics; borders, corner pieces; bird motifs, etc. 64pp. 9⅜ x 12¼.
21995-X Pa. $2.75

ART NOUVEAU: AN ANTHOLOGY OF DESIGN AND ILLUSTRATION FROM THE STUDIO, edited by E.V. Gillon, Jr. Graphic arts: book jackets, posters, engravings, illustrations, decorations; Crane, Beardsley, Bradley and many others. Inexhaustible. 92pp. 8⅛ x 11.
22388-4 Pa. $2.50

ORIGINAL ART DECO DESIGNS, William Rowe. First-rate, highly imaginative modern Art Deco frames, borders, compositions, alphabets, florals, insectals, Wurlitzer-types, etc. Much finest modern Art Deco. 80 plates, 8 in color. 8⅜ x 11¼.
22567-4 Pa. $3.50

HANDBOOK OF DESIGNS AND DEVICES, Clarence P. Hornung. Over 1800 basic geometric designs based on circle, triangle, square, scroll, cross, etc. Largest such collection in existence. 261pp.
20125-2 Pa. $2.75

VICTORIAN HOUSES: A TREASURY OF LESSER-KNOWN EXAMPLES, Edmund Gillon and Clay Lancaster. 116 photographs, excellent commentary illustrate distinct characteristics, many borrowings of local Victorian architecture. Octagonal houses, Americanized chalets, grand country estates, small cottages, etc. Rich heritage often overlooked. 116 plates. 11⅜ x 10. 22966-1 Pa. $4.00

STICKS AND STONES, Lewis Mumford. Great classic of American cultural history; architecture from medieval-inspired earliest forms to 20th century; evolution of structure and style, influence of environment. 21 illustrations. 113pp.
20202-X Pa. $2.50

ON THE LAWS OF JAPANESE PAINTING, Henry P. Bowie. Best substitute for training with genius Oriental master, based on years of study in Kano school. Philosophy, brushes, inks, style, etc. 66 illustrations. 117pp. 6⅛ x 9¼. 20030-2 Pa. $4.50

A HANDBOOK OF ANATOMY FOR ART STUDENTS, Arthur Thomson. Virtually exhaustive. Skeletal structure, muscles, heads, special features. Full text, anatomical figures, undraped photos. Male and female. 337 illustrations. 459pp.
21163-0 Pa. $5.00

AN ATLAS OF ANATOMY FOR ARTISTS, Fritz Schider. Finest text, working book. Full text, plus anatomical illustrations; plates by great artists showing anatomy. 593 illustrations. 192pp. 7⅞ x 10¾. 20241-0 Clothbd. $6.95

THE HUMAN FIGURE IN MOTION, Eadweard Muybridge. More than 4500 stopped-action photos, in action series, showing undraped men, women, children jumping, lying down, throwing, sitting, wrestling, carrying, etc. "Unparalleled dictionary for artists," American Artist. Taken by great 19th century photographer. 390pp. 7⅞ x 10⅝. 20204-6 Clothbd. $12.50

AN ATLAS OF ANIMAL ANATOMY FOR ARTISTS, W. Ellenberger et al. Horses, dogs, cats, lions, cattle, deer, etc. Muscles, skeleton, surface features. The basic work. Enlarged edition. 288 illustrations. 151pp. 9⅜ x 12¼. 20082-5 Pa. $4.50

LETTER FORMS: 110 COMPLETE ALPHABETS, Frederick Lambert. 110 sets of capital letters; 16 lower case alphabets; 70 sets of numbers and other symbols. Edited and expanded by Theodore Menten. 110pp. 8⅛ x 11. 22872-X Pa. $3.00

THE METHODS OF CONSTRUCTION OF CELTIC ART, George Bain. Simple geometric techniques for making wonderful Celtic interlacements, spirals, Kells-type initials, animals, humans, etc. Unique for artists, craftsmen. Over 500 illustrations. 160pp. 9 x 12. USO 22923-8 Pa. $4.00

SCULPTURE, PRINCIPLES AND PRACTICE, Louis Slobodkin. Step by step approach to clay, plaster, metals, stone; classical and modern. 253 drawings, photos. 255pp. 8⅛ x 11. 22960-2 Pa. $5.00

THE ART OF ETCHING, E.S. Lumsden. Clear, detailed instructions for etching, drypoint, softground, aquatint; from 1st sketch to print. Very detailed, thorough. 200 illustrations. 376pp. 20049-3 Pa. $3.75

CONSTRUCTION OF AMERICAN FURNITURE TREASURES, Lester Margon. 344 detail drawings, complete text on constructing exact reproductions of 38 early American masterpieces: Hepplewhite sideboard, Duncan Phyfe drop-leaf table, mantel clock, gate-leg dining table, Pa. German cupboard, more. 38 plates. 54 photographs. 168pp. 8⅜ x 11¼. 23056-2 Pa. $4.00

JEWELRY MAKING AND DESIGN, Augustus F. Rose, Antonio Cirino. Professional secrets revealed in thorough, practical guide: tools, materials, processes; rings, brooches, chains, cast pieces, enamelling, setting stones, etc. Do not confuse with skimpy introductions: beginner can use, professional can learn from it. Over 200 illustrations. 306pp. 21750-7 Pa. $3.00

METALWORK AND ENAMELLING, Herbert Maryon. Generally coneeded best all-around book. Countless trade secrets: materials, tools, soldering, filigree, setting, inlay, niello, repoussé, casting, polishing, etc. For beginner or expert. Author was foremost British expert. 330 illustrations. 335pp. 22702-2 Pa. $3.50

WEAVING WITH FOOT-POWER LOOMS, Edward F. Worst. Setting up a loom, beginning to weave, constructing equipment, using dyes, more, plus over 285 drafts of traditional patterns including Colonial and Swedish weaves. More than 200 other figures. For beginning and advanced. 275pp. 8¾ x 6⅜. 23064-3 Pa. $4.50

WEAVING A NAVAJO BLANKET, Gladys A. Reichard. Foremost anthropologist studied under Navajo women, reveals every step in process from wool, dyeing, spinning, setting up loom, designing, weaving. Much history, symbolism. With this book you could make one yourself. 97 illustrations. 222pp. 22992-0 Pa. $3.00

NATURAL DYES AND HOME DYEING, Rita J. Adrosko. Use natural ingredients: bark, flowers, leaves, lichens, insects etc. Over 135 specific recipes from historical sources for cotton, wool, other fabrics. Genuine premodern handicrafts. 12 illustrations. 160pp. 22688-3 Pa. $2.00

THE HAND DECORATION OF FABRICS, Francis J. Kafka. Outstanding, profusely illustrated guide to stenciling, batik, block printing, tie dyeing, freehand painting, silk screen printing, and novelty decoration. 356 illustrations. 198pp. 6 x 9. 21401-X Pa. $3.00

THOMAS NAST: CARTOONS AND ILLUSTRATIONS, with text by Thomas Nast St. Hill. Father of American political cartooning. Cartoons that destroyed Tweed Ring; inflation, free love, church and state; original Republican elephant and Democratic donkey; Santa Claus; more. 117 illustrations. 146pp. 9 x 12.
22983-1 Pa. $4.00
23067-8 Clothbd. $8.50

FREDERIC REMINGTON: 173 DRAWINGS AND ILLUSTRATIONS. Most famous of the Western artists, most responsible for our myths about the American West in its untamed days. Complete reprinting of *Drawings of Frederic Remington* (1897), plus other selections. 4 additional drawings in color on covers. 140pp. 9 x 12.
20714-5 Pa. $3.95

EARLY NEW ENGLAND GRAVESTONE RUBBINGS, Edmund V. Gillon, Jr. 43 photographs, 226 rubbings show heavily symbolic, macabre, sometimes humorous primitive American art. Up to early 19th century. 207pp. 8⅜ x 11¼.
21380-3 Pa. $4.00

L.J.M. DAGUERRE: THE HISTORY OF THE DIORAMA AND THE DAGUERREOTYPE, Helmut and Alison Gernsheim. Definitive account. Early history, life and work of Daguerre; discovery of daguerreotype process; diffusion abroad; other early photography. 124 illustrations. 226pp. 6⅙ x 9¼. 22290-X Pa. $4.00

PHOTOGRAPHY AND THE AMERICAN SCENE, Robert Taft. The basic book on American photography as art, recording form, 1839-1889. Development, influence on society, great photographers, types (portraits, war, frontier, etc.), whatever else needed. Inexhaustible. Illustrated with 322 early photos, daguerreotypes, tintypes, stereo slides, etc. 546pp. 6⅛ x 9¼. 21201-7 Pa. $5.95

PHOTOGRAPHIC SKETCHBOOK OF THE CIVIL WAR, Alexander Gardner. Reproduction of 1866 volume with 100 on-the-field photographs: Manassas, Lincoln on battlefield, slave pens, etc. Introduction by E.F. Bleiler. 224pp. 10¾ x 9.
22731-6 Pa. $5.00

THE MOVIES: A PICTURE QUIZ BOOK, Stanley Appelbaum & Hayward Cirker. Match stars with their movies, name actors and actresses, test your movie skill with 241 stills from 236 great movies, 1902-1959. Indexes of performers and films. 128pp. 8⅜ x 9¼. 20222-4 Pa. $2.50

THE TALKIES, Richard Griffith. Anthology of features, articles from Photoplay, 1928-1940, reproduced complete. Stars, famous movies, technical features, fabulous ads, etc.; Garbo, Chaplin, King Kong, Lubitsch, etc. 4 color plates, scores of illustrations. 327pp. 8⅜ x 11¼. 22762-6 Pa. $6.95

THE MOVIE MUSICAL FROM VITAPHONE TO "42ND STREET," edited by Miles Kreuger. Relive the rise of the movie musical as reported in the pages of Photoplay magazine (1926-1933): every movie review, cast list, ad, and record review; every significant feature article, production still, biography, forecast, and gossip story. Profusely illustrated. 367pp. 8⅜ x 11¼. 23154-2 Pa. $7.95

JOHANN SEBASTIAN BACH, Philipp Spitta. Great classic of biography, musical commentary, with hundreds of pieces analyzed. Also good for Bach's contemporaries. 450 musical examples. Total of 1799pp.
EUK 22278-0, 22279-9 Clothbd., Two vol. set $25.00

BEETHOVEN AND HIS NINE SYMPHONIES, Sir George Grove. Thorough history, analysis, commentary on symphonies and some related pieces. For either beginner or advanced student. 436 musical passages. 407pp. 20334-4 Pa. $4.00

MOZART AND HIS PIANO CONCERTOS, Cuthbert Girdlestone. The only full-length study. Detailed analyses of all 21 concertos, sources; 417 musical examples. 509pp. 21271-8 Pa. $6.00

THE FITZWILLIAM VIRGINAL BOOK, edited by J. Fuller Maitland, W.B. Squire. Famous early 17th century collection of keyboard music, 300 works by Morley, Byrd, Bull, Gibbons, etc. Modern notation. Total of 938pp. 8⅜ x 11.
ECE 21068-5, 21069-3 Pa., Two vol. set $15.00

COMPLETE STRING QUARTETS, Wolfgang A. Mozart. Breitkopf and Härtel edition. All 23 string quartets plus alternate slow movement to K156. Study score. 277pp. 9⅜ x 12¼.
22372-8 Pa. $6.00

COMPLETE SONG CYCLES, Franz Schubert. Complete piano, vocal music of Die Schöne Müllerin, Die Winterreise, Schwanengesang. Also Drinker English singing translations. Breitkopf and Härtel edition. 217pp. 9⅜ x 12¼.
22649-2 Pa. $4.50

THE COMPLETE PRELUDES AND ETUDES FOR PIANOFORTE SOLO, Alexander Scriabin. All the preludes and etudes including many perfectly spun miniatures. Edited by K.N. Igumnov and Y.I. Mil'shteyn. 250pp. 9 x 12.
22919-X Pa. $5.00

TRISTAN UND ISOLDE, Richard Wagner. Full orchestral score with complete instrumentation. Do not confuse with piano reduction. Commentary by Felix Mottl, great Wagnerian conductor and scholar. Study score. 655pp. 8⅛ x 11.
22915-7 Pa. $11.95

FAVORITE SONGS OF THE NINETIES, ed. Robert Fremont. Full reproduction, including covers, of 88 favorites: Ta-Ra-Ra-Boom-De-Aye, The Band Played On, Bird in a Gilded Cage, Under the Bamboo Tree, After the Ball, etc. 401pp. 9 x 12.
EBE 21536-9 Pa. $6.95

SOUSA'S GREAT MARCHES IN PIANO TRANSCRIPTION: ORIGINAL SHEET MUSIC OF 23 WORKS, John Philip Sousa. Selected by Lester S. Levy. Playing edition includes: The Stars and Stripes Forever, The Thunderer, The Gladiator, King Cotton, Washington Post, much more. 24 illustrations. 111pp. 9 x 12.
USO 23132-1 Pa. $3.50

CLASSIC PIANO RAGS, selected with an introduction by Rudi Blesh. Best ragtime music (1897-1922) by Scott Joplin, James Scott, Joseph F. Lamb, Tom Turpin, 9 others. Printed from best original sheet music, plus covers. 364pp. 9 x 12.
EBE 20469-3 Pa. $6.95

ANALYSIS OF CHINESE CHARACTERS, C.D. Wilder, J.H. Ingram. 1000 most important characters analyzed according to primitives, phonetics, historical development. Traditional method offers mnemonic aid to beginner, intermediate student of Chinese, Japanese. 365pp.
23045-7 Pa. $4.00

MODERN CHINESE: A BASIC COURSE, Faculty of Peking University. Self study, classroom course in modern Mandarin. Records contain phonetics, vocabulary, sentences, lessons. 249 page book contains all recorded text, translations, grammar, vocabulary, exercises. Best course on market. 3 12" 33⅓ monaural records, book, album.
98832-5 Set $12.50

THE BEST DR. THORNDYKE DETECTIVE STORIES, R. Austin Freeman. The Case of Oscar Brodski, The Moabite Cipher, and 5 other favorites featuring the great scientific detective, plus his long-believed-lost first adventure — 31 New Inn — reprinted here for the first time. Edited by E.F. Bleiler. USO 20388-3 Pa. $3.00

BEST "THINKING MACHINE" DETECTIVE STORIES, Jacques Futrelle. The Problem of Cell 13 and 11 other stories about Prof. Augustus S.F.X. Van Dusen, including two "lost" stories. First reprinting of several. Edited by E.F. Bleiler. 241pp. 20537-1 Pa. $3.00

UNCLE SILAS, J. Sheridan LeFanu. Victorian Gothic mystery novel, considered by many best of period, even better than Collins or Dickens. Wonderful psychological terror. Introduction by Frederick Shroyer. 436pp. 21715-9 Pa. $4.00

BEST DR. POGGIOLI DETECTIVE STORIES, T.S. Stribling. 15 best stories from EQMM and The Saint offer new adventures in Mexico, Florida, Tennessee hills as Poggioli unravels mysteries and combats Count Jalacki. 217pp. 23227-1 Pa. $3.00

EIGHT DIME NOVELS, selected with an introduction by E.F. Bleiler. Adventures of Old King Brady, Frank James, Nick Carter, Deadwood Dick, Buffalo Bill, The Steam Man, Frank Merriwell, and Horatio Alger — 1877 to 1905. Important, entertaining popular literature in facsimile reprint, with original covers. 190pp. 9 x 12. 22975-0 Pa. $3.50

ALICE'S ADVENTURES UNDER GROUND, Lewis Carroll. Facsimile of ms. Carroll gave Alice Liddell in 1864. Different in many ways from final Alice. Handlettered, illustrated by Carroll. Introduction by Martin Gardner. 128pp. 21482-6 Pa. $1.50

ALICE IN WONDERLAND COLORING BOOK, Lewis Carroll. Pictures by John Tenniel. Large-size versions of the famous illustrations of Alice, Cheshire Cat, Mad Hatter and all the others, waiting for your crayons. Abridged text. 36 illustrations. 64pp. 8¼ x 11. 22853-3 Pa. $1.50

AVENTURES D'ALICE AU PAYS DES MERVEILLES, Lewis Carroll. Bué's translation of "Alice" into French, supervised by Carroll himself. Novel way to learn language. (No English text.) 42 Tenniel illustrations. 196pp. 22836-3 Pa. $2.50

MYTHS AND FOLK TALES OF IRELAND, Jeremiah Curtin. 11 stories that are Irish versions of European fairy tales and 9 stories from the Fenian cycle — 20 tales of legend and magic that comprise an essential work in the history of folklore. 256pp. 22430-9 Pa. $3.00

EAST O' THE SUN AND WEST O' THE MOON, George W. Dasent. Only full edition of favorite, wonderful Norwegian fairytales — Why the Sea is Salt, Boots and the Troll, etc. — with 77 illustrations by Kittelsen & Werenskiöld. 418pp. 22521-6 Pa. $4.00

PERRAULT'S FAIRY TALES, Charles Perrault and Gustave Doré. Original versions of Cinderella, Sleeping Beauty, Little Red Riding Hood, etc. in best translation, with 34 wonderful illustrations by Gustave Doré. 117pp. 8⅛ x 11. 22311-6 Pa. $2.50

MOTHER GOOSE'S MELODIES. Facsimile of fabulously rare Munroe and Francis "copyright 1833" Boston edition. Familiar and unusual rhymes, wonderful old woodcut illustrations. Edited by E.F. Bleiler. 128pp. 4½ x 6⅜. 22577-1 Pa. $1.50

MOTHER GOOSE IN HIEROGLYPHICS. Favorite nursery rhymes presented in rebus form for children. Fascinating 1849 edition reproduced in toto, with key. Introduction by E.F. Bleiler. About 400 woodcuts. 64pp. 6⅞ x 5¼. 20745-5 Pa. $1.00

PETER PIPER'S PRACTICAL PRINCIPLES OF PLAIN & PERFECT PRONUNCIATION. Alliterative jingles and tongue-twisters. Reproduction in full of 1830 first American edition. 25 spirited woodcuts. 32pp. 4½ x 6⅜. 22560-7 Pa. $1.00

MARMADUKE MULTIPLY'S MERRY METHOD OF MAKING MINOR MATHEMATICIANS. Fellow to Peter Piper, it teaches multiplication table by catchy rhymes and woodcuts. 1841 Munroe & Francis edition. Edited by E.F. Bleiler. 103pp. 4⅝ x 6.
22773-1 Pa. $1.25
20171-6 Clothbd. $3.00

THE NIGHT BEFORE CHRISTMAS, Clement Moore. Full text, and woodcuts from original 1848 book. Also critical, historical material. 19 illustrations. 40pp. 4⅝ x 6. 22797-9 Pa. $1.25

THE KING OF THE GOLDEN RIVER, John Ruskin. Victorian children's classic of three brothers, their attempts to reach the Golden River, what becomes of them. Facsimile of original 1889 edition. 22 illustrations. 56pp. 4⅝ x 6⅜.
20066-3 Pa. $1.50

DREAMS OF THE RAREBIT FIEND, Winsor McCay. Pioneer cartoon strip, unexcelled for beauty, imagination, in 60 full sequences. Incredible technical virtuosity, wonderful visual wit. Historical introduction. 62pp. 8⅜ x 11¼. 21347-1 Pa. $2.50

THE KATZENJAMMER KIDS, Rudolf Dirks. In full color, 14 strips from 1906-7; full of imagination, characteristic humor. Classic of great historical importance. Introduction by August Derleth. 32pp. 9¼ x 12¼. 23005-8 Pa. $2.00

LITTLE ORPHAN ANNIE AND LITTLE ORPHAN ANNIE IN COSMIC CITY, Harold Gray. Two great sequences from the early strips: our curly-haired heroine defends the Warbucks' financial empire and, then, takes on meanie Phineas P. Pinchpenny. Leapin' lizards! 178pp. 6⅛ x 8⅜. 23107-0 Pa. $2.00

THE BEST OF GLUYAS WILLIAMS. 100 drawings by one of America's finest cartoonists: The Day a Cake of Ivory Soap Sank at Proctor & Gamble's, At the Life Insurance Agents' Banquet, and many other gems from the 20's and 30's. 118pp. 8⅜ x 11¼. 22737-5 Pa. $2.50

THE MAGIC MOVING PICTURE BOOK, Bliss, Sands & Co. The pictures in this book move! Volcanoes erupt, a house burns, a serpentine dancer wiggles her way through a number. By using a specially ruled acetate screen provided, you can obtain these and 15 other startling effects. Originally "The Motograph Moving Picture Book." 32pp. 8¼ x 11. 23224-7 Pa. $1.75

STRING FIGURES AND HOW TO MAKE THEM, Caroline F. Jayne. Fullest, clearest instructions on string figures from around world: Eskimo, Navajo, Lapp, Europe, more. Cats cradle, moving spear, lightning, stars. Introduction by A.C. Haddon. 950 illustrations. 407pp. 20152-X Pa. $3.50

PAPER FOLDING FOR BEGINNERS, William D. Murray and Francis J. Rigney. Clearest book on market for making origami sail boats, roosters, frogs that move legs, cups, bonbon boxes. 40 projects. More than 275 illustrations. Photographs. 94pp. 20713-7 Pa. $1.25

INDIAN SIGN LANGUAGE, William Tomkins. Over 525 signs developed by Sioux, Blackfoot, Cheyenne, Arapahoe and other tribes. Written instructions and diagrams: how to make words, construct sentences. Also 290 pictographs of Sioux and Ojibway tribes. 111pp. 6⅛ x 9¼. 22029-X Pa. $1.50

BOOMERANGS: HOW TO MAKE AND THROW THEM, Bernard S. Mason. Easy to make and throw, dozens of designs: cross-stick, pinwheel, boomabird, tumblestick, Australian curved stick boomerang. Complete throwing instructions. All safe. 99pp. 23028-7 Pa. $1.75

25 KITES THAT FLY, Leslie Hunt. Full, easy to follow instructions for kites made from inexpensive materials. Many novelties. Reeling, raising, designing your own. 70 illustrations. 110pp. 22550-X Pa. $1.25

TRICKS AND GAMES ON THE POOL TABLE, Fred Herrmann. 79 tricks and games, some solitaires, some for 2 or more players, some competitive; mystifying shots and throws, unusual carom, tricks involving cork, coins, a hat, more. 77 figures. 95pp. 21814-7 Pa. $1.25

WOODCRAFT AND CAMPING, Bernard S. Mason. How to make a quick emergency shelter, select woods that will burn immediately, make do with limited supplies, etc. Also making many things out of wood, rawhide, bark, at camp. Formerly titled Woodcraft. 295 illustrations. 580pp. 21951-8 Pa. $4.00

AN INTRODUCTION TO CHESS MOVES AND TACTICS SIMPLY EXPLAINED, Leonard Barden. Informal intermediate introduction: reasons for moves, tactics, openings, traps, positional play, endgame. Isolates patterns. 102pp. USO 21210-6 Pa. $1.35

LASKER'S MANUAL OF CHESS, Dr. Emanuel Lasker. Great world champion offers very thorough coverage of all aspects of chess. Combinations, position play, openings, endgame, aesthetics of chess, philosophy of struggle, much more. Filled with analyzed games. 390pp. 20640-8 Pa. $4.00

DRIED FLOWERS, Sarah Whitlock and Martha Rankin. Concise, clear, practical guide to dehydration, glycerinizing, pressing plant material, and more. Covers use of silica gel. 12 drawings. Originally titled "New Techniques with Dried Flowers." 32pp. 21802-3 Pa. $1.00

ABC OF POULTRY RAISING, J.H. Florea. Poultry expert, editor tells how to raise chickens on home or small business basis. Breeds, feeding, housing, laying, etc. Very concrete, practical. 50 illustrations. 256pp. 23201-8 Pa. $3.00

HOW INDIANS USE WILD PLANTS FOR FOOD, MEDICINE & CRAFTS, Frances Densmore. Smithsonian, Bureau of American Ethnology report presents wealth of material on nearly 200 plants used by Chippewas of Minnesota and Wisconsin. 33 plates plus 122pp. of text. 6⅛ x 9¼. 23019-8 Pa. $2.50

THE HERBAL OR GENERAL HISTORY OF PLANTS, John Gerard. The 1633 edition revised and enlarged by Thomas Johnson. Containing almost 2850 plant descriptions and 2705 superb illustrations, Gerard's Herbal is a monumental work, the book all modern English herbals are derived from, and the one herbal every serious enthusiast should have in its entirety. Original editions are worth perhaps $750. 1678pp. 8½ x 12¼. 23147-X Clothbd. $50.00

A MODERN HERBAL, Margaret Grieve. Much the fullest, most exact, most useful compilation of herbal material. Gigantic alphabetical encyclopedia, from aconite to zedoary, gives botanical information, medical properties, folklore, economic uses, and much else. Indispensable to serious reader. 161 illustrations. 888pp. 6½ x 9¼. USO 22798-7, 22799-5 Pa., Two vol. set $10.00

HOW TO KNOW THE FERNS, Frances T. Parsons. Delightful classic. Identification, fern lore, for Eastern and Central U.S.A. Has introduced thousands to interesting life form. 99 illustrations. 215pp. 20740-4 Pa. $2.75

THE MUSHROOM HANDBOOK, Louis C.C. Krieger. Still the best popular handbook. Full descriptions of 259 species, extremely thorough text, habitats, luminescence, poisons, folklore, etc. 32 color plates; 126 other illustrations. 560pp. 21861-9 Pa. $4.50

HOW TO KNOW THE WILD FRUITS, Maude G. Peterson. Classic guide covers nearly 200 trees, shrubs, smaller plants of the U.S. arranged by color of fruit and then by family. Full text provides names, descriptions, edibility, uses. 80 illustrations. 400pp. 22943-2 Pa. $4.00

COMMON WEEDS OF THE UNITED STATES, U.S. Department of Agriculture. Covers 220 important weeds with illustration, maps, botanical information, plant lore for each. Over 225 illustrations. 463pp. 6⅛ x 9¼. 20504-5 Pa. $4.50

HOW TO KNOW THE WILD FLOWERS, Mrs. William S. Dana. Still best popular book for East and Central USA. Over 500 plants easily identified, with plant lore; arranged according to color and flowering time. 174 plates. 459pp. 20332-8 Pa. $3.50

DRIED FLOWERS, Sarah Whitlock and Martha Rankin. Concise, clear, practical guide to dehydration, glycerinizing, pressing plant material, and more. Covers use of silica gel. 12 drawings. Originally titled "New Techniques with Dried Flowers." 32pp. 21802-3 Pa. $1.00

ABC OF POULTRY RAISING, J.H. Florea. Poultry expert, editor tells how to raise chickens on home or small business basis. Breeds, feeding, housing, laying, etc. Very concrete, practical. 50 illustrations. 256pp. 23201-8 Pa. $3.00

HOW INDIANS USE WILD PLANTS FOR FOOD, MEDICINE & CRAFTS, Frances Densmore. Smithsonian, Bureau of American Ethnology report presents wealth of material on nearly 200 plants used by Chippewas of Minnesota and Wisconsin. 33 plates plus 122pp. of text. 6⅛ x 9¼. 23019-8 Pa. $2.50

THE HERBAL OR GENERAL HISTORY OF PLANTS, John Gerard. The 1633 edition revised and enlarged by Thomas Johnson. Containing almost 2850 plant descriptions and 2705 superb illustrations, Gerard's Herbal is a monumental work, the book all modern English herbals are derived from, and the one herbal every serious enthusiast should have in its entirety. Original editions are worth perhaps $750. 1678pp. 8½ x 12¼. 23147-X Clothbd. $50.00

A MODERN HERBAL, Margaret Grieve. Much the fullest, most exact, most useful compilation of herbal material. Gigantic alphabetical encyclopedia, from aconite to zedoary, gives botanical information, medical properties, folklore, economic uses, and much else. Indispensable to serious reader. 161 illustrations. 888pp. 6½ x 9¼. USO 22798-7, 22799-5 Pa., Two vol. set $10.00

HOW TO KNOW THE FERNS, Frances T. Parsons. Delightful classic. Identification, fern lore, for Eastern and Central U.S.A. Has introduced thousands to interesting life form. 99 illustrations. 215pp. 20740-4 Pa. $2.75

THE MUSHROOM HANDBOOK, Louis C.C. Krieger. Still the best popular handbook. Full descriptions of 259 species, extremely thorough text, habitats, luminescence, poisons, folklore, etc. 32 color plates; 126 other illustrations. 560pp. 21861-9 Pa. $4.50

HOW TO KNOW THE WILD FRUITS, Maude G. Peterson. Classic guide covers nearly 200 trees, shrubs, smaller plants of the U.S. arranged by color of fruit and then by family. Full text provides names, descriptions, edibility, uses. 80 illustrations. 400pp. 22943-2 Pa. $4.00

COMMON WEEDS OF THE UNITED STATES, U.S. Department of Agriculture. Covers 220 important weeds with illustration, maps, botanical information, plant lore for each. Over 225 illustrations. 463pp. 6⅛ x 9¼. 20504-5 Pa. $4.50

HOW TO KNOW THE WILD FLOWERS, Mrs. William S. Dana. Still best popular book for East and Central USA. Over 500 plants easily identified, with plant lore; arranged according to color and flowering time. 174 plates. 459pp. 20332-8 Pa. $3.50

THE STYLE OF PALESTRINA AND THE DISSONANCE, Knud Jeppesen. Standard analysis of rhythm, line, harmony, accented and unaccented dissonances. Also pre-Palestrina dissonances. 306pp. 22386-8 Pa. $4.50

DOVER OPERA GUIDE AND LIBRETTO SERIES prepared by Ellen H. Bleiler. Each volume contains everything needed for background, complete enjoyment: complete libretto, new English translation with all repeats, biography of composer and librettist, early performance history, musical lore, much else. All volumes lavishly illustrated with performance photos, portraits, similar material. Do not confuse with skimpy performance booklets.

CARMEN, Georges Bizet. 66 illustrations. 222pp. 22111-3 Pa. $3.00
DON GIOVANNI, Wolfgang A. Mozart. 92 illustrations. 209pp. 21134-7 Pa. $2.50
LA BOHÈME, Giacomo Puccini. 73 illustrations. 124pp. USO 20404-9 Pa. $1.75
AÏDA, Giuseppe Verdi. 76 illustrations. 181pp. 20405-7 Pa. $2.25
LUCIA DI LAMMERMOOR, Gaetano Donizetti. 44 illustrations. 186pp.
22110-5 Pa. $2.00

ANTONIO STRADIVARI: HIS LIFE AND WORK, W. H. Hill, et al. Great work of musicology. Construction methods, woods, varnishes, known instruments, types of instruments, life, special features. Introduction by Sydney Beck. 98 illustrations, plus 4 color plates. 315pp. 20425-1 Pa. $4.00

MUSIC FOR THE PIANO, James Friskin, Irwin Freundlich. Both famous, little-known compositions; 1500 to 1950's. Listing, description, classification, technical aspects for student, teacher, performer. Indispensable for enlarging repertory. 448pp. 22918-1 Pa. $4.00

PIANOS AND THEIR MAKERS, Alfred Dolge. Leading inventor offers full history of piano technology, earliest models to 1910. Types, makers, components, mechanisms, musical aspects. Very strong on offtrail models, inventions; also player pianos. 300 illustrations. 581pp. 22856-8 Pa. $5.00

KEYBOARD MUSIC, J.S. Bach. Bach-Gesellschaft edition. For harpsichord, piano, other keyboard instruments. English Suites, French Suites, Six Partitas, Goldberg Variations, Two-Part Inventions, Three-Part Sinfonias. 312pp. 8⅛ x 11.
22360-4 Pa. $5.00

COMPLETE STRING QUARTETS, Ludwig van Beethoven. Breitkopf and Härtel edition. 6 quartets of Opus 18; 3 quartets of Opus 59; Opera 74, 95, 127, 130, 131, 132, 135 and Grosse Fuge. Study score. 434pp. 9⅜ x 12¼. 22361-2 Pa. $7.95

COMPLETE PIANO SONATAS AND VARIATIONS FOR SOLO PIANO, Johannes Brahms. All sonatas, five variations on themes from Schumann, Paganini, Handel, etc. Vienna Gesellschaft der Musikfreunde edition. 178pp. 9 x 12. 22650-6 Pa. $4.50

PIANO MUSIC 1888-1905, Claude Debussy. Deux Arabesques, Suite Bergamesque, Masques, 1st series of Images, etc. 9 others, in corrected editions. 175pp. 9⅜ x 12¼. 22771-5 Pa. $4.00

INCIDENTS OF TRAVEL IN YUCATAN, John L. Stephens. Classic (1843) exploration of jungles of Yucatan, looking for evidences of Maya civilization. Travel adventures, Mexican and Indian culture, etc. Total of 669pp.
20926-1, 20927-X Pa., Two vol. set $6.00

LIVING MY LIFE, Emma Goldman. Candid, no holds barred account by foremost American anarchist: her own life, anarchist movement, famous contemporaries, ideas and their impact. Struggles and confrontations in America, plus deportation to U.S.S.R. Shocking inside account of persecution of anarchists under Lenin. 13 plates. Total of 944pp. 22543-7, 22544-5 Pa., Two vol. set $9.00

AMERICAN INDIANS, George Catlin. Classic account of life among Plains Indians: ceremonies, hunt, warfare, etc. Dover edition reproduces for first time all original paintings. 312 plates. 572pp. of text. 6⅛ x 9¼.
22118-0, 22119-9 Pa., Two vol. set $8.00
22140-7, 22144-X Clothbd., Two vol. set $16.00.

THE INDIANS' BOOK, Natalie Curtis. Lore, music, narratives, drawings by Indians, collected from cultures of U.S.A. 149 songs in full notation. 45 illustrations. 583pp. 6⅝ x 9⅜. 21939-9 Pa. $6.95

INDIAN BLANKETS AND THEIR MAKERS, George Wharton James. History, old style wool blankets, changes brought about by traders, symbolism of design and color, a Navajo weaver at work, outline blanket, Kachina blankets, more. Emphasis on Navajo. 130 illustrations, 32 in color. 230pp. 6⅛ x 9¼. 22996-3 Pa. $5.00
23068-6 Clothbd. $10.00

AN INTRODUCTION TO THE STUDY OF THE MAYA HIEROGLYPHS, Sylvanus Griswold Morley. Classic study by one of the truly great figures in hieroglyph research. Still the best introduction for the student for reading Maya hieroglyphs. New introduction by J. Eric S. Thompson. 117 illustrations. 284pp. 23108-9 Pa. $4.00

THE ANALECTS OF CONFUCIUS, THE GREAT LEARNING, DOCTRINE OF THE MEAN, Confucius. Edited by James Legge. Full Chinese text, standard English translation on same page, Chinese commentators, editor's annotations; dictionary of characters at rear, plus grammatical comment. Finest edition anywhere of one of world's greatest thinkers. 503pp. 22746-4 Pa. $5.00

THE I CHING (THE BOOK OF CHANGES), translated by James Legge. Complete translation of basic text plus appendices by Confucius, and Chinese commentary of most penetrating divination manual ever prepared. Indispensable to study of early Oriental civilizations, to modern inquiring reader. 448pp.
21062-6 Pa. $3.50

THE EGYPTIAN BOOK OF THE DEAD, E.A. Wallis Budge. Complete reproduction of Ani's papyrus, finest ever found. Full hieroglyphic text, interlinear transliteration, word for word translation, smooth translation. Basic work, for Egyptology, for modern study of psychic matters. Total of 533pp. 6½ x 9¼.
EBE 21866-X Pa. $4.95

BUILD YOUR OWN LOW-COST HOME, L.O. Anderson, H.F. Zornig. U.S. Dept. of Agriculture sets of plans, full, detailed, for 11 houses: A-Frame, circular, conventional. Also construction manual. Save hundreds of dollars. 204pp. 11 x 16.
21525-3 Pa. $6.00

HOW TO BUILD A WOOD-FRAME HOUSE, L.O. Anderson. Comprehensive, easy to follow U.S. Government manual: placement, foundations, framing, sheathing, roof, insulation, plaster, finishing — almost everything else. 179 illustrations. 223pp. 7⅞ x 10¾.
22954-8 Pa. $3.50

CONCRETE, MASONRY AND BRICKWORK, U.S. Department of the Army. Practical handbook for the home owner and small builder manual contains basic principles, techniques, and important background information on construction with concrete, concrete blocks, and brick. 177 figures, 37 tables. 200pp. 6½ x 9¼.
23203-4 Pa. $4.00

THE STANDARD BOOK OF QUILT MAKING AND COLLECTING, Marguerite Ickis. Full information, full-sized patterns for making 46 traditional quilts, also 150 other patterns. Quilted cloths, lamé, satin quilts, etc. 483 illustrations. 273pp. 6⅞ x 9⅝.
20582-7 Pa. $3.50

101 PATCHWORK PATTERNS, Ruby S. McKim. 101 beautiful, immediately useable patterns, full-size, modern and traditional. Also general information, estimating, quilt lore. 124pp. 7⅞ x 10¾.
20773-0 Pa. $2.50

KNIT YOUR OWN NORWEGIAN SWEATERS, Dale Yarn Company. Complete instructions for 50 authentic sweaters, hats, mittens, gloves, caps, etc. Thoroughly modern designs that command high prices in stores. 24 patterns, 24 color photographs. Nearly 100 charts and other illustrations. 58pp. 8⅜ x 11¼.
23031-7 Pa. $2.50

IRON-ON TRANSFER PATTERNS FOR CREWEL AND EMBROIDERY FROM EARLY AMERICAN SOURCES, edited by Rita Weiss. 75 designs, borders, alphabets, from traditional American sources printed on translucent paper in transfer ink. Reuseable. Instructions. Test patterns. 24pp. 8¼ x 11.
23162-3 Pa. $1.50

AMERICAN INDIAN NEEDLEPOINT DESIGNS FOR PILLOWS, BELTS, HANDBAGS AND OTHER PROJECTS, Roslyn Epstein. 37 authentic American Indian designs adapted for modern needlepoint projects. Grid backing makes designs easily transferable to canvas. 48pp. 8¼ x 11.
22973-4 Pa. $1.50

CHARTED FOLK DESIGNS FOR CROSS-STITCH EMBROIDERY, Maria Foris & Andreas Foris. 278 charted folk designs, most in 2 colors, from Danube region: florals, fantastic beasts, geometrics, traditional symbols, more. Border and central patterns. 77pp. 8¼ x 11.
USO 23191-7 Pa. $2.00

Prices subject to change without notice.
Available at your book dealer or write for free catalogue to Dept. GI, Dover Publications, Inc., 180 Varick St., N.Y., N.Y. 10014. Dover publishes more than 150 books each year on science, elementary and advanced mathematics, biology, music, art, literary history, social sciences and other areas.